CRYSTAL PALACE F.C.
1969–2021

COMPLETE BIASED COMMENTARY

Written and illustrated by Chris Winter
Foreword by Attilio Lombardo

RED POST PRESS

First edition published in 2021 by

Red Post Press

ISBN 978–0–9516636–7–7

Contents

Note: Throughout the text I refer to what used to be the four tiers of the Football League according to the terminology of the season in question. The Premier League replaced the First Division in 1992, and was temporarily rebranded as the Premiership between 1993 and 2007. Thus in 1992 the old Second Division became known as the First Division before itself being renamed the Championship in 2004. I hope that helps.

*Dedicated to Lenny Hill
and to all Palace fans, past present and future*

Foreword by Attilio Lombardo

CRYSTAL PALACE represented for me a great opportunity from all points of view: a radical change on a cultural level, an opportunity to play in a league different from the Italian one, to be an integral part of the Premier League and to get to know a world unknown to me except through pictures on TV. Therefore I hoped to be a useful player for the club, especially with my background at SAMPDORIA and JUVENTUS.

Through the warmth that people sent me I experienced indescribable emotion. I remember my first game in Liverpool against EVERTON and the victory with my first goal and the penalty I won which was converted by BRUCE DYER. I remember my goal in the derby against WIMBLEDON where I found myself submerged by the embrace of a fan who entered in the field, and I remember also the opportunity to become a player-manager with the difficult task of trying to keep us in the Premier League.

I have only beautiful and exciting memories of my time at CRYSTAL PALACE, I lived my adventure with great motivation, I discovered the great passion of the fans and the great respect from my teammates. Living in the CRYSTAL PALACE world means loving all the people.

ATTILIO LOMBARDO

Attilio Lombardo

Introduction

For several decades I have had the privilege of providing live match commentaries from within Selhurst Park to patients in Mayday Hospital, and latterly to blind and partially sighted fans at the ground, and there is no shame in admitting that my description of the action in front of me has always been utterly biased, hence the title and the tone of this book. As well as covering the events of each season from 1969 onwards, I also reflect on my favourite players in each position in the final chapters and have chosen my dream team from everyone who has played for Palace during that time.

If football gets its talons into you at any age, the first experience of a live game is something that will stay with you forever, and mine was Crystal Palace against Carlisle, in the Second Division in 1968. I don't remember whether I had badgered my stepfather Len, or whether it was his idea to take me along to see our local team, and I doubt if I had even heard of Palace, but like any other ten-year-old I knew all the big names of the day, players like George Best and Bobby Charlton, and had seen and loved the film of England winning the World Cup at Wembley. Everyone else at the time claimed that they supported either Manchester United or Chelsea, but from that distant Saturday afternoon onwards one of my few certainties has been that I am a Palace fan.

It probably helped that the score that day was 5–0, but what stuck with me was the atmosphere of being among the crowd, unlike anything I had experienced before, and the fact that everyone there was having so much fun. Best of all was the moment when 'Glad All Over' came on the tannoy, and all around the ground hands stretched out and pummelled the advertising boards in unison. I soon joined in, and like any other Palace fan have been pounding out those two beats ever since

This book is a compilation of two previous volumes covering the periods 1969–1990 and 1990–2011, with new chapters to bring the story up to date, and with some corrections and additions to the earlier text and illustrations. My purpose in writing it is not to produce a statistical record but rather to set down my own veracious but subjective memories of the last 52 years, and my thoughts on the characters involved. Some of what I have written you might agree with, most of it you probably won't, since we all see the game in different ways, but I simply hope that you will recognise the sentiments that lie behind what amounts to a labour of love, and that you find plenty in the words and pictures to bring back fond memories of your own.

Finally, thanks are due to many people for their support and encouragement during the production of this and earlier volumes: Keith Andrews, Richard Avison, Jo Brand, Steve Browett, Andy Bull, Michael De Luca, Roger Dickson, Carol Hobley, Dave Keeley, Ian King, Attilio Lombardo, Jayne Love, Don Madgwick, David Peach, Norman Turpin, Luca Vialli, Ian Weller, Barbara Winter, Bud Winter, Ellie Winter, and to all the players who have entertained, infuriated and delighted me over the years.

1969–70

'I'm feelin' glad all over, so glad you're mine'
Dave Clark & Mike Smith

By the end of that 1968–69 season Palace had won promotion to Division One for the first time ever, and although by then I was as ecstatic as anyone else among the thousands running on to the pitch after beating Fulham, I probably didn't quite understand quite how momentous that was in the context of Palace's history. What a glorious feeling that must been for the fans who had been following Palace for so many years in the lower divisions, who probably never dreamed for a moment that the day would come when they would be up there competing with the elite.

Arthur Wait

One might have assumed that the most sensible priority of a newly promoted club would be to go out and buy a couple of players with First Division experience to help to dig in, especially since this was to be Crystal Palace's first ever glimpse of the top flight, but their immediate concern was to finish the building of a new stand at breakneck speed, where once had been a dangerous mound of earth. Constructed opposite Archibald Leitch's original 1920s stand – itself not one of the Scottish architect's most elegant designs – the new structure was functional in the extreme, but it was an impressive feat to throw it up over the summer nonetheless. Arthur Wait had been chairman since 1958, raising Palace up from the Fourth Division, and didn't have to worry about getting the builders in, as he was the builder, so he had every right to name this utilitarian new stand in his own honour.

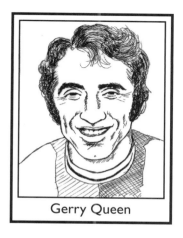

Gerry Queen

With several Scots already in the team that had won promotion, and with transfer funds still limited, manager Bert Head returned to Scotland to sign three more players, Roger Hynd, Gerry Queen and Per Bartram, as well buying Alan Pinkney from Exeter City. Queen was intended to be a direct replacement for Bobby Woodruff as centre forward, and Hynd was to accompany John McCormick in central defence, allowing Mel Blyth more of a midfield role. Apart from these two changes, it was essentially the same team that had won promotion who lined up for Palace's first ever game in the First Division, against no less a side than the waning Manchester United. After finishing 11th. in the league the previous season, Matt Busby had handed over team affairs to the ill-fated Wilf McGuiness, and the team for his first game in charge was still packed with household names, the front line consisting of Willie Morgan, Brian Kidd, Bobby Charlton, Denis Law and George Best. Although still a glamorous side, it is clear in retrospect that by this time United's best days were behind them. However, it was still an achievement for a mostly unmodified Second Division team such as Palace to earn a 2–2 draw in front of a record-breaking crowd of 48,610, after twice going ahead with goals from Mel Blyth and, on his debut, Gerry Queen. A comfortable home victory against Sunderland was followed by a good performance at Everton, despite losing 2–1, and it appeared that Palace might be surprisingly at home in such company, as at least defensively they were looking fairly capable.

Mark Lazarus

The pattern for the season began to emerge in the next game, however, when the opponents were again Sunderland – destined for relegation that season – this time at Roker Park. Just a week after beating them 2–0, Palace concentrated on earning an away point, and despite never being troubled by an attack that had so far failed to score in four games, were content to come away with a goalless draw. Bobby Woodruff was back in the side in place of the injured Gerry Queen, and the Dane Per Bartram came on as substitute for Cliff Jackson; the fact that these four strikers only managed 17 goals between them all season explains why Palace struggled to survive. Jackson and Woodruff were clearly nearing the end of their careers, and this was to be the last season in Division One for each of them. Gerry Queen, although not without both skill and speed, appeared to be typical of the old fashioned inside forward, and would have benefitted from playing alongside someone with a bit more muscle, while Bartram, the Danish international intended to fill that role, had problems initially with his work permit, being classified as an alien, and having to report regularly to the police. When he did come into the team, he proved a disappointment, and only played a few games before returning to Morton the following season.

Hence, although Palace were able to achieve a good number of draws against good sides, they only managed five more victories all season, albeit with two of them being against recent champions Manchester City. The defence was still being held together by the good form of McCormick and the heroics of John Jackson in goal, and Kember was superb in midfield, but nothing too much was happening up front. The calendar year of 1969 ended with an appalling run of 10 games during which Palace won only three points, scoring six goals and conceding 23, and bracketed by 5–1 home defeats at the hands of Arsenal at the start of November and Chelsea on Boxing Day, when the crowd of 49,498 set another new record. The team selection became even more cautious, with Woodruff and Lazarus departing for Cardiff and Orient respectively, and Phil Hoadley coming into the side together with the reliable David Payne. With injuries to Tony Taylor, Roger Hoy and Cliff Jackson, Bert Head was also forced to use reserve players such as Trevor Dawkins and Len Tomkins, and Palace went into the new year third from bottom, above Sunderland and Sheffield Wednesday, but still looking certainties for relegation. A 3–2 defeat at West Bromwich Albion in the new year left them in the bottom two and surely doomed.

Things began to look up, however, when Bert Head persuaded Bobby Tambling, one of Chelsea's greatest ever goal scorers, to come to Selhurst on loan for three games. Then, after unsuccessfully pursuing several forwards, including Jimmy Greaves, he signed the Scottish international Jim Scott from Newcastle. Although he failed to score in his first 11 games, Scott's inclusion alongside Tony Taylor balanced the forward line, and Palace began to look more of a team as they forced valuable draws at St. James' Park, Old Trafford and Molineux, three of the most intimidating grounds for away teams. They also managed two wins in a row for the only time all season, when they beat both Manchester City and Southampton in the space of four days. The most notable achievement during this period, however, was the victory over Spurs in the FA Cup 4th round. After holding them 0–0 at White Hart Lane, Palace won the replay the following Wednesday night against a side which contained seven full international players, including Greaves, Alan Gilzean, and Alan Mullery, as well as a youngster in his first season, Steve Perryman. Although Spurs, along with Arsenal and Manchester United, were to finish only in a middle of the table position at the end of that season, they were still one of the best sides around, and Palace fully deserved to win what remains the best cup tie seen at Selhurst Park, with a

goal from Gerry Queen, and the usual flat-out performance from Roger Hoy. Somehow, after that, it seemed inevitable that Palace would stay up, and despite going out of the Cup to Chelsea, and losing a crucial 'four-pointer' at home to Sheffield Wednesday, they completed the season by beating Manchester City again, the only double that year. Palace eventually escaped relegation by just a single point, an outcome that had seemed most improbable at the turn of the year.

Jim Scott

A significant factor in Palace's survival was the form of Mel Blyth, who deposed Roger Hynd as John McCormick's partner in central defence, creating a combination that was to last for the next two and a half seasons. The most worrying thing, though, was that the team had clearly not progressed since winning promotion, and of the new players, Hynd had added little, Bartram and Pinkney had failed to make any impression, whilst Queen found himself rather isolated up front. The core of the team which had come up were still playing well enough, namely John Jackson, McCormick and Kember, but unlike fellow newcomers Derby County, their natural home looked to be the Second Division.

Despite some poor football on the pitch, the club was very successful at cultivating a friendly atmosphere and a feeling of homeliness in the days before the segregation of rival fans, and the Whitehorse Lane end, with supporters of both teams mixing quite happily, became the natural area for young fans to stand, without having to be designated as such. That this no longer happens at football grounds is a great pity, and one thing for which one can be forgiven a pang of nostalgia. There is a temptation to become misty-eyed about the passing of the great players and the great teams, which implies that the game has become inferior and that there aren't the characters now that there were in the 60's and 70's. I don't hold that view, as players like George Best and Rodney Marsh stood out as exceptions at the time, and although so much around the edges of the game has changed, some of it even for the better, on the pitch we still have the mavericks, the showmen, the heroes and the villains, and we always will have.

1970-71

It was clear from the previous season that Bert Head would have to spend some money on a new centre forward, and he went for an uncharacteristic touch of glamour in the shape of Chelsea's Alan Birchenall, rated at £100,000, who came in a package with Bobby Tambling. The other significant purchase was that of Peter Wall from Liverpool, who immediately consigned left back John Loughlan to the reserves. With Birchenall's arrival, there was no place for Cliff Jackson, and he returned to his native West Country, with Torquay. Mel Blyth's good run at the end of the previous season and the maturing of Phil Hoadley also meant that Roger Hynd was no longer needed, and he moved on to have a fine career at Birmingham, while more surprising was the loss of the very versatile squad player Roger Hoy to Luton.

draws in the first eight games found themselves sitting third in the league, behind Leeds United and Manchester City, a high point from which the slide was to be relentless. However, at this point the team were earning some deserved praise for the quality of their football, and the close-season signings were proving to be good ones. Alan Birchenall was exactly the kind of partner that Gerry Queen needed, and for the first part of the season at least the combination of Tambling's attacking instincts on the wing, Birchenall's strength in the air and Gerry Queen's speed proved quite effective, if not prolific.

Bobby Tambling

Phil Hoadley

Before a ball had been kicked, the newspapers had front page stories about Palace's new wages and bonus scheme, which gave rise to speculation that their players could become the game's highest earners, with up to £300 in their weekly pay packet! Whatever the true figures, Palace made a tremendous start to the new season, and after four wins and three

Just as important was the extra dimension to Palace's defensive thinking added by left back Peter Wall. Although not a regular first team choice at Liverpool, some of that club's class had rubbed off on him, and he impressed as a cool, skilful player with the confidence to play the ball out of defence, and a touch of arrogance which could inspire his colleagues.

It appeared that Bert Head had transformed last season's no-hopers into a genuine First Division side by adding just three players, and although the core of the side remained intact, they were at this stage all playing to their limits. In October of 1970, after consecutive victories against Southampton and West Bromwich Albion at home, and by a single goal at Old Trafford to spoil Bobby Charlton's 500th game for United, the top six of the first division contained four London clubs – Arsenal, Spurs, Palace and Chelsea – along with Leeds and Manchester City, and for the first time Palace fans felt they really did belong in the elite. Confirmation that Palace's league position was no fluke came when they faced Arsenal in the 4th round of the League Cup. The Gunners were to win the FA Cup and Football League double that season, so it was a great feat for Palace, after forcing a 0–0 draw at Selhurst Park, to win the replay at Highbury, albeit against the run of play, with goals from Gerry Queen and a Bobby Tambling penalty.

John Sewell

an undeserved defeat. When the ball fell loose to John Sewell inside his own half, it looked as if the captain too had given up all hope, for instead of trying to find a team mate up front, he simply clogged the ball up field as hard as he could, to the groans of the home crowd. The ball dropped gently towards the Leeds goal, where Gary Sprake, with nobody else within 30 yards of him, prepared to take the simplest of catches inside the left-hand post. One moment the ball was safely in his hands, and the next it was behind him, in the net. Sprake looked around, searching desperately for the unseen force which had sucked the ball from his grasp, but there was no one but himself to blame. Those of the crowd who had left the ground a couple of minutes early had missed the finest moment of comedy they were ever likely to see at Selhurst Park, but luckily for them – if not for the hapless goalkeeper – the slapstick was repeated on television every week until the end of the season. There is a photograph taken from behind the goal, which shows the keeper's gloved hands firmly behind the ball as he catches it, and this was probably one of the many incidents that suggested the later title of Gary Sprake's authorised biography, 'Careless Hands'.

It appeared that things were going Palace's way, because this game came just two days after a memorable home match against Leeds United, at that time two points clear at the top of the table. Despite matching Leeds for most of the game, Palace were unable to break through the miserly defence, and found themselves a goal down with less than a minute left and heading for

Tony Taylor

Although still on the heels of the leaders, the team was soon to be affected by injuries to Queen, Tambling and Payne, and the productive partnership of Birchenall and Queen was never able to recover its early promise. Jim Scott's form in place of Tambling was a disappointment, and with Gerry Humphries and Trevor Dawkins pressed into service, a run of four games during December and January saw the team unable to score a single league goal, and knocked out of the FA Cup by Chelsea, always a particularly bitter pill to swallow. Things improved slightly after the purchase of an established goal scorer, Bolton's Terry Wharton, and home victories followed against Liverpool and Ipswich. The Liverpool result, with Gerry Queen scoring the only goal, stood as Palace's first and only victory over them until a famous day nearly 20 years later. Thus, with two thirds of the season gone, Palace were still lying quite handy in 9th. position, with an outside chance still of qualifying for Europe, and everything to play for. With the European possibilities in mind, a friendly game was arranged against the leaders of the Dutch League, PSV Eindhoven. It was certainly no disgrace to lose 4–2 against such a good side, but for some reason the effect on Palace was devastating. In the following eight games they only earned themselves one point, and after the home defeat by Coventry Bert Head allowed himself a rare public outburst when he claimed that several of his players were performing as if the season was over, which of course proved to be the case, only John Jackson escaping his wrath. One incident summed up the peculiar lack of passion in the team, when Alan Birchenall picked up a ball in the opponent's half of the field and, showing a good deal of skill, dribbled past several tackles as he looked in vain for a team mate sufficiently interested to receive a pass, eventually taking it all the way back to John Jackson in his own area.

After such a good start to the season, it was especially disappointing to witness such a decline, and it looked as though many of the players knew that they could achieve no more. John Sewell, certainly, was at the end of his career, and injury had affected John McCormick and David Payne, as well as Queen and Tambling, but the slide from third in the league to a final, humiliating 6–0 defeat at Southampton was incomprehensible. The only consolation was that Palace finished in their highest ever league position, 18th. in the First Division, and comfortably clear of the two relegation places.

Terry Wharton

Some self-respect was recovered after the season's end with good performances against Inter Milan and Cagliari in the Anglo-Italian Tournament, and the Palace fans, ever optimistic in the face of all the contradictory evidence, looked forward to next season in the knowledge that their team was now well and truly established in Division One.

Bert Head obviously shared the fans' optimism, since no new players arrived during the summer, the only departure being that of John Sewell to Orient just before the start of the season. This brought about the conversion of David Payne from midfield to right back, which seemed a reasonable ploy since Payne had lost some speed but had the experience to adapt well to a new role. Steve Kember, at the height of his powers, was the logical choice to take over as captain, and with this almost unchanged line up, Palace faced Newcastle in the first game of the season.

Bert Head

The major change that had taken place, though, was the introduction of a new playing strip – no doubt inspired by the pre-season efforts against Dutch opposition – consisting of two broad vertical bands of claret and blue on a white shirt. This was clearly based on the design used by Johann Cruyff's Ajax of Amsterdam, but instead of making the team look slick and Continental, it made the players look strangely lopsided. A conscious attempt had obviously been made to drag Palace's image into the modern era of the 70's, but the previous design of claret with thin light blue stripes was far preferable.

The previously spare and sophisticated matchday programme underwent a radical change too, being replaced by surely one of the worst programme designs in history. The cover featured a generic drawing of a goalkeeper smiling wanly as the ball sails past him and into the net, patently not Jacko.

Bobby Kellard

The game against Newcastle gave their new signing Malcolm McDonald his first chance in the First Division, but he was unable to bludgeon his way through a well organised Palace defence, and Steve Kember's brief career as captain began with a 2–0 victory. It was too early to assume that Palace could recover their excellent form of a year before, but the signs were good. The dramatic loss of form over the next eight games, then, is hard to explain. The only answer I can offer is that too many of the players, those with years of experience as much as those who had won promotion two years earlier, felt that they had arrived as First Division regulars and had become complacent, with the result that Bert Head was no longer able to motivate them. Over the next few weeks, as the team struggled to win just one point from eight games, it seemed that the harder they tried the worse they played, and the fans started to express their impatience more than they ever had before. Bearing in mind that the home gates were still averaging nearly 30,000, they clearly had a perfect right to expect a lot more for their money.

On the Sunday morning following a 3–0 defeat at Spurs, the board met and demanded that the manager should take decisive action to reverse the decline. Within a week, Bert Head had sold his two most valuable assets: Steve Kember to Chelsea for a record fee of £170,000, and Alan Birchenall to Leicester. The justification for this was that the money would be used to inject a new spirit into the team with the purchase of half a dozen new players, in a most dramatic shake-up of staff. Three others to have played their last games for Palace were Phil Hoadley, sold to Orient, the disappointing Jim Scott, and Terry Wharton. The fans, already critical of the sale of Kember in particular, were even more bemused when the new blood was announced.

John Hughes

Each day the newspapers reported a new signing: the first was Bobby Kellard, familiar enough to most from his previous spell at the club, and a straightforward replacement for Steve Kember in midfield, but John Craven, Sammy Goodwin and Bobby Bell were far from household names. Indeed, Goodwin had been making a living as a car salesman while playing part-time for Airdrie! The final two newcomers, arriving a month later, sounded distinctly more exciting: the Celtic pair John Hughes and Willie Wallace, both forwards with Scottish international caps and European experience.

With the loss of Kember, John Jackson briefly became team captain, but by November this duty had passed to Bobby Kellard, one of the games natural skippers. With so many new players thrown together at one time, it was something of a surprise to defeat Everton 2–1, the goal coming from a young and enthusiastic Ross Jenkins, playing only his fourth game in the first team. By the time of the home fixture with Sheffield United in December, results had started to improve, and Palace were playing like a team again, albeit with a definite defensive bias. It must be remembered that Sheffield United were at this time lying near the top of the First Division, and after beating Ipswich 7–0 were being spoken of as a major new force in the game. The 5–1 victory that ensued was certainly the highlight of the entire season for Palace fans, and nobody who was there on that day, or who saw the highlights on television, will ever forget the two goals scored by John Hughes, who surprisingly only scored twice more in his 23 games for Palace. 'Yogi', as he had been known at Celtic, was so named because of his size and strength, and without ever having much speed, he had the ability to shake off defenders through sheer physical power, while keeping his head down and the ball always under close control. There was something immediately likeable about him, and he became a hero overnight with his performance that day. His first goal was a gem in its own right, a diagonal solo run from the halfway line completed with a strong left foot shot to put Palace 2–0 up after only 7 minutes. It was his second goal, however, and Palace's fourth, which ensured his place in history. Picking the ball up on the left, following a free kick for yet another foul on him, he seemed to move in slow motion as he lumbered inside, dipping his shoulders to shrug off a couple of challenges before working his way into a position some 35 yards from goal. Without breaking stride, he swung his massive right leg at the ball and produced a shot of such power and accuracy that it was in the net almost before the helpless goalkeeper could

Willie Wallace

react. Palace's other scorers that day were Tony Taylor, John McCormick and Gerry Queen, and although Willie Wallace failed to complete a unique nap hand for the Scots, he also looked good on a day when everything went right for his new team.

As well as being a splendid performance, perhaps more important was the fact that the result lifted Palace off the bottom of the table, and in the process vindicated Bert Head's faith in his new players, and in particular his persistent policy of looking to Scotland for fresh blood. Unfortunately, Yogi Hughes was injured towards the end of that match, and only managed a further five games during the rest of the season. It was a campaign which turned out to be the usual hard slog to avoid relegation, which they did by once again finishing third from bottom, but clear by four points. Despite this struggle, the second half of the season kept the fans more interested than had been the case the previous year, and in the end, survival was considered a fine achievement after such a dreadful start. Of the new players, Bobby Kellard was an unqualified success, with the fighting spirit that had been so lacking the year before, and John Craven showed occasional bursts of skill which promised better to come.

This had been the year of a well-publicised referee's clampdown, a good idea in theory, but turned into a farce by the inflexibility of the authorities. Referees, who will always be considered inconsistent if the rules allow for interpretation, were suddenly given strict instructions as to what constitutes foul play, and for a while defenders were unable to tackle from behind, however cleanly. Rather than trying to attract referees of a higher calibre, and with more natural authority, the league effectively took some of the responsibility away from them, and the result was confusion all round, for players were now finding themselves penalised for playing the way they had been doing for years. The overall effect, far from encouraging skilful football – as had been the intention – was that teams developed more efficient strategies for cheating, following the fine example set by the Don Revie's Leeds United.

1972-73

Before the season began there was no end of transfer speculation in the press, although most of it was due to Palace having earned a reputation for throwing money around, and therefore being linked with every player going. There was no doubt, however, that a new centre forward was a priority, considering that the top scorer the previous season had been the ageing Bobby Tambling, with just 11 goals in all competitions. Of the other forwards, John Craven had done best with eight goals, but Queen and Wallace were clearly below par. Bert Head claimed that during the summer he had been pursuing a total of 22 players, and among those he was apparently on the verge of signing were Stan Bowles, Alan Gowling and Derek Johnson, as well as England regular Alan Mullery. Nevertheless, come the kick-off, the only significant changes to the side were the inclusion of Alan Pinkney in place of Sammy Goodwin in midfield, and Ross Jenkins replacing Gerry Queen. The playing strip had been modified with the addition of a white stripe down the middle, and a new badge in a supposedly high-tech design.

The league, determined to further pursue the war on foul play announced a new penalty points system, which at least had the merit of bringing some consistency to what had seemed fairly arbitrary refereeing the year before. Something I have yet to see anyone booked for is the offence, carrying one penalty point, of 'a player using the shoulders of his own team colleague to assist in the heading of the ball', so this practice at least must have been successfully stamped out.

Palace's start this time was not disastrous, although suggesting yet another season spent in the bottom half of the table. With four draws and a defeat in the first five games, again the problem looked to be one of scoring goals, but perhaps the most worrying incident was the broken leg sustained by Peter Wall in the 1–1 draw against his old club, Liverpool. This was, in effect, the end of his season, and although he was loaned to Orient for rehabilitation once the break had mended, it was to be another two and a half years before he regained a regular place in the side.

Alan Pinkney

The left back position went at first to the 18-year-old Bill Roffey, and then Tony Taylor was moved back from midfield to defence, fairly successfully. By now, just four years after promotion, the only five survivors from that team made up the entire defence: John Jackson, David Payne, Tony Taylor, John McCormick and Mel Blyth.

Following a single goal defeat of Manchester City, courtesy of an own goal and Jackson's penalty save from Francis Lee, came a 2–1 victory over Newcastle, and at the beginning of September Palace were sitting comfortably in 10th position, a significant improvement on the previous year. The Newcastle game featured a remarkable goal for Palace which, as it turned out, used up their quota of luck for the next two months.

Willie Wallace lost control of the ball in the penalty area, but as he chased after it he stumbled into a defender, who could hardly believe it when the referee awarded a penalty. Although absolutely nobody agreed, the decision stood, and it was left to Palace's captain Bobby Kellard to take the spot kick. As he ran up, he slipped over and miskicked the ball completely with his left foot. This sent a clump of earth towards the goal, at the same time diverting the ball slowly into the net, with the goalkeeper McFaul utterly flummoxed.

The following Tuesday, a dire performance at home to Fourth Division Stockport County ended Palace's interest in the League Cup, and five straight league defeats sent them to the very bottom of the table. During this time, including two Texaco Cup games against Hearts, Palace went six games without scoring, and despite losing out to Manchester United for the signature of the £200,000 striker Ted MacDougall, Bert Head made it clear that he was about to make some big money signings.

Charlie Cooke

The weeks that followed echoed the shake-up of the previous autumn, with Palace's transfer record broken twice: first by Iain Philip, a 21-year-old costing £115,000 from Dundee, and then Don Rogers, coming from Swindon for £150,000. Paddy Mulligan and Charlie Cooke also joined from Chelsea, and with John McCormick being dropped in favour of Bobby Bell, half the team was changed in a stroke. With Mulligan immediately installed as captain, a disgruntled Bobby Kellard demanded a transfer and was soon dropped, as were Wallace, Tambling and Jenkins.

Before the arrival of Rogers, Palace were unlucky to lose 3–2 to Arsenal in a home game, with all three Arsenal goals considered highly dubious, and none more so than Charlie George's penalty. Paul Hammond, playing only his second game in goal in place of the injured Jackson, held on to the ball at the second attempt and seemed to have saved the penalty, but the referee considered that the ball had crossed the line, and Palace were denied a crucial point. Although the television evidence was inconclusive, it was one of those games where Palace certainly deserved a result which would have lifted them off the bottom of the First Division, but it was not until Don Rogers' arrival that there seemed any hope of a genuine revival. Rogers was already famous, having scored two goals for Swindon in the 1969 League Cup final against Arsenal, but the big clubs had remained unconvinced that he could step up in class, and consequently he had remained a star of the lower divisions until re-joining his old boss Bert Head at Palace. Any doubts about him were quickly dispelled in his first appearance, when he scored the goal against Everton which gave Palace only their third victory from 16 games. This goal was the first of many in exactly the same mould, racing onto a through ball from John Craven from his own half and beating the defender for speed before drawing the goalkeeper, looking up and placing the ball sweetly past him and into the net. Although he did score the odd scrambled goal, these solo efforts became his trademark, and as a crowd pleaser he was one of the best in the game. His heroic status was confirmed in the famous 5–0 defeat of Manchester United a few weeks later. This was the first game for another new signing, Alan Whittle from Everton, and he was to score a single goal alongside a brace each by Rogers and Paddy Mulligan. Arthur Wait described the losing team as 'The worst United side I have ever seen', and it gave the board at Old Trafford the final excuse that they needed to get rid of their latest manager, Frank O'Farrell, and replace him with Tommy Docherty.

Ray Bloye

At last able to score goals and augmented by the signing of Millwall's highest ever goal scorer, Derek Possee, Palace managed some good results which suggested the possibility of survival, but what the fans were unaware of at the time was that Bert Head's days were numbered. Ray Bloye, a front man for the business consortium Matthews Holdings, had been installed earlier in the season as vice-chairman, and despite his unconvincing protestations that

'when I joined the club as a Director, I had neither the ambition nor the intention to become Chairman', by November the old Chairman Arthur Wait had become Life President, and Bloye's firm were firmly in control. It was not until the following March that it was announced that Bert Head was to be kicked upstairs, becoming General Manager until the end of the season, but it had been planned for some time. At this stage Palace were still one place away from relegation, and it seems remarkable that Head wasn't allowed to see out the last few weeks of the season in charge, but Bloye clearly felt that he could buy instant success, and so Malcolm Allison arrived, heralded as the saviour of Crystal Palace.

In a touching show of loyalty, Bert Head and his assistant Terry Long introduced Allison to the crowd before the home game against Chelsea, and for an afternoon at least Palace could hail the new Messiah. The 2–0 victory over Chelsea was Palace's first against a London club in all their time in the First Division, and Jim Cannon had an outstanding debut in defence, marking Peter Osgood out of the game as well as rushing forward to head in the second goal. However, Palace were unable to win again until the last game of the season at Manchester City, and despite achieving a better points total than in either 1971 or 1972, relegation finally became reality after four seasons of almost constant struggle.

1973–74

Malcolm Allison wanted to save not only Crystal Palace, but English football, yet he will be remembered mostly for what is called 'flamboyance' – his big cigar, big hat and a big mouth.

It was a surprise, given Palace's recent image, that no new players arrived during the summer, and the major change was one of presentation. The claret and blue, which had been a part of Palace's playing strip since the club was founded, was replaced by scarlet and royal blue stripes, a change anticipated by the cover of the previous season's programme, where a primary red stood for claret, which was more difficult to print. In this spirit of rebranding, the nickname was changed from The Glaziers to The Eagles, a nod to the Portuguese giants Benfica, and a new crest designed accordingly, which mercifully retained a depiction of the original Crystal Palace building itself. Another gimmick, thankfully a short-lived one, was the printing of bogus nicknames in the programme alongside each player's name, so Tony Taylor became 'The Road Runner', Alan Whittle 'The Hustler', and so on, titles which also embellished their track-suit tops.

With Allison in charge, Palace were guaranteed more publicity than any other Second Division club, and the consensus before the season began was that a side containing so many well-known names would bounce straight back into Division One. In typical Allison style, after losing the first game 4–1 at home to Notts County, the manager confidently predicted that 'we won't just get promotion, we'll win the Second Division championship', and he clearly believed it.

Alan Whittle

Malcolm Allison

Encouraged by the promise shown by Jim Cannon, Allison gave sporadic first team chances to other youth team players Nicky Chatterton and Dave Swindlehurst, and kept faith in Bill Roffey as cover for the injured Paddy Mulligan. Martin Hinshelwood, who had played 16 games the season before despite a recurring back injury, was joined for a few games by his brother Paul, at that time an aspiring centre forward, but without doubt the most controversial choice was that of Paul Hammond in goal in place of John Jackson. Allison insisted that Hammond deserved his place on merit, but it seems more likely that the manager was determined to break with the old regime regardless, and Jackson was the ultimate symbol of that recent past, although most fans will agree that he kept Palace in Division One far longer than they deserved. After two games during which Hammond was mercilessly barracked by sections of the crowd, Jackson had a run of five games back in goal, but after being blamed for two of Cardiff's goals in a 3–3 draw, he was dropped again, and soon afterwards moved to Orient, an undignified end to his glorious Palace career. By this time, Orient were managed by former Palace trainer George Petchey, coached by Terry Long, and now had five ex-Palace players in the side, Jackson and Roffey joining David Payne, Gerry Queen and Phil Hoadley. Ironically, Orient went desperately close to winning promotion themselves at the end of the season, while Palace went rapidly downhill.

John Craven

Following that Cardiff game, and with his team badly adrift at the bottom of the Second Division, Allison made his first two signings – Derek Jeffries and Roy Barry – and threw them together in central defence, dropping both Mel Blyth and Iain Philip. Jeffries had been one of Allison's proteges at Maine Road, and as a 15-year-old he had described him as 'one of the best prospects

since Bobby Moore'. Certainly, he looked a cut above the usual centre half in terms of skill, but his new partner was a classic example of a 'stopper'. Roy Barry, a Scot, was a hard man who had recovered from a badly broken leg and regained his place at Coventry only to lose it, strangely enough, to John Craven, who Allison had rejected as a forward. Barry's arrival left no place for Bobby Bell, and after failing to attract any interest on the transfer market he went to try his luck in South Africa.

Derek Jeffries

The new-look defence, with Mulligan having apparently recovered from his knee injury, didn't really improve matters, though, and with Whittle and Possee having failed to score a single goal between them, Allison's next move was for Southend winger Peter Taylor, which signalled the start of a steady improvement. Until now, Palace had been playing without true wingers, since Don Rogers had dropped back to a deeper position, in keeping with Allison's philosophy, the cornerstone of which was a belief in the short pass. Taylor's great strength was his crossing ability, and although he didn't score too many goals in his first season, he had a hand in the majority of Palace's goals, and gave the fans something to get excited about once again. Until now, Possee and Whittle had received most balls with their backs to the goal, and were failing to make clear chances for themselves, but now Peter Taylor was getting behind defences and lashing in the kind of crosses which neither Don Rogers nor Charlie Cooke had been capable of. Unfortunately, Possee and Whittle were two of the shortest forwards in the league, and were hardly a menace to defenders in the air, so Allison signed Derek Hill, a centre forward from Ipswich, who did a lot of the donkey work up front without managing to score. With two new forwards in the side, Cooke and Tambling were released, and Palace made their final signings for the season, Jeff Johnson and Stewart Jump.

Rogers, and the 1–0 victory began an astonishing run of thirteen games with just two defeats, which miraculously lifted them at one stage to fourth from bottom, one place clear of relegation. Derek Possee returned from injury to score eight goals in ten games, and despite a vote of confidence from the board, Malcolm Allison not only survived, but seemed vindicated. However, the recovery proved to have come too late after such a diabolical start, and Palace were finally relegated for the second year running, despite playing some genuinely good football and attracting large crowds. The tragedy was that if Allison had compromised his ideals even slightly, then they might have avoided the drop, but pragmatism wasn't in his make-up, as was evident throughout his management career.

Jeff Johnson

On Boxing Day of 1973, Palace suffered the humiliation of losing 3–0 to the exiles at Orient, and went into the new year still in bottom place, with Malcolm Allison doggedly defending his conviction that Palace would turn the corner, and refusing to resign. The first day of 1974 saw Palace line up against West Bromwich Albion with only two survivors from the season's first game, Paul Hammond and Don

1974-75

Despite relegation, Malcolm Allison had at last got his players performing approximately according to his theories, and there was no doubt in anybody's mind that Palace's stay in the Third Division would be brief, given the improved quality of football seen in the latter half of the season. Although the team began this new campaign with very little difference in personnel – only Derek Possee had gone, inevitably to Brisbane Road – some very significant changes were imminent, which were to have a lasting effect on the club.

Mel Blyth

A couple of good early results were a 6–2 defeat of Swindon and an impressive 5–1 victory over Watford in the League Cup, which was Palace's best game to date under Allison. It seemed that confidence in a quick return to Division Two was reasonable, but the manager surprised everyone by releasing two players who one would have thought were crucial to the side. Mel Blyth, who had re-established himself in central defence, and who was the final link with Bert Head's promotion winners of 1969, was sold to Southampton, and Don Rogers, easily Palace's top scorer in each of his two seasons, moved up two divisions to join Queens Park Rangers. The

two players who moved in the opposite direction from Loftus Road were Terry Venables, a famous player well past his prime, and a young Welsh centre back, Ian Evans. Malcolm Allison, justifying his decision to release Blyth, succeeded in damning him with faint praise, but was certainly accurate in the comparison with his replacement: 'Mel is a very competent all-round defender but I felt we needed more power in the air and in this respect Ian Evans is brilliant.' Regarding Don Rogers, the implication was that the much younger Peter Taylor, already being noticed by the England manager Don Revie, had overshadowed Rogers since his arrival, and the opportunity to sign Venables – a good friend of Allison's – would be of more benefit to the club. In fact, Allison already had Venables earmarked as a potential coach, but his sixteen appearances as a player helped to consolidate Palace's position amongst the Third Division leaders.

Venables' playing style had always been in accordance with Allison's ideals, relying on accurate passing and conservation of energy, but his physical limitations made things very difficult for him in the rough and tumble of the lower divisions and he wisely decided to finish his playing days at the surprisingly young age of 31, and concentrate on his burgeoning career in management. Indeed, shortly after leaving QPR for Palace, there was speculation that he might return to replace the Rangers manager Gordon Jago, but Venables quickly pledged his future to Selhurst Park, happy for the moment to work as Malcolm Allison's assistant. The signing of the 22-year-old Ian Evans turned out to be Allison's best transfer manoeuvre for Palace, and he immediately became the first choice in the middle of the defence, teaming up with Derek Jeffries once Roy Barry had lost his place after a sudden attack of pleurisy.

Undoubtedly the inspiration for the side was Peter Taylor, who scored for the England Under-21's on his debut, and went on to play for the senior side while still in the Third Division with Palace, but another player who made an important contribution was Mark Lindsay, one of several youth players thrown into the first team by Allison.

Len Chatterton

Lindsay was used mainly in a defensive midfield position, and occasionally as a genuine sweeper, and was central to Palace's success in the first part of the season. He was quick to the loose ball and accurate in his passing, and exemplified the policy at that time of building attacks from deep positions. Sadly, he lost his form after a good start and was superseded at first by Nicky Chatterton, the groundsman's son, and then by Martin Hinshelwood, both of whom were colleagues of Lindsay in the youth team, and both prone to repeated injuries. At one stage of the season, with Jim Cannon and Dave Swindlehurst established in the side, the average age of the outfield players was under 21, a reflection of the manager's abiding belief in youth. Swindlehurst, who had started only four first team games the year before, eventually emerged as the best option

at centre forward, seeing off Mick Hill and the briefly on-loan Wyn Davies, and went on to finish joint top scorer with 15 goals. He had apparently conquered his terrible pre-match nerves thanks to Allison's novel psychological approach, and another player to benefit from this emphasis on a positive mental attitude was Paddy Mulligan, who won his place back from Stewart Jump after being inspired by a series of films on sports psychology from America. It wasn't long, though, before Peter Wall was back in the reckoning, this time after a bout of hepatitis, and Mulligan's patchy Palace career ended with him moving on to West Bromwich Albion.

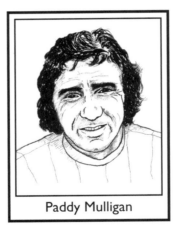
Paddy Mulligan

Despite an excellent start to the season, which saw Palace on top of the division at the beginning of October after four straight wins, results began to dip as winter approached, and a sequence of seven games with only one victory pushed them down to sixth place, although still well in touch. Malcolm Allison was clear about the reason for this decline, blaming the poor state of the pitches for reducing matches to lotteries, and advocating a winter break in the season. He showed his true colours with the splendid cry of 'How can you expect an artist to work in these conditions?', in spite of which his next purchase was the artisan Phil Holder from Spurs. Holder's efforts, tireless though they were, could not help to raise Palace into a promotion place, and they eventually finished in a disappointing fifth position, although only a few points away from third place. In the end, it was the form away from home against eminently beatable sides that let them down, together with too many drawn games at home, and

Phil Holder

once again a lot of entertaining football had led nowhere. Yet despite this, the crowd had stayed loyal, averaging around 17,000, which was exceptional for the Third Division, and Allison's flair for publicity undoubtedly endeared him to the fans, regardless of his conspicuous lack of success. In the final game of the season, with their Promotion chance gone, Palace lost in front of a miserable crowd of 2,025 at Tranmere, who were already relegated to the Fourth Division. Not a game worthy of too much interest, perhaps, except that it saw the debut of another youngster, the 16-year-old left back Kenny Sansom, who was to develop into one of the outstanding players of all time for both Crystal Palace and England.

1975–76

'Palace and Derby. That's my forecast for the Cup Final on May 1st.'
Malcolm Allison

Once again Palace were among the favourites for promotion, and this time it looked a certainty for most of the season, after five straight wins had given them their best start ever. The foundation of their success was an excellent defence, comprised of the rejuvenated Peter Wall, now playing at right back, Jim Cannon at left back, Ian Evans with Derek Jeffries in the centre and goalkeeper Paul Hammond back in the team after losing his place temporarily to Tony Burns. Peter Taylor, Nicky Chatterton,

Nicky Chatterton

Martin Hinshelwood and Phil Holder made up the midfield, while up front Dave Swindlehurst had a new partner in David Kemp. Kemp had been signed from non-league Slough Town, leaving the transfer-listed Alan Whittle scrapping unhappily in the reserves, and he made a good start for Palace, scoring seven goals in the first eight games, but it was Ian Evans who earned the headlines with a wonderful hat-trick against Colchester. This was quite a feat for any Palace player, let alone a defender, and it was the first since Barry Dyson's

in 1966. Indeed, since Evans the only defenders to score hat-tricks for Palace are Dean Gordon and Danny Butterfield, and this illustrates the value of his contribution to attack as well as to a sound defence. Like most footballers, Evans obeyed a catalogue of superstitions, a particularly revolting one being the habit of always chewing the same bit of gum throughout the game, which involved sticking it on the bench at half-time and popping it back in his mouth for the second half. One of the less obscure footballer's superstitions is the habit of not having a haircut during a cup run, a tradition which died out during the spikey-topped 1980s, but which was widespread in the shaggy '70s. This meant some pretty dishevelled hairstyles in the Palace team this season, because this was the year of the great cup run, the abiding symbol of which was 'Mal's Fedora'.

By the time of the first round of the FA Cup, Palace were already clear at the top of the Third Division, having only lost once in 18 games, and must have fancied their chances at home to Isthmian League side Walton & Hersham. Victory was achieved only narrowly, with David Kemp scoring from close range against several of his former Slough teammates, and on that evidence few people would have imagined that Palace would progress to the semi-finals. That they did so well owed something to the fact that they were drawn away from home in every round from then on, since Palace's away form in the league that season was spectacular, and they actually ended the season with more points earned on their travels than at home. With Palace now a feared team, sides would come to Selhurst Park determined to go away with a point, but on their own grounds they found they could not match Palace when it came to an open game of football. Having beaten Millwall after a replay in the second round, the third round of the cup saw the 2–1 defeat of another non-league side, Scarborough, but not too many people would have shared Malcolm Allison's optimism when the draw for the fourth round paired his team with First Division Leeds United, at Elland Road. David Swindlehurst's headed goal from Taylor's free kick completed a genuine piece of giant-killing, and this victory gave the team fresh confidence after a surprising loss of form in the league during December, although Palace had built up such an impressive lead that despite four consecutive defeats they still entered the new year on top of Division Three.

Dave Swindlehurst

Allison's hunger for publicity was never more evident, and he was constantly pictured in a variety of poses, from brandishing his big cigar and daft hat to sharing a bath with Fiona Richmond, then notorious as a purveyor of soft porn. The fans had been used to media exposure since Allison's arrival but now, with the players having made a record, and cheap replicas of the fedora on sale, all sorts of people were professing themselves lifelong supporters, and a whole generation of Croydon schoolboys were suddenly

proudly sporting red and blue scarves. Victory in the fifth round was somehow inevitable, and it came against Chelsea at Stamford Bridge.

Palace took a 2–0 lead through Taylor and Chatterton before Chelsea drew level, only for Taylor to score an unforgettable winner direct from a free kick. By now, Alan Whittle had fought his way back into the side, and it was his last ever goal for Palace that won the sixth-round tie against the leading Second Division side Sunderland, and put them into the semi-final for the first time in their history. The players had got there by quite simply playing a quality of football that their more illustrious opponents – Leeds, Chelsea and Sunderland – couldn't hope to match, and allied to excellent tactical organisation was the total belief in themselves that made Palace special, which is why Malcolm Allison will always command affection from the fans who were around then.

Tony Burns

Despite these famous victories Palace had now slipped down the league table to third place after too many mediocre home performances, and they also suffered the loss of Martin Hinshelwood for the rest of the season, hospitalised for a cartilage operation. Hinshelwood was never truly fit ever again, and although he played a handful of games over the next two seasons, he was eventually forced to retire from the game at the age of 24. It is quite difficult to assess his influence on the team, because although he was by no means spectacular, he was a dedicated disciple of Allison and Venables, and was arguably the most intelligent member of Palace's midfield.

Martin Hinshelwood

As Palace prepared for their semi-final, against Southampton at Stamford Bridge, Malcolm Allison made another of his confident predictions: 'Palace and Derby. That's my forecast for the Cup Final on May 1st.", and he went on to tempt fate by looking forward to appearing in next season's European Cup-Winners' Cup. Although Southampton were pressing for promotion from the Second Division, many people made Palace favourites to reach the final, comparing their cup run with that of the Saints, who had taken the easier route of overcoming Aston Villa, Blackpool, West Brom and Bradford. Far from being overconfident, on the day the Palace players were paralysed by nerves, and they performed nowhere near their

best. After Peter Taylor had gone off injured early on, there was no source of inspiration, and Southampton won rather comfortably, by two goals to nil, surprised at the absence of any threat to their own goalmouth.

The feeling of anti-climax was certainly felt very strongly by the fans at the game, who had come to believe in Allison's prophecies, and the same sense of disappointment spread throughout the players, who completely lost any sense of purpose in the remaining league games. They won only one out of seven, and amazingly missed out on promotion once again, having looked the biggest certainties ever earlier in the season. Needing to win the final two games to go up, Palace could only draw 0–0 at home to a mediocre Chesterfield, and it was hard for the fans to swallow the fact that the season had so quickly turned so sour. If Palace had reached the Cup Final, then Malcolm Allison's extravagant boasts would have been acceptable, but I suspect that a quieter approach, of the kind favoured by Steve Coppell in 1990, might have seen them at least concentrate harder on their league position, and gain something from an extraordinary season. As it was, Allison's three years ended with him leaving 'by mutual consent' and being succeeded naturally by his deputy, Terry Venables. Although known as a showman himself, Venables had until now appeared thoughtful and dignified in comparison to Big Mal, and he was now ready for the next step towards his ultimate goal, the job of England manager.

1976-77

In many ways, Malcolm Allison's most tangible achievement at the club was the development of a strong youth policy, which began to bear fruit just as he left, enabling Terry Venables to enjoy the benefit and much of the kudos. The first of the crop to make the first team was Kenny Sansom, who had looked outstanding in the few games he had played after Palace's semi-final defeat, and Venables immediately installed him as first choice left back. Cannon moved into the centre alongside Evans, precipitating the departure of Derek Jeffries back up North to Chester, and Peter Wall made up a back four that was among the best the club has had. Venables declared his intentions for the future by predicting early on some others of the youth team players likely to break into the first team during the season, naming Neil Smillie, Vince Hilaire, Ian Walsh and Peter Caswell. In addition, Paul Hinshelwood, who had already been converted from a centre forward to a full back in the reserves, was being groomed to take over from Peter Wall. As it was, he came into the side sooner than expected, but as a midfield replacement for his brother Martin.

Yet another change of playing strip saw the adoption of another supposedly continental style, the diagonal red and blue sash across a white shirt replacing the previous design, which was apparently 'too drab and dark, especially under floodlights'. I don't remember anyone complaining about it, and I suspect that the change had more to with the new manager's commercial instincts. Venables' obsession with continental football also manifested itself in an exaggerated version of Allison's passing game, which frustrated the fans, with each move being built slowly and deliberately from the back, and possession being paramount. In a way, the departure of the more flamboyant Peter Taylor to

Spurs can be seen as a necessary part of the Venables plan, and although the fans were sad to see him go, he was obviously too talented to stay in the Third Division, having already won four England caps, and he went with their blessing. Alan Whittle had left for Orient and David Kemp was soon to move on to Portsmouth, but Venables had already signed a couple of unknown players as potential replacements – the not very loveable rogues, Barry Silkman and Rachid Harkouk.

Harkouk was a wayward attacker with an occasionally explosive shot, which earned him the inevitable nickname of 'Rash the Smash', while Silkman was an out and out winger who had fallen out with his last manager at Hereford, John Sillett, who had wanted him to work on running back, covering and tackling rather than concentrating on attack, and Silkman never did take to that particular aspect of the game.

Rachid Harkouk

In contrast to the wonderful start to the 1975–76 season, early results were rather disappointing and for most of the season it looked as though Palace would end up missing out on promotion once again, although this time the results at home were excellent. In an extremely closely matched division, though, there were rarely less than ten sides within a few points of a promotion place, and Palace were always threatening to put together a string of results, it being widely acknowledged that they were potentially a cut above the rest.

Ricky Heppolette

In the FA Cup, the first round went to two replays against Brighton, the eventual victory coming by a single goal at the neutral ground of Stamford Bridge, and after a comfortable 4–0 result over non-league Enfield, Palace had to travel to face Liverpool in the third round. This time there were no brash predictions of an upset, but Palace organised themselves well and were considered unfortunate to come away only with a goalless draw, largely thanks to a series of good saves by Ray Clemence. Despite Palace leading 1–0 in the replay, Liverpool eventually went through 3–2, and the fans chorus of 'we can concentrate on the league now' was for once a wise thought. By now Venables had added the experienced George Graham to the midfield, enabling Paul Hinshelwood to finally take up his duties at right back, and the reserve team forward Steve Perrin had

come in to partner Swindlehurst up front. An experiment with the Indian born Ricky Heppolette proved a flop, though, which meant that Holder and Chatterton kept their places in a reliable, if rather dull midfield. Graham's ability to control the game at his own painfully slow pace served Palace well, and it was his influence which helped to improve their position at the start of new year into fifth place.

Barry Silkman

Scoring goals was proving to be somewhat of a problem, with Perrin being too similar to Swindlehurst in his rather lumbering style, and it was the purchase of Jeff Bourne from Derby County which in the end proved to be the season's turning point. The fee for Bourne came from the sale of goalkeeper Paul Hammond to Tampa Bay Rowdies in the North American Soccer League, where he joined Mark Lindsay, and the fact that Venables felt compelled to justify the £30,000 outlay illustrates that the days of the big money signings were way past, and that Ray Bloye was not prepared to invest in the team, despite having enjoyed bigger crowds than most in the Third Division. Bourne came to Palace rather overweight from being out of the team at Derby, but once he was fit he made a crucial contribution to the promotion effort, scoring nine goals in his fifteen games, and complementing Swindlehurst nicely. He inspired Palace's best two victories of the season, 5–0 against Swindon and 4–0 against Sheffield Wednesday, and suddenly promotion became a possibility, if still a slim one.

Steve Perrin

Venables was livid when a rearranged game at Port Vale was played on a waterlogged pitch, after the earlier fixture had been postponed at very short notice due to illness and injury among the opposition. Vale won 4–1 with George Graham sent off in a bad-tempered game, and once again Palace were written off for the season with four games remaining and six points to make up on third placed Wrexham. However, two of the four games were against the Welsh side themselves, and after winning at Chesterfield, and at home to Wrexham and Lincoln City, Palace's final game of the season saw them travelling to the Racecourse Ground in midweek needing to win by two clear goals to even have a chance of going up. Since Wrexham had not lost at home all season, the odds looked very much against Palace.

The manner of Palace's victory that evening is still hard to believe. After Swindlehurst and Perrin had made it 2–0 to Palace, Wrexham woke up and fought back to 2–2, which remained the score line until the last minute of the game. When Harkouk scored Palace's third on the stroke of full time, it still didn't seem to matter much to the celebrating Welsh supporters, but straight from the restart, and in injury time, Jeff Bourne – fittingly – made the score 4–2 and completed an unforgettable night. I only wish I could claim I was there, but the elation I felt when hearing the score on the radio must have been magnified in the hearts of those at the game, and many were moved to tears at the remarkable manner of the victory, and at the prospect of promotion from the Third Division, although this was still not certain. Wrexham were completely shattered by the result, and although they could still have gone up at Palace's expense, they lost their final game against the champions Mansfield, and Terry Venables won promotion to Division Two in his first season as a manager, one of the few honours he ever achieved in English football.

1977-78

Of the three promoted teams, it was the champions, Mansfield, who fared worst in the Second Division, ultimately being relegated after just one season. Palace and Brighton, always very closely matched, both looked at home straight away, and in the end it was the Seagulls, a team which Alan Mullery had built around Mark Lawrenson and the talented Peter Ward, who narrowly missed promotion to the First Division. It is of note that from 1974 to 1981, over a period of seven seasons, Palace and Brighton were always in the same division as each other, winning promotion at the same time as they progressed from the Third to the First. The rivalry that has built up between the two sets of supporters was fuelled when old enemies Venables and Mullery had a public slanging match after a particularly bad-tempered cup game the previous season, the Brighton manager calling Palace a team of 'animals', and Mullery has been despised ever since at Selhurst Park, not least for his vulgar gestures to the Palace fans.

Terry Venables

It was Palace who started the season best, winning their first two games against Millwall and Mansfield, and moving into third place with seven games played.

Venables gave further indication of his faith in the players who had won the FA Youth Cup by introducing two more of them into the team alongside Sansom, namely Peter Nicholas and Vince Hilaire.

Peter Nicholas

Nicholas was at this stage perceived as a defender and only played a couple of early games as cover for injured players, but Hilaire was given a good run as an inside forward rather than the more orthodox winger he was to become. A surprise inclusion for the team against Mansfield was Martin Hinshelwood, who had supposedly retired the year before, but who had been kept on the staff to help with coaching. With George Graham and Phil Holder both injured, Venables was forced to press Hinshelwood into the midfield and he played well, even scoring a goal, before being substituted late in the game.

Having beaten Brentford over two legs in the first round of the League Cup, Palace were given a chance for revenge over the FA Cup winners Southampton in the second round, but threw it away by missing a penalty in a goalless draw during which the referee sent off Phil Boyer for head-butting Jim Cannon, and Cannon for retaliating.

In the replay at The Dell, which went to extra time, Southampton were leading 2–1 when Palace were awarded a penalty on the stroke of full time. Jeff Bourne's spot kick was saved but George Graham followed up to put the ball in the net for the equaliser. As the players left the field, most of them shared the belief of the crowd that 2–2 was the final score, but it transpired that the referee had disallowed the goal, ruling that full time was up the moment the goalkeeper had saved the original shot. Never one to take defeat graciously, Terry Venables had a good old moan about being cheated by the referee, although he had in fact made the correct decision.

George Graham

Putting this setback behind them, Palace went on to beat Sheffield United and leaders Bolton in the league, despite George Graham being sent off again, to stay in touch at the top. The programme for the next game, against Fulham, included an item about Ian Evans, who had by now played 13 times for Wales and was looking forward to the imminent World Cup qualifier against Scotland, for which he was an automatic choice. The Fulham game changed the whole direction of Palace's season, and brought Evans' career for both Palace

and Wales to a cruel end. The once great George Best was now playing for Fulham, and when he and Evans went for a loose ball around the halfway line they arrived at exactly the same time; the cracking of bone produced an unmistakable sound that could be heard by all 28,343 people in the crowd. Best was unscathed, but Ian Evans had sustained a double fracture to his right leg which put him in hospital for months.

The loss of Evans affected Palace's form very badly, and their position deteriorated steadily to that of a mid-table side, which on reflection turned out to be a blessing for Venables, giving him a very convenient opportunity to experiment with his young players. He was constantly being asked why he didn't buy anyone to strengthen the team and push for promotion, and he was always clear with his reply: Bloye wouldn't give him any money. He believed, however, that the youth team, now heading towards a second successive FA Youth Cup victory, would form the basis of his side for next season, and with the breathing space created by having earned points early on, he devoted the rest of the year to his experiments. The first task, though, was to replace Evans at centre back, because the optimistic forecasts of an early recovery were soon found to be far from true. Peter Wall played there for a few games, and then Mel Blyth came back from Southampton on a three-month loan, forming a nostalgic link with the days of Bert Head, which now seemed light years away. Next into the number six shirt was Peter Nicholas, soon to be succeeded by Billy Gilbert, who formed a partnership with Jim Cannon that was to last for the next six years.

Venables knew that the current team would not last too long in the First Division if they were elevated too soon, so he was ruthless in his purge of anyone who wasn't either young enough or good enough to have a part to play for the next few years, and started to trim his squad in preparation for next season. The first to go was Jeff Bourne, who signed for Dallas Tornado, followed by Peter Wall and Stewart Jump. Steve Perrin was then sold to Plymouth for £35,000, and Neil Smillie and Tony Burns went to America on loan for the rest of the season. To replace Burns, Venables invested £40,000 in Aston Villa's John Burridge, the ultimate goalkeeping clown and Bruce Grobbelaar's role model, who instantly became popular with the fans after years of enduring the grim countenances of Burns and Hammond.

Sansom remained. The celebrity status of Terry Venables was being enhanced with a TV serialisation of his 'Hazell' books, co-written with Gordon Williams, and at the same time as he was coining it in from that, the board of directors were busy concocting a deal with Sainsburys, which the subsequent chairman Ron Noades implied lined their own pockets at the club's severe long-term expense. Several of the young players were already representing their countries at youth level, and were showing great promise for the future, and everything seemed on the up and up. The great surprise, given this anticipation of imminent success, was that it actually happened.

Billy Gilbert

Palace's final position of ninth in Division Two was a good one considering the experimental nature of the team and their extreme youth, especially when one realises that five of the players – Nicholas, Gilbert, Hilaire, Murphy and Fenwick – were combining their first team duties with playing in the Youth Cup. Venables had done well to completely transform the team bequeathed to him by Malcolm Allison, without having been able to spend much money, and after two years only Chatterton, Cannon, Swindlehurst and

1978–79

It is worth taking a close look at the team that won promotion at the end of this season in some detail, because as well as being the best ever seen at Palace, it was certainly the most settled, with the smallest number of players to be used in the course of the season – only 18, including Barry Silkman's one appearance as a substitute. The oldest player in the squad at the start of the season was goalkeeper John Burridge, at 26. As well as being a dedicated crowd pleaser – he would endeavour to make the most straightforward save look spectacular – he kept the defence going throughout the game with constant shouted instructions, and his enthusiasm for the game was contagious. Right back Paul Hinshelwood was a much better player in that position than as a striker, and was still only 22, while Sansom at left back was so exceptionally gifted that he was already in the reckoning for a place in the England team at the age of 19. In central defence Jim Cannon, already in his seventh season in the first team, was not yet 25, but was a seasoned old pro compared to his 18-year-old partner Billy Gilbert, whose physical toughness belied his youth. Three more teenagers, Murphy, Nicholas and Hilaire, combined with 24-year-old Nicky Chatterton in midfield, and the top scorer for the past three seasons, Dave Swindlehurst, was still only 21.

With Harkouk having gone to Q.P.R. and Silkman shortly to join Malcolm Allison at Plymouth, the attack was augmented by the £180,000 signing of Mike Elwiss from Preston, who kept Ian Walsh out of the side for the first dozen games. Elwiss was the latest and most promising in a growing list of partners up front for Swindlehurst, succeeding Mick Hill, Dave Kemp, Steve Perrin and Jeff Bourne. He had once been on the verge of signing for Liverpool four years earlier while at Doncaster, but the deal fell through when the club bumped up his price at the last minute. Although not a very prolific goal scorer to start with, Elwiss was a skilful ball player of the type Venables always admired, and his influence resulted in Palace's neat passing moves being extended into the penalty area, with speculative long-range shots becoming a rarity. Although most people expected Palace to be among the front runners once again, even the fans were surprised at how well the season began, with their team quickly going to the top of the table and remaining unbeaten for 11 games. Evidence that this was to be Palace's lucky season came in the 1–1 home draw with West Ham, with Billy Gilbert's fluked goal from his own half reminiscent of John Sewell's famous punt against Leeds years earlier.

John Burridge

In the League Cup it took First Division Aston Villa two replays to get past Palace, with the final 3–0 score line at Coventry's neutral ground being easily the heaviest defeat of the season, and the only time all year that John Burridge let in more than two goals. Indeed, it is unlikely that Palace's defensive record for the season – 24 goals conceded in 42 league games – will ever be equalled, and has certainly never been approached since. To attribute Palace's success simply to the defence, though, would be a mistake, because the essence of their game was controlled possession in every area of the field, Venables' European dream realised in the English Second Division. In midfield the cocksure Jerry Murphy was already a master of first-time control and accurate passing, and Peter Nicholas, although less adventurous with the ball, invariably found himself in the right position to either attack or defend. The genuine element of flair came from Vince Hilaire, outrageously skilful although inconsistent, and always looking for the chance to get the ball at his feet and go past the full back.

The final component which made the midfield complete was the signing of Steve Kember from Leicester, which meant Chatterton finally moving on to Millwall. Kember's return to Selhurst Park after seven years away turned out to be an inspired move, but in fact Venables only intended to buy him and defender Tony Hazell as squad members, to cover for likely injuries to the younger players. Kember's experience and undiluted passion for the game was exactly what the other players needed to sustain their impetus to the end of the season, and with George Graham unable to regain his first team place, Kember was able to help Palace into the First Division for the second time in his career. The surprising thing was the lack of injuries throughout the season, and despite Hinshelwood being out for two months after a cartilage operation, with Terry Fenwick substituting at right back, the major problem was a similar injury to Mike Elwiss half way through the season, from which he never fully recovered.

Having started the season so well, a slight dip in results after Christmas, with seven draws from nine games, served as a warning

against complacency, and a promising FA Cup run was thwarted in the fifth round with a surprising home defeat at the hands of Wolves. Come the spring, however, the young players blossomed again, with Ian Walsh proving an admirable replacement for Elwiss up front, and the defence becoming even meaner, conceding only five goals in the final 17 games. Remarkably, with only three games to go, Palace were occupying their lowest position of the whole season – fourth behind Stoke, Brighton and Sunderland – and with no apparently easy fixtures remaining. Venables had been saying all season that with no outstanding team in the Division nothing would be decided until the final kick, and so it proved.

Paul Hinshelwood

The 2–0 home victory over a very ordinary Notts County was comprehensive enough, but it was the next game, at Orient's cramped Brisbane Road ground, that was to prove crucial, for a defeat would in the event have condemned Palace to another frustrating year in Division Two. The latter half of the season had taught the players to fight for possession when they weren't being given space by the opposition and this quality, typified by Steve Kember more than anyone, enabled them to scrape through a tense game and hang on to the narrow lead provided by Swindlehurst's goal.

That victory, under such pressure against a good side, boosted their confidence and that of the fans, so that when it came to the last game – a rearranged fixture against Burnley on the Friday night before the Cup Final – an amazing crowd of 51,482 turned out to witness another piece of Selhurst Park history, a crowd figure that will never be equalled. Promotion was still not certain, with at least a point needed to climb above Sunderland in third place, but in the event the passionate atmosphere, enhanced as always under the floodlights, inspired Palace to play as well as they had all year. This was a bit of a surprise, given that the imperative was simply not to lose, which can very often result in turgid games.

delirious. Time had shrunk, and the ten-year-old boy innocently cheering Mark Lazarus on his lap of honour against Fulham in 1969 had become a twenty year old celebrating the same feeling of pure joy. Palace had made it to Division One by sticking uncompromisingly to the principles introduced by Malcolm Allison five years earlier, although his teams had never quite been able to put them into practice. Whereas some of Allison's players would not be convinced of the value of patience and cautious possession, Venables was able to start from scratch with his youngsters, and he deserved a great deal of credit for constructing a team in his own image, playing in a style that was unique among the lower divisions.

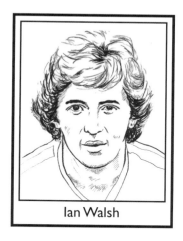

Ian Walsh

Ian Walsh's precisely aimed header put Palace ahead and when Swindlehurst made it 2–0 from distance we all knew that we were worthy champions ahead of Brighton and Stoke. The players and the ecstatic fans celebrated promotion together and I set off on my moped, replaying the goals in my head and feeling dangerously

1979-80

At long last, having made it to the First Division on a shoestring, Ray Bloye granted his manager some money to spend, and Venables could hardly contain his relief at being able to buy two 'big name' players. Gerry Francis, erstwhile England captain, had always been prone to injury but was still regarded as one of the country's most sophisticated midfield players, while Mike Flanagan – a prolific scorer for Charlton – was also renowned for a punch-up on the pitch with his bearded partner Derek Hales. It is difficult to imagine now, but at this time Flanagan was being touted as a possibility for the England team. In fact his style was very similar to that of the luckless Mike Elwiss, but without that player's cutting edge, and he eventually found his best position later in his career in QPR's midfield. Flanagan, then, started the season in place of Ian Walsh up front, and Francis took over from Kember, who Venables did not consider up to playing in Division One, having served his purpose.

Mike Flanagan

These two additions to the side did nothing to disrupt the cohesion of the team, and the quality of football played in the first couple of months of the season quickly dispelled the doubts that many people had about

the true worth of Venables' young stars. Vince Hilaire, in particular, was looking exceptional and thriving on the service from an occasionally brilliant Francis. Jerry Murphy, reaching his peak tragically early in his career, epitomised the energy-saving approach to midfield play so favoured by Venables. Kenny Sansom, having played his first game for England in the post-season home international game against Wales, was already acknowledged as peerless in that position, and even Jim Cannon was looking like a player of international class.

Early results tended to suggest a difficult time ahead, with draws against Manchester City, Southampton and Middlesbrough followed by another stalemate in the League Cup against Stockport, twice Palace's conquerors in that competition during the 1970s. Suddenly though, everything clicked and within a week they had beaten Derby County 4–0, and then slaughtered Stockport 7–0 in the home leg of the cup tie, with Flanagan scoring twice in each game. These two results set up a run of games during which Palace beat Aston Villa, Stoke and finally Ipswich, to end September at the top of Division One, along the way earning Terry Venables a bottle of whisky. The victory over Ipswich, still one of the division's better teams, was the apogee of what Palace had been working towards since Allison's time: every player was constantly thinking about his position in relation to the play, and each seemed able to find space and time to control the ball and pass accurately to a team mate. The principle seems very simple, but only Liverpool were able to perfect it consistently in England at the time, making it virtually impossible for lesser players to compete on equal terms. And although it might be heretical to say so, at times it became very boring. When the system worked, however, good results kept the fans happy, and Palace's result against Ipswich was executed with such efficiency that the score might well have been extended. Particularly enjoyable was the fourth goal, started and finished by a rampant Jim Cannon, having the time of his life; he won the ball in his own half, laid it out to the left, and timed his run into the box perfectly to meet the cross with a sweet volley.

Jim Cannon

lavish praise: whilst that is undoubtedly true of Sansom, it does not explain why the combined wisdom of Terry Venables and his lieutenant Gerry Francis could not keep them on a straight course towards the success of which they were surely capable. One thing is certain, that there was only one way to go, and Palace went that way with a vengeance for the next five years, with little respite and precious little to cheer.

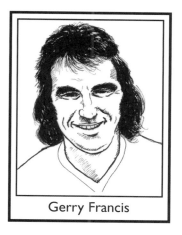

Gerry Francis

In moving to the top of the table with such style, the amount of publicity in the media reached a new level, beyond even Malcolm Allison's wildest dreams, and whichever hack coined the phrase 'The Team of the Eighties' provided his fellows with an easy reference point for whatever they wrote about Palace for the next decade, most of it snide. At the time, though, the comment was all favourable, and it was easy to believe that Venables was in charge of a team capable of challenging the likes of Liverpool and Nottingham Forest at their own game. Dreams of the championship, and at the very least qualifying for Europe, were commonplace, and I have yet to hear a satisfactory theory for why everything went quite so badly wrong. The usual explanation is that the players were too green to handle the considerable pressure of success and

Directly after reaching the heights by beating Ipswich, Palace stumbled to a run of five games without a win, and although still playing well enough, the extravagant claims of greatness became tempered. The 'Team of the Eighties' tag was still in vogue, though, and two excellent victories followed: against Manchester City, now managed by Malcolm Allison, and – for the only time to date in the league – against Terry Neill's Arsenal. The City game was the most entertaining of the season, with extensive coverage on TV, and reaffirmed Palace's reputation as a genuine force in the First Division. Also notable was a 1–0 victory over Brian Clough's Nottingham Forest team, then the reigning European Champions. By now, though, Palace had fallen down to eighth position, and the players were beginning to believe too much in their own publicity. They couldn't understand why the points weren't just falling into their laps, considering how very good they apparently were, and having lost only six of their previous 60 league matches, a run of four defeats from five games came as a new and totally devastating experience to them. Although Venables had taught his players to stay calm and patient when in control of a game, he hadn't equipped them to cope with the crisis of confidence that defeat can bring, and they never again came to resemble the precocious team that had strolled to the top of the league just a couple of months previously.

After being knocked out of the FA Cup at the third attempt by Swansea City, the end of the season became as dull and disappointing as the start had been bright and promising. The best late performance came in the 1–1 draw at Arsenal, where Sansom scored his only goal of the season and Pat Jennings saved a penalty from Gerry Francis, but with only one victory in the last ten games Palace collapsed to finish 13th in the table, still their highest position ever. The backlash had begun, but worse, far worse was to come.

Jerry Murphy

Already Kenny Sansom was talking about getting away, and his club form at least was in decline, and Jerry Murphy, not for the last time, appeared indifferent to what was happening. With goals becoming a rare commodity Dave Swindlehurst was made the scapegoat, and after being dropped in favour of Ian Walsh he was transferred to Derby County. He actually became a more dangerous player after leaving Selhurst Park, but it must be said that at the time he did look rather stale.

During the summer Terry Venables pulled off one of the worst transfer deals ever, with Ken Sansom moving to Arsenal in return for Clive Allen and Paul Barron. The 19-year-old Allen had yet to play for the Gunners since his move from QPR, but was valued at £1 million, and goalkeeper Barron was supposedly worth £400,000. John Burridge was a far better keeper, but was in dispute over pay, and was relegated to the reserves. The new partnership of Flanagan and Allen stimulated the feeble imaginations of the tabloid papers, and the two strikers were more memorable dressing up as the music-hall act for the cameras than they ever were on the pitch, only playing 17 games together in all.

After two early setbacks, being beaten by Liverpool and Spurs, a 5–2 victory over Middlesbrough gave considerable encouragement, with Clive Allen scoring a hat-trick and in the process playing his best ever game in Palace colours. Any fancy ideas were quickly stifled, though, by a sequence of seven league defeats on the trot, Palace's worst run since 1925 and one which was sadly to be repeated later in the season.

By now the relationship between the manager and the board of directors had deteriorated to the point where Venables could no longer see a future for himself at the club, and although he stayed until the end of October he had already lost whatever commitment he may have had. The fans, needless to say, were kept in the dark as to the real reasons for his disenchantment, but one can surmise that Ray Bloye's tightfistedness when it was obvious that the squad needed strengthening had become intolerable after four years with hardly any money being spent, a period during which it must have been absolutely rolling in. Burridge's supposed falling-out with Venables was a red herring, as the two

men were shortly reunited at QPR, and in retrospect one could see that Bloye himself was preparing to cut and run, having brought the club to the brink of financial ruin.

Paul Barron

When Venables finally resigned, to pursue his plastic fantasy at Loftus Road, readers of the programme for the next home game, against Leicester, were able to read – in his own words – the thoughts of Chairman Bloye: his regret at losing Venables after all he had done for the club. The text of the chairman's message was printed in the space reserved for the manager's regular platitudes, and the words 'Terry Venables' appear, like Banquo's ghost, behind a most unappealing picture of Bloye. The man temporarily in charge of the winning team that day was a long-serving member of the coaching staff – Ernie Walley – but Bloye made it clear that '..we will appoint Terry's successor as soon as possible. We want a young man with a progressive outlook.' This certainly appeared to put Walley out of the reckoning, but Jim Cannon led a deputation demanding that the board give him the job, and Ernie Walley was officially appointed to the dubious position of 'Caretaker Manager'.

The new man certainly had the confidence of the players, since he had looked after many of them in their days with the youth team, but despite three wins and a draw from five games – their best spell of a miserable season – they stayed firmly anchored to the foot of the table. The fans foresaw little joy under Walley's management, and were clamouring for the return of Malcolm Allison, recently sacked by Manchester City but still a popular figure with those who had so enjoyed the cup run of 1976. He was the complete opposite of the dour and uncharismatic Walley and their wish came true at the beginning of December when once again Bloye asked Allison to save his bacon. John Burridge, Mike Flanagan and Terry Fenwick bailed out to join Venables at QPR, and were replaced in the team by the second-string players Terry Boyle and Tony Sealey. With a badly depleted and demoralised squad, and no chance of spending any money on new players, Allison was left with a hopeless task and Palace managed only a single victory under his brief stewardship. Within a year they had gone from a team of bright, talented and above all confident players to become disillusioned and completely aimless.

Ernie Walley

With crowd revenue steadily dropping and relegation looking a certainty, Bloye couldn't get rid of the club quickly enough and didn't have to be asked twice when Ron Noades made him an offer. Like the Tory government blaming their Labour predecessors for all their troubles, Noades quickly set about establishing what a mess he had inherited. One wonders why a shrewd businessman would have bought such a clapped-out heap of a club if it really was in such a state, and whether the 'Wimbledon Supremo' Noades was conned. One area of operation which had certainly collapsed was that of youth team development, which had been so beneficial to the club just a few years before but which was now moribund. Quite apart from the state of the finances this was the most damaging legacy of Bloye's reign, and for the next five years the only home-grown players to make any impact in the first team were Steve Lovell, Shaun Brooks and Gary Stebbing.

Noades wanted to rebuild Crystal Palace in Wimbledon's image, and the first step was to import Dario Gradi as Malcolm Allison's replacement. Sacking Allison was unpopular in any case, but after Gradi had supervised seven straight defeats – and effectively relegation from Division One – he had no chance of winning the crowd's support. Peter Nicholas, about the only player to emerge with any credit from this period, wisely accepted Arsenal's offer to stay in the First Division and in return Palace took on the former local schoolboy star David Price, who had by now become an enthusiastic but ineffective plodder. Making their debuts at the same time were Tommy Langley, off-loaded by Venables from QPR, and Brian Bason, but none of the new players could do anything to rescue the season, and it was a very tough time to be a Palace fan.

David Price

Palace didn't gain their first win of 1981 until beating Birmingham 3–1 in April, but by then relegation had become a mathematical certainty with five games still to play, and no team can ever have had fewer excuses for going down than Palace had that year. Of the four managers, Venables, Allison and Gradi had enjoyed one win each in charge, with Walley seeing his team victorious on three occasions. The home crowd of 9,820 who witnessed that rare win against Birmingham, and two equally rare goals from Langley, was the worst since 1968, but once again worse was to come, and this time everybody somehow knew it.

1981–82

The name of Tommy Langley has become like some jaded comedian's meaningless catch phrase, a cheap way to get a laugh, but I am prepared to defend him nonetheless. His playing style epitomised Palace's collective approach for the whole season, with endeavour being the only quality in evidence, and with few results. Although he only scored three goals all season no one has tried harder than Langley did for Palace, and for that at least he deserved praise rather than the vilification he received. To say that he was simply useless doesn't tell the whole story, because he was a player who had been extremely good as a youngster at Chelsea and he knew that he wasn't doing himself justice with his performances at Palace. It must be very frustrating for a striker in particular when he knows that he can do so much better, and since goals are such a clear measure of success or failure it is easy to lose confidence completely. Langley chased everything, but there was little purpose to Palace's play and it was hard to tell what role he was being asked to perform, since he lacked the strength of a classic centre-forward; his partner Walsh was similarly lightweight, and with Clive Allen having returned to QPR to re-join Venables there was now nobody in the team who knew where the goal was.

The deal which took Allen to QPR involved Steve Wicks – a central defender – moving the other way, and this was another bit of transfer business from which Palace came off badly, after losing the best part of £1 million with the cut-price sale of Flanagan and Francis. With Cannon and Gilbert still a solid partnership in central defence the signing of Wicks seemed a peculiar one at a time when the desperate need was for a striker and a left back, and as things turned out Wicks was injured for most of his short time at Selhurst Park.

Palace at least had the satisfaction of winning a few games early on, which they had forgotten how to do in the woeful season before, but they were dreadfully short of attacking ideas. The midfield of Neil Smillie, David Price, Jerry Murphy and Vince Hilaire was neither robust enough to win the ball or confident enough to use it to any great effect. Gradi's team were given an early opportunity to put one over on Venables' renegades – Burridge, Fenwick, Francis, Flanagan, Allen and Sealy – but on the brand new artificial pitch at Loftus Road an awful game was won not by the best team, but by the least worst. It was incredible to me that it took the Football League nearly ten years to decide that the arguments in favour of all-weather surfaces were far outweighed by those against, chief of which was the rotten entertainment value to the spectator.

Complementing the overall naffness of the team during this season was the match-day programme, once again sporting a cartoon cover. One can recognise some of the characters depicted in uncharacteristic action poses – Langley, Barron and Walsh amongst them – and Dario Gradi looking worried as usual, but I always wondered why the long-forgotten Iain Philip stands with his fists clenched in triumph, although

Tommy Langley

I assume that Jim Cannon is the artist's intended victim.

Shaun Brooks

It was clear before too long that although Gradi was unlikely to repeat Malcolm Allison's feat of immediate relegation to the Third Division, neither was his team going to do any better than finish in a moderate mid-table position. The fans were prepared to be patient, realising as they did that Gradi had hardly any resources at his disposal and the weakest first team squad for years, but Ron Noades was less forgiving. Following three narrow defeats by Derby, Luton and Blackburn, Gradi was sacked after less than ten months in charge, a period during which he had been forced to sell Peter Nicholas, Gerry Francis, Clive Allen and Tony Sealy, replacing them with David Price, Brian Bason, Billy Hughes and Wicks, who had only played four games. It is unsurprising, then, that most fans felt inclined to blame Noades rather than Gradi for the state of things, and it took many years for him to earn any sort of grudging respect. Ironically, Gradi had made his best signing by far just a couple of weeks before his dismissal, when he bought Bristol City's Kevin Mabbutt, brother of the Spurs player Gary and equally likeable. A

less shrewd investment was Steve Galliers, who had served under Gradi and Noades at Wimbledon, but who failed to import that team's aggression to Palace's midfield in the few games he played before returning to Plough Lane.

David Giles

Short of bringing back Malcolm Allison for a third time, the next most popular choice as manager was Steve Kember, a Palace man through and through who had played in the two promotion sides of 1969 and 1979, and who was now in charge of the youth team. Kember made a good start to the job, with a draw and two wins, but he wasn't able to raise his players above the mediocre, despite the efforts of Mabbutt. If Murphy and Hilaire had been playing at anything like their best then I am sure that Mabbutt would have flourished, but he found himself too often having to drop a long way back to find the ball, and was too rarely in scoring positions. In order to try and put some pace into the forward line, Kember made what looked like a very good signing, that of David Giles from Swansea. Giles had been called the Welsh Keegan, simply because of his hairstyle, but he was in fact a fairly straightforward winger, which left the central midfield looking weaker than ever. Murphy had completely lost his way, neither Smillie or Hilaire were ball-winners, Price was injured for most of the rest of the season and Shaun Brooks hadn't really progressed from being a very good England schoolboy. The only time that the midfield began to look more solid was when the return of Wicks allowed Jim Cannon to move forward; this was only a temporary measure though, with Wicks bizarrely moving back to QPR at a loss as soon as results started to improve. It is ironic that the one position that Kember was never able to fill adequately, apart from centre-forward, was that of an aggressive midfielder in the No.4 shirt, for which he would have been the ideal candidate.

that should have been Palace's, and it was QPR who progressed, eventually losing to Spurs in the final.

By now Mabbutt was completely alone up front, with Walsh having been sold to Swansea and Langley utterly ineffective, but he was looking better and better in a declining team, and seemed to be the only hope for the future – if only Palace would buy another striker to help him out. From being fairly comfortable in the middle of the table, Palace slipped steadily towards the relegation zone, and it wasn't until they beat Wrexham in the penultimate game of the season that safety was assured. After another miserable season many fans wanted Ron Noades to go, but of course it was Steve Kember who got the push, after just six months in the job.

Kevin Mabbutt

The one bright spot of the season was reaching the Sixth round of the FA Cup, Palace's best run since the semi-final year of 1976, and the furthest they were to go in the competition for the whole of the 1980s. This time there was no First Division opposition to overcome, and having scraped past Enfield, Bolton and Orient, they faced Venables' hated QPR team for a place in the last four. Such a prize would possibly have saved Kember's managerial skin, but Clive Allen cruelly scored a late winner in a game

Proof, if any were needed, that Ron Noades was some way out of touch with the feelings of the supporters came when he announced the name of the new manager: Alan Mullery, without doubt the most unpopular choice one could imagine. Mullery had been manager of the Brighton side which finished runners-up in Division Two to Palace in 1979, and then moved on to Charlton, from where Noades headhunted him after a year. This left Palace's South London neighbours to soldier on under the unknown Lennie Lawrence, for which they must have been eternally grateful. The bad blood between Palace and Brighton had been at its worst during Mullery's time on the South Coast, and from the moment his appointment was announced the majority of fans – myself included – were convinced that the Chairman had made a dreadful mistake. Noades obviously saw in Mullery the charisma which Gradi and Kember lacked, and an ego to match his own, but he never for a moment threatened to endear himself to Palace fans.

of a series of forgettable forwards he was to buy over the next two years. He also bought Gary Williams, a left back who had been with him at Brighton, and with Neil Smillie joining the Seagulls at the same time there was a place in midfield for Kember's last signing, Henry Hughton. As many people predicted, Kevin Mabbutt made a good start by scoring five goals in the first six games, and Palace earned some respectable results at last. But the essential problem remained, with neither Edwards or Langley doing much to help Mabbutt, and the goals soon dried up.

Alan Mullery

Ron Noades

Mullery's first act as manager was to recognise the need for a big striker to replace Langley, but the player he signed was Wrexham's Ian Edwards, the first

Mullery had declared his intention of buying a new centre-back to allow Cannon to play in midfield but that purchase never materialised, and Cannon's partnership with Billy Gilbert stayed intact for another season. Although Cannon was playing as well as ever, the defence as a whole were looking less and less able to prop up the team, and Hinshelwood and Gilbert had lost their appetite for the game. Gary Williams was soon forced to retire after having a knee operation, and the South African teenager Gavin Nebbeling was drafted into the defence, while the young goalkeeper David Fry came into the side in place of Paul Barron, sold to West Bromwich Albion. Steve Lovell was tried in midfield, but lost his place once Jerry Murphy started coming back to his best form, and was sold on to Millwall where he immediately started scoring goals!

Steve Lovell

Shaun Brooks was unhappy at being left out by Mullery and was put on the transfer list, and all in all it was obvious to the fans that they were paying to watch a very miserable bunch of players. By now, though, the number of punters prepared to stump up for that dubious pleasure had dwindled severely; the home gates had fallen within two years from regularly pushing 30,000 to the point where 10,000 was now considered a good crowd, and Ron Noades' pledge to turn the club around within a year was proving as absurd as it had always seemed. Perhaps the most despicable public act by Noades – considering his criticism of the previous regime – was the dismantling of the youth team, who were suddenly withdrawn from their league in the middle of the season. This was justified by Noades as a necessary cost-cutting measure, but as well as being a prematurely cruel blow to several young hopefuls it seemed doubly stupid for a club whose greatest success to date had been built on a strong and active youth policy.

This period of Palace's history was without doubt the most depressing ever, and if it was difficult to understand why any of us kept going to the matches in the early part of the season, it was impossible to comprehend once Kevin Mabbutt was out of the team. The meagre crowd had taken to Mabbutt in a big way, and it was a genuine tragedy for them and for the team when a bad pelvic injury put him out of the game for a large part of the season, enabling the unimproved Langley back into the side. At about the same time Palace's only other striker – Ian Edwards – fractured a cheekbone; he was quickly replaced by the former Spurs player, Chris Jones, bought from Manchester City, but Jones was even slower and less prolific than Edwards, scoring only three goals in 22 games before moving on to Charlton. The next journeyman to try his luck up front was Ally Brown, the West Bromwich Albion striker who had formed a good partnership at the Hawthorns with Cyril Regis, but who had now lost his place to an exciting young forward called Garry Thompson.

Brown proved to be no more incisive than Langley, Edwards or Jones, and it was only when a half-fit Kevin Mabbutt came back into the team that Palace were able to put together a crucial series of four home wins on the trot to save them from the drop to Division Three; indeed, it wasn't until the very last game of the season – a postponed match against Burnley – that such a fate was avoided. The two teams had met in similar circumstances only four years earlier, in the game which gave Palace the Second Division Championship, but the implications of the result this time around were vastly different. Burnley had already beaten Palace in the League and the FA

Cup, and had reached the last four of the League Cup by beating Spurs at White Hart Lane. They eventually went out to Liverpool despite winning the second leg of the semi-final, and they had some outstanding young players such as Trevor Steven, Mike Phelan and Brian Laws, but by the end of the season they found themselves in 21st. position and needing to beat Palace to stay up. Every other team had completed their fixtures, and it came down to a straight fight for the third relegation place, with Palace only needing a draw to escape – a dramatic scenario which enticed over 22,000 to Selhurst Park, easily the biggest crowd for two years. For Mullery and Noades the prospect of Third Division football was too awful to contemplate, since there were now very few assets left to sell off; Barron had gone and Gilbert, Murphy and Hilaire no longer appealed as bright young things. Defeat by Burnley would have had serious long-term consequences for the club, but Ian Edwards returned from injury and with his last touch for Crystal Palace scored the goal that provided ill-deserved salvation for another year.

if he could possibly believe the patent nonsense he was talking when he declared: 'I feel that the squad Alan Mullery and Ken Shellito have developed is capable of achieving our target for next season of promotion to Division One.'

Henry Hughton

The last word on this abysmal season goes to Ron Noades, who leaves us to wonder

1983-84

It was obvious – even to Mullery – that the present squad would struggle again, albeit in a particularly poor Second Division, and his summer clear-out meant the departure of Paul Hinshelwood, David Price, Ally Brown, Chris Jones, Tommy Langley, Ian Edwards and David Fry. Fry's replacement was Arsenal's George Wood, who was joined by some other experienced old professionals – John Lacy, Andy McCulloch and Les Strong. McCulloch was intended to partner Mabbutt in the forward line, but Mabbutt again sustained a serious injury – this time tearing his knee ligaments in a pre-season friendly – and wasn't able to play again until after Christmas. Mullery had also bought two other forwards, Tony Evans and Stan Cummins, but still found it necessary to take John Fashanu on loan, with a view to signing him permanently. At this time, Fashanu was very much in the shadow of his more famous brother (as were Hughton and Mabbutt) and after playing just two clumsy games for Palace he was sent back to Norwich. His reincarnation a couple of years later at Millwall surprised everyone, and not even Mullery's sternest critic could blame him for failing to spot a future England player.

The one new signing who did look particularly good was Stan Cummins, who his former manager Jackie Charlton had said – with his usual hyperbole – would one day play for England. He was certainly the best new player to arrive at the club since Kevin Mabbutt, but he suffered the same bad luck with injuries, only managing to play in fits and starts.

John Lacy

After a very slow beginning in the League, with only two points from five games, Palace could at least look forward to progressing beyond the first round of the League Cup, having comfortably beaten Peterborough 3–0 in the first leg. In the return game, however, Palace contrived to lose to the Fourth Division side by the same scoreline and were then knocked out on penalties, to earn themselves fines and a public scolding from Mullery. That outburst proved to be Mullery's most effective motivational act in his entire two years at Selhurst Park, because his team went on to win their next three league games, something unheard of since that famous victory against Ipswich – almost exactly four years earlier – and the ensuing hullabaloo.

George Wood

The curious thing about Palace during this period was that they didn't seem to be playing to any recognisable plan, and were limping along from game to game relying more than ever on Vince Hilaire to make things happen. The success of Watford in Division One, and of Dave Bassett's Wimbledon team, was inspiring furious debate about the merits of the direct, long ball game, and upsetting the purists, but Mullery resisted adopting such tactics. He still believed that his ragged troops could carry on playing the passing game established by Venables, and in an attempt to recapture some of that former glory he brought Peter Nicholas back from Arsenal. The deal was an unusual, initially temporary arrangement, and Ron Noades appealed to the fans for money to finance the transfer. If they didn't quite dig into their pockets as he had hoped, at least most of them felt that Nicholas' return was exactly what was needed to bring about an improvement in results, but his influence was strangely negligible. He had obviously matured as a player whilst at Arsenal, but however well he played he couldn't raise the performance of his team mates sufficiently, and long before the end of the season it was clear that he had lost heart. Nicholas also missed a month of the season after being injured whilst playing for Wales, and at one stage so many of the first team squad were injured that debuts were given to two 17-year-olds, David Lindsay and Wayne Martin. This severely weakened team ended 1983 with just one point earned from seven games, and slipped from being fairly comfortable in the middle of the table towards the relegation area, above only Derby, Swansea and Cambridge.

As soon as Cannon, Nicholas and Mabbutt – arguably Palace's three best players – returned to the side, though, they started playing for the first time under Mullery

with a bit of discipline and vigour, and the first few weeks of 1984 brought their best results of the entire season. The third round of the FA Cup paired Palace with First Division Leicester City, but the strike force of Gary Lineker and Alan Smith could find no way past Billy Gilbert – once again playing at his best – who then went on to put Palace through with the winning goal. They were drawn at home again in the next round to West Ham, then occupying fourth place in Division One, and put up their best show yet to draw 1–1 in a game which they fully deserved to win. Sadly, Palace didn't play nearly so well in the replay a few days later and the Hammers won 2–0, but it was good to see a bit of self-confidence creeping in.

Andy McCulloch

Similarly, in the League, there were two particularly pleasing results against Newcastle and Middlesbrough. Newcastle had bought Kevin Keegan to help them win promotion, and their team also contained Terry McDermott, Peter Beardsley and Chris Waddle, so it was a surprise that Palace were such convincing 3–1 winners, and that they played so well. The next game, against Boro, was always likely to be tough one, but was made even harder after both

Gilbert and Mabbutt were sent off before half time. However, the nine remaining players did themselves proud, and the policy of passing to Vince Hilaire on the wing at every opportunity paid off when he was brought down for a penalty, from which Peter Nicholas scored the winner.

Tony Evans

Just for a while it looked as though Mullery had at last got the machine working properly, but Mabbutt had come back from injury far too soon and was forced to miss a further two months of the season, which coincided with another slump in results. With Giles and McCulloch also injured, Alan Mullery's last signing for Palace – Phil Barber, bought from Aylesbury for £7,000 – was thrown into the team sooner than expected at the age of 19, briefly forming a lightweight partnership up front with Stan Cummins. He looked alright, but nothing special, and Palace ended another season with the usual problem remaining unsolved: that despite a sound defence, in which Gilbert had been outstanding, they simply couldn't score. For such an experienced striker, McCulloch's haul of four goals all season was pathetic, and the top scorer with seven goals – Tony Evans – had already been sold to Wolves.

Relegation had never really been a live possibility, but was only completely out of the question with two games to go, and Ron Noades was forced to accept, after two miserable years, that Alan Mullery really didn't have a clue. As soon as the season finished Noades sacked his fourth manager in as many years, and not a single tear was shed for the departing Mullery. A few days later the new manager was announced as Dave Bassett, the charmless cockney who had dragged Wimbledon up from the Fourth to the Second Division in successive seasons, and who clearly had a talent for getting mediocre footballers to play to their strengths – surely the right man for the job at Palace! It was a big decision for Bassett to leave Wimbledon at such an exciting time, and he quickly realised it was the wrong one when he arrived at Selhurst Park and looked around him. Whatever horrors he saw left no doubt in his mind, and only four days after being appointed he turned straight round and went back to Plough Lane, leaving the Palace faithful more suspicious of Noades and his methods than ever. Inevitably, Malcolm Allison was one of the first names to be suggested as the new man at the top, along with Steve Kember, Brian Horton and Lou Macari, but in the end the surprising choice of Steve Coppell and Ian Evans delighted everyone. Coppell was still only 28 years old but his playing career had been truncated by injury, whilst Ian Evans was still massively popular with the fans, reminding them of happier times. In complete contrast to the reaction to Mullery's appointment, the Palace supporters were behind Coppell from the moment he came, because he had earned universal respect as a player, and as a spokesman for the PFA, of the kind that his predecessor never could.

1984-85

Steve Coppell had worn the No.7 shirt for Manchester United and England with great success, and it is not surprising that he was to see this position as a key one in rebuilding the team, signing the Scottish winger Alan Irvine from Everton. His assessment of where the weaknesses lay was spot on, and for the first time since the days of Kenny Sansom, Palace tried using a natural left back in the No.3 shirt, with Brian Sparrow coming from Arsenal. Trevor Aylott was signed from Luton as a direct replacement for McCulloch, and with Giles having gone during the summer, Coppell signed another forward, Tony Mahoney from Brentford, although it never became clear what his position was meant to be.

Brian Sparrow

The really significant departures, of course, were Billy Gilbert and Vince Hilaire, whose contracts had expired and who were therefore at liberty to move wherever they wished. Inspired by Peter Nicholas' stated desire to leave the club, they at last decided to give up waiting for things to improve at Palace, and went to Portsmouth and Luton respectively, leaving an uncommitted Nicholas and Jerry Murphy behind, with

Jim Cannon, as the last reminders of the halcyon days under Venables. With Gilbert gone, and Lacy of little use, Coppell signed Arsenal's central defender Chris Whyte, an excellent footballer who regrettably only played 17 games before returning to Highbury.

Trevor Aylott

At once the philosophical difference between Mullery and Coppell became evident, with the new manager's team starting from the premise of a solid and logical shape, and players being used in very specific roles, contrasting with Mullery's confused and aimless formations. Behind the scenes, Noades was claiming that the club was now heading in the right direction financially, denying accusations that Palace lacked ambition, although he did appeal for a millionaire to take over as Chairman and inject some cash for new players. He had in mind someone like Elton John, but the closest we got was a rumour about one of Status Quo, which came to nothing. Another good sign was that Alan Smith's youth team had been reconstituted, and two 15-year-olds – Richard Shaw and John Salako – were soon making names for themselves.

On the field, Coppell's newly wrought team made a poor start to the season, and very soon found themselves in the bottom three, with the manager fairly happy with his defence and midfield, but bemoaning 'the age old problem of getting the ball in the onion bag'. Trevor Aylott was carrying on where Langley, McCulloch, Jones and Brown had left off and Mabbutt's by now predictable injury problem was once again keeping him out of the team, leaving Cummins and Mahoney to forage up front to little effect. Cummins, who had looked as if he could have been such a good player, was apparently homesick in London and moved back to Sunderland, and with Whyte moving back to Arsenal shortly afterwards, this gave Gavin Nebbeling an extended run in the centre of defence alongside Jim Cannon, who had by now passed Terry Long's club appearance record.

Apart from the perennial problem of scoring goals, the midfield formation was unbalanced, with Irvine, Stebbing and Nicholas all being exclusively right-sided players, and Murphy as the only left-footer. This was remedied when Phil Barber, who was bought originally as a centre forward, replaced Stebbing in the team and took up a position wide on the left, releasing Murphy to his more natural central position. The immediate effect was an unbeaten run of eight games, with the best result a 3–1 win at Grimsby, who had recently knocked Everton out of the League Cup, and who were one of the Second Division's better sides. Palace's second goal that night was scored by a player making the first League appearance of his career, the 20-year-old striker Andy Gray, signed recently from Dulwich Hamlet. Gray had once been at Selhurst Park as a schoolboy, and had later joined Brentford as an apprentice before an ominous personality clash with the manager seemed to put an end to his

chances in the professional game. Coppell, still with little money to spend, had been scavenging around the local non-league teams for talent, and as well as cleverly spotting Gray's potential had also bought Steve Galloway from Sutton. Galloway did well in the reserves, scoring plenty of goals, but his way into the first team was blocked at first by Andy Gray, and ultimately by Ian Wright. Coppell was also persuaded to give a trial to Tony Finnigan – a friend of Gray's – and was sufficiently impressed to take him on as well, thus strengthening the squad at minimal cost.

Gary Stebbing

The run of improved results came to an emphatic end when Palace lost 5–0 at Oxford, followed a few weeks later by a home defeat at the hands of Millwall in the League Cup and – especially humiliating – another 5–0 drubbing at home to Wimbledon, an abysmal performance which was Palace's lowest point under Steve Coppell. His decisive response was to drop Nebbeling and Aylott, bringing in Stebbing and Finnigan in their places, but he knew that the main problem was a weakness in midfield caused by Peter Nicholas' acrimonious departure to Luton. Henry Hughton was a versatile player, having played in midfield, as centre back, right and left back, and even in goal when George Wood was injured against Shrewsbury, but he wasn't the answer to this particular problem. To fill the gap, Coppell spotted another bargain, and signed the undervalued Kevin Taylor From Derby. His inclusion in the team alongside Murphy restored the familiar symmetry to the midfield, but the signing that really proved to be Palace's short-term salvation was that of the giant centre half Micky Droy from Chelsea. Despite his long experience in the First Division, not too many people expected very much from the 33-year-old. but he confounded everyone by transforming Palace's defence and emanating an aura of effortless self-confidence that settled all those around him. You simply knew that Droy would win everything in the air, and his trips forward for free kicks and corners – he scored in his first game – were reminiscent of Ian Evans at his troublesome best.

time made Palace's own position fairly safe. By the end of the season they had climbed to 15th. in a 22-team division, well clear of relegation, and Coppell had started to lay the foundations for a successful future despite home crowds of frequently less than 5,000.

Micky Droy

The most satisfying result for the few remaining fans was the 2–1 victory over Portsmouth which helped ruin the chances of Billy Gilbert and Vince Hilaire returning to Division One, and at the same

1985–86

When Jerry Murphy left Palace in the summer of 1985, after being a regular in the team for the past seven seasons, he was still only 25 years old and should have been approaching his peak, so why he was allowed to go on a free transfer is a mystery, especially so since Coppell had at times managed to get him to play with a new robustness. Perhaps the manager saw that Murphy could never really supply the fighting qualities that were to become so important to his team in the long, hard slog out of the Second Division, or perhaps the player simply didn't fancy being forced to work so hard for his living. Along with Murphy went Tony Mahoney and sadly, Kevin Mabbutt, whose latest attempt at a comeback had lasted just three full games, and who finally had to submit to repeated injury. Mahoney's replacement in the squad was a similarly anonymous left-sided forward called Andy Higginbottom, while Murphy's place went to Steve Ketteridge, who had looked particularly good when helping Wimbledon to destroy Palace the previous winter. The other player to come to Selhurst Park was a young non-league forward from a club few people had heard of – Ian Wright from Ten-Em-Bee – and Micky Droy was persuaded to postpone devoting himself to his second-hand car business for another year, signing a new contract for the season.

Palace quickly gave notice that they were at last coming good with some promising early league results, and a fine League Cup victory over Lennie Lawrence's expensively reconstructed Charlton side, who were on their way to Division One. The prize for beating Charlton was a second round draw against Coppell's old team, Manchester United, and he was justifiably proud of the way Palace played over the two legs, despite losing both games by a single goal. Although United's First Division class was obvious in both games, they were never allowed to take things easy for a moment, and the most significant effect on the Palace players was that they really started to believe in their ability to work together as a team.

Steve Ketteridge

Ron Noades was also delighted with the home crowd of 21,506 – the best for two years – and gate receipts generally began to improve slightly as the season went on, although not enough to provide any more transfer money. Having stopped the financial rot, Ron Noades now came up with his latest brainchild for making money, not only for Palace, but for all participating clubs. Top Score was a hideously complicated football pool to be operated by 86 of the 92 League clubs, and although few people thought it could ever work, Noades claimed that it would soon challenge the position of the major pools companies, the profit being ploughed back into the game. Typical of the scheme was the way that the Palace players – in the absence of any bona fide shirt sponsorship – sported a panel stitched onto their kit advertising Top Score and entreating the punters to 'Play 6 from 49', a phrase which at the time failed to lodge itself in the consciousness of the nation; the competition finally folded after only three months.

Tony Finnigan

With the emergence of Andy Gray as an unpredictable and dangerous goal scorer, and Alan Irvine's steady supply of testing crosses from the right, Palace's style was now becoming geared towards relentless attack, and Phil Barber topped the Division Two scoring table by the end of August with six goals from the first five games. The defence had become rather leaky, though, with the two full back positions proving a bit of a problem for Coppell. He tried David Lindsay in place of Sparrow for a while, but then decided to add some experience by buying Paul Brush from West Ham, relegating Sparrow to the odd appearance in midfield. Neither Hughton or Locke were entirely convincing at right back, and the young Irishman Ken O'Doherty was given a run at No.2, but whatever deficiencies there were in that position were compensated for by the fact that Cannon and Droy in the middle were as solid as any defensive partnership in the division. Being built like a munitions works, Droy rarely had to resort to foul play to win a challenge, but he was sent off in the home game against Millwall which, with Palace

a goal behind, looked like resulting in their fourth defeat in five games. Not for the last time that season, though, Palace came from behind to win with goals from Barber and Gray, further evidence that Coppell had put some heart back into the team.

Paul Brush

Three weeks after that Millwall game Palace once again found themselves trailing at home – this time 2–1 to Oldham – when Ian Wright came on as substitute for the ineffective Trevor Aylott. Wright had already scored several good goals for the reserves, but didn't yet look strong enough for the first team in his few appearances as substitute. His last-minute winning goal against Oldham, after Kevin Taylor's well hit equaliser, was headed in from such an unlikely position that it gave the impression of being a bit of a fluke. However, Wright was to score three more winning goals in the No.12 shirt throughout the rest of the season, and he quickly progressed from being 'super-sub' to claim his place in the team alongside Andy Gray, a partnership that at its best was the most exciting I have seen.

With Kevin Taylor back in midfield after injury, Palace put together an excellent sequence of four wins and a draw in November, the highlight of which was a 3–1 victory at Leeds United. With neither Gray nor Wright playing at Elland Road, Tony Finnigan alone was on the receiving end of the Yorkshire folk's traditional racism, but although he only scored three goals all season he saved two of them especially for that day, admitting that his anger at the crowd's behaviour had helped to fire him up.

Kevin Taylor

Palace couldn't sustain the form to really challenge for promotion, and in particular were too often found wanting at home, losing to poor teams like Huddersfield, Hull and Shrewsbury, and more reasonably to Wimbledon and Norwich, after which they were never within spitting distance of the top three. By the last third of the season a good team pattern had emerged, with Finnigan dropping from midfield to right back, Nebbeling standing in very successfully for the injured Droy, and Irvine, Taylor, Ketteridge and Barber supplying Gray and Wright up front, Aylott finally having been dropped. The last month of the season saw the team earn some excellent results, once again putting paid to Portsmouth's ambitions by beating

them 2–1, cruising to a 3–0 victory over Leeds, and putting four past Barnsley, Palace's best score for over three years. In fact the season's total of 57 League goals was the best since 1977, and from now on the fans could expect to see plenty of goals from Palace, whatever happened at the other end. The final position of fifth in the table was cause for celebration after so long spent struggling, and a year later would have earned Palace a place in the new play-off system for promotion, but Coppell was happy enough knowing that, by anyone's standards, he was succeeding as a manager.

Ron Noades chose a good time to announce the next money-making venture, with a new feeling of optimism on the terraces, and the Lifeline scheme was a success straight away. With half of the subscription money going back to members in the form of weekly prizes, they were happy to donate the rest to the club, whose solemn promise was that it would be used exclusively to buy new players, and whether Palace's ensuing success can be directly attributed to Lifeline or not, at least that is how it was perceived. Of course, the more significant source of income was the rent obtained from Charlton Athletic, forced to share Selhurst Park after being sold out by their own directors, and despite which they were promoted to Division One as runners-up to Norwich. The only evidence of their presence was a portacabin tucked away in the corner of the ground, and while the arrangement made not a scrap of difference to the Palace fans, for the Valley faithful it was a rotten way to be treated, and it was to be another seven years before they were able to return home.

1986-87

Palace now found themselves in the unaccustomed position of being fancied for promotion, and that looked an accurate assessment when they won their first three games, two of them away from home. The first 'Lifeline' signing was the Millwall winger Anton Otulakowski, who immediately came into the team on the left, mirroring Irvine's role on the right. This meant Phil Barber reverting to centre forward and Andy Gray dropping to substitute, a strange decision since Gray had apparently established himself towards the end of the previous season, and combined particularly well with Wright. Coppell perhaps felt that Barber's graft was more valuable than Gray's erratic brilliance, and his selection of Phil Barber ahead of other, more gifted players is something for which he earned much criticism.

Phil Barber

Having only just scraped past Third Division Bury in the second round of the League Cup, Palace were once again drawn against First Division opposition – Brian Clough's Nottingham Forest – and relished the challenge after having done so well against Manchester United the year before. In fact they surpassed that performance in the home leg, drawing 2–2 after twice being ahead, and then lost the away leg by a single late goal from Clough's son. They really did play some excellent football over the two games, and Forest could not have complained had Palace gone through to the next round rather than them.

Mark Bright

Shortly after losing to Forest, Micky Droy went to Brentford on a free transfer and Gavin Nebbeling came back into the side, but the most significant change was up front, with Mark Bright being signed from Leicester. Bright's first game was a dramatic affair against Ipswich, and he scored Palace's first goal on a day when Ian Wright's last-minute equaliser earned them a 3–3 draw, after an inexplicable run of five defeats had landed them back in the middle of the table. Soon afterwards, an injury to Otulakowski – from which he never recovered – allowed Barber back into the team on the left, and it was at the same time that Andy Gray began to stake his own claim for a midfield place, where his perverse talent was to eventually settle. Starting with a 5–1 destruction of Hull City, Palace embarked on a run of games that took them past Christmas and into the New Year with five wins out of six, and once again they were back in contention at the top of the table. With confidence at a peak, the prospect of meeting Forest again in the FA Cup third round was one that they looked forward to without fear, and they played superbly to win by a single goal from Alan Irvine. Palace's £40,000 signing Gary O'Reilly made an impressive debut in this game, replacing Nebbeling, but the star for Palace was Tony Finnigan, a forward turned midfielder, turned right back, who now played the game of his life at left back to obliterate Forest's most dangerous player, Franz Carr. Dreams of a glorious cup run were swiftly shattered in the next round at White Hart Lane, though, when Spurs won easily by four goals, one of them a beautifully finished close range own goal from one of their former players, Gary O'Reilly.

Gary O'Reilly

The next few weeks were worrying ones for everyone connected with Palace, when it became known that the Wimbledon chairman, Sam Hammam, had approached Ron Noades with a view to merging the two clubs. All sorts of scenarios were invented, such as the two managers job-sharing, the names being combined, and only the best players from each team being kept on, but Noades disclaimed any such ideas,

assuring anyone who believed him that all the moves had come from Hammam's direction. It later transpired that Steve Coppell was very much against any form of merger, but nevertheless Noades took the entirely honourable course of printing a questionnaire in the programme for the game against Blackburn, and promising to abide by the opinion of the fans. With the results of the survey demonstrating the strength of feeling – the fans voting nine to one against a merger – the scheme was immediately scuppered, and the team celebrated by pummelling Birmingham 6–0. Gray's outstanding performance, coming through from midfield to score one and set up two other goals, finally sealed his place in the team at the expense of Ketteridge, who later moved on to that traditional home for old Palace players, Leyton Orient. From then on, Palace were always just outside the play-off positions, eventually missing out by one place, and in the final analysis it was again inconsistency at home that cost them the few crucial points, with earlier defeats by Shrewsbury and Grimsby being especially damaging.

It was interesting, after the 0–0 draw with Plymouth, that Steve Coppell drew attention to their uncomplicated long ball game, and contrasted it with what he saw as Palace's more subtle approach through midfield. The polarisation of opinion on this issue had become such that too many commentators on the game started from the position of putting a team into one category or another, and let that dictate how they perceived the game. Palace themselves fell foul of this lazy approach, becoming branded as 'Route One' merchants, when in fact Coppell's teams always placed great importance on the use of wingers, and were most effective when first Irvine, then Redfearn, then McGoldrick were on song. It may be true that the defenders on the whole lacked the ability of someone like Alan Hansen to bring the ball forward, but that isn't the same thing at all as the gung-ho tactics then favoured by Wimbledon, and so despised elsewhere.

Andy Gray

The last home match of the season had all the makings of a great game, with Palace wanting to win to give themselves a chance of making the play-offs, and Portsmouth needing victory to go up as champions. With Gilbert and Hilaire once again on the opposing side, the biggest crowd of the season witnessed Palace outplay Pompey and win with a goal from substitute John Salako, although Ian Wright's final touch gave him the credit. As it turned out, Portsmouth still went up and Palace stayed down, but the result emphasised that at their best Palace could match anyone in the Second Division, and would surely be the team to catch in next year's race for promotion.

1987-88

This was the season that Palace really became a joy to watch, and the crowds came back accordingly, largely thanks to the emergence of Mark Bright and Ian Wright as truly great goal scorers. Having failed narrowly to make the play-offs the previous season it was surprising that Coppell chose to sell two such important team members as Alan Irvine and Kevin Taylor, the former going to Dundee United and the latter to Scunthorpe after his wife apparently insisted on moving back up north. Their replacements, however, succeeded in improving the team significantly, and illustrated Coppell's ability to spot talented players from the lower divisions. The more expensive of the two was Neil Redfearn, costing £85,000 from Doncaster, but it was Geoff Thomas, a £55,000 signing from Crewe Alexandra who was to prove such a bargain. Neither of them had any trouble adapting to the higher grade and they slotted into the team's established pattern with ease.

Gavin Nebbeling

After a couple of shaky draws and a defeat at Barnsley, Palace struck a seam of form that lifted them, after seven games, to the top of the division. The most spectacular victory was in the game at Birmingham, who Palace once again beat 6–0, and perhaps the best performance came in the 4–1 defeat of West Bromwich Albion. Mark Bright was now the top scorer in Division Two, with eight goals in six games, but the most promising aspect of Palace's game was the midfield partnership of Andy Gray and Geoff Thomas, both playing with great confidence, constantly spraying the ball out wide to Redfearn and Salako and getting it forward to Wright and Bright. With Thomas running non-stop to win possession, Gray was given a lot of freedom to get forward and this first part of the season produced the most consistently dynamic and exhilarating football seen for a long while. Just when things were going so well Palace were knocked back, first by injury, and then by internal strife. After beating Reading 3–2, Palace suddenly found themselves without the services of five defenders: Brush, Finnigan, Stebbing and O'Reilly all had long term injuries while Jim Cannon was forced to miss four games, his first absence from the team for over three years. With a makeshift back four of O'Doherty, Nebbeling, Thomas and young Richard Shaw, Palace lost their next two games, against Ipswich and – inevitably – Shrewsbury, although they easily overcame Newport County over two legs in the League Cup.

More destructive was the fact that Andy Gray's opinion of his own worth had now expanded to the point where he made it known that he had outgrown Crystal Palace, and in effect invited bigger clubs to come and get him, which Aston Villa's Graham Taylor duly did. Although Coppell wanted to keep such an obviously talented player, the turmoil which Gray caused to team morale was intolerable, and Coppell was ultimately glad to get shot of him. It transpired that Jim Cannon in particular could not abide Gray's arrogance, and whether the tales of them coming to blows are true or not, it is not hard to imagine. According to some stories, George Wood was also involved in whatever was going on, and it is interesting that within six months all three players had left the club. The sale of Gray for the absurdly low fee of £150,000 left a gap in midfield that was never adequately filled, and I maintain that had the partnership of Gray and Thomas stayed intact, then Palace would have won promotion that year, although I have no doubt that Coppell did the right thing at the time. The player bought to replace Gray, for the same amount of money, was Southend's Glenn Pennyfather; a busy grafter who lacked inspiration, Pennyfather shared the position for the rest of the season with another hard working but unspectacular player, the former Yeovil part-timer Alan Pardew.

David Burke

A more successful purchase was that of left back David Burke from Huddersfield, and with Stebbing replacing the disappointing O'Doherty at right back, Palace settled down once again to record six wins from seven games, which put them back into contention in fourth place. The first game of that run was against Plymouth, with Andy

Gray making his penultimate appearance and playing a major part in the 5–1 victory, but the hero was Ian Wright, who became Palace's first hat-trick scorer since Mike Flanagan in 1980. Once again Palace were drawn against Manchester United in the League Cup at Old Trafford, and despite going two down pulled a goal back through O'Doherty, and again pleased Coppell by looking the better side for much of the game.

Perry Suckling

The most dramatic match of the season was the one at Maine Road, where Palace won 3–1 after the Manchester City goalkeeper Eric Nixon was sent off, and Mark Bright scored two goals but came away with a broken arm, which kept him out for the next six games. Bright was still injured for the game against his old team Leicester, but after being 3–1 up Palace threw the game away to draw 4–4; the blame was put squarely on the shoulders of George Wood, who had recently been criticised by the fans for giving away several vital goals, and who only played once more before moving to Cardiff. His final appearance was against Newcastle in the FA Cup, where Palace were knocked out by a goal from the latest Geordie sensation Paul Gascoigne, despite controlling most of the game. Gascoigne had not yet become a demi-god, and was still mortal flesh, although plenty of it.

With Wood ruthlessly dropped from the team, Coppell went out and spent £100,000 on Perry Suckling, Manchester City's reserve keeper, who immediately reduced the number of goals conceded, keeping Palace on the edge of the promotion race until the very last game of the season. They also qualified for a half-baked tournament at Wembley to mark the League's centenary, and although they were knocked out on penalties by Sheffield Wednesday it at least gave the players probably the only chance of playing at Wembley that they would ever get.

into the lead from Burke's free kick, and then Thomas's second goal sent the crowd into ecstasy when word got around that Millwall had drawn level at The Den. In reality the Lions had lost 4–1, and by all accounts seem to have taken things very easy indeed, although nobody dared to make the obvious accusation. For the third year running Palace had just missed out, and the great worry was that Bright and Wright – who had scored an astonishing 48 goals between them – would surely be tempted to make their own way directly to Division One, where they clearly belonged. That Steve Coppell had turned Palace into a club deserving of the loyalty of such players is testament both to his skills as a manager and his personal qualities.

Glenn Pennyfather

Palace approached the last few games with the final play-off place still in their sights; after beating Blackburn 2–0, with Perry Suckling saving a penalty from Steve Archibald, and losing 1–0 at Leeds, they knew exactly what was needed from the final game at home to Manchester City. If Palace could win, then the champions Millwall only needed to force a draw at home to Blackburn for Palace to qualify for the play-offs. Nebbeling headed Palace

1988-89

To find Jim Cannon's name missing from the team sheet after 15 years took some getting used to, but it was no great surprise. He could have probably played on for another year or so, but Coppell's ambitions for Crystal Palace required him to take a longer-term view and improve each position wherever possible. Many people felt that Cannon was badly treated, but Coppell had shown his ruthless streak before – in the case of George Wood – and knew that he had to replace parts before they were worn out. The fans' loyalty to, and affection for Cannon made it difficult for the new man to win them over, but Jeff Hopkins – for whom Palace paid £250,000 to Fulham – undoubtedly improved the team and eventually did a grand job as captain at the end of the season.

Neil Redfearn

Less easy to understand was the release of Tony Finnigan to Blackburn, because although Palace had bought John Pemberton as a specialist right back, Finnigan had proved himself more than reliable in all sorts of positions and would have been extremely useful later on in midfield. To cover that area, Coppell had bought Dave Madden, who together with Pardew looked destined for the reserves,

but who ended up as one of the heroes the following spring.

Palace were reasonably pleased with their first result, a 1–1 draw with the eventual champions Chelsea, but with Nebbeling injured and Hopkins serving a suspension, Geoff Thomas was forced back into defence for the second game, a 2–0 defeat at home to Watford. Pardew thus came into the midfield with Pennyfather, and although he would never have been first choice he managed to stay there for virtually the rest of the season. Watford's victory was a quite convincing one, and for a few months they looked certain to bounce straight back to Division One; in the end they finished a place behind Palace in fourth, and lost out in the play-offs, demonstrating what a very long season it was in the Second Division.

By the time of the next game, against Walsall, both Glenn Pennyfather and Perry Suckling had been forced out with injuries, but Brian Parkin was an able deputy in goal, and with Hopkins and O'Reilly now back together in central defence, Thomas was again able to move forward into the midfield. Coppell's indecision about his wingers continued with Barber soon winning back his place from Salako, who in turn frequently came on as substitute for Redfearn, who began to feel aggrieved.

After six league games, Palace had yet to win, were in 20th. position, and even Mark Bright hadn't scored a goal; perhaps Cannon's leadership had been more important to the wellbeing of the team than Coppell had realised. Then, for no apparent reason, everything clicked into place and Palace won seven of their next eight games, including both legs of the League Cup tie against Swindon, and a 4–1 defeat of Plymouth which Palace so dominated that they could easily have scored ten. The one defeat came at Ewood Park, where after apparently cruising to another three points they managed to lose 5–4 to Blackburn, beginning the persistent worries about the frail nature of Palace's defence.

Jeff Hopkins

Despite Redfearn's important part in Palace's revival, he was still miffed at being substituted in earlier games, and Steve Coppell reluctantly granted his transfer request, whilst making it clear that he didn't want him to go. It seemed peculiar behaviour by Redfearn at the time, and I wondered whether he regretted throwing away the chance of making it to the First Division at the time, although he finally got there with Oldham. Into Redfearn's place came Alex Dyer, recently bought from Hull, for whom he had played especially well in recent games against Palace. It was intended that Dyer should play wide on the left, but he filled the gap on the right wing until Eddie McGoldrick's arrival, and his five goals in as many games included one direct from a corner to beat Birmingham, before injury put him out for the rest of the season. Also ruled out from then on was Geoff Thomas, who had justified the decision to appoint him as captain in only his second year, but whose insistence

on maximum physical exertion for every minute of every game put him into hospital for a hernia operation. Pennyfather came back into midfield, and with two thirds of the season gone Palace were still nicely placed within three points of the play-offs, and poised for the run-in, as well as nearly reaching Wembley in the Full Members Cup, now called the Simod Cup. After knocking out Walsall, Southampton, Luton and Middlesbrough – winning this last game 3–2 after being 2–1 down with two minutes left – Palace had to travel to Nottingham Forest for the semi-final, and were not disgraced in losing 3–1 after David Burke was harshly sent off.

After this, their league form stuttered slightly, with Bournemouth inflicting only the second home defeat of the season, and it looked as though Palace had blown it once again, dropping below half way in the table. The turning point came at Vicarage Road, with Barber's superbly taken goal wreaking revenge on Watford, and a run of nine wins from eleven games put Palace right back into contention at the top. Come the final game of the season they still had a slim chance of grabbing the second automatic promotion place from Manchester City, the equation being that Palace needed to win by five goals against Birmingham, and City had to lose at Bradford. Palace were in rampant, irresistible form, but a large number of drunks had come down in fancy dress to celebrate Birmingham's relegation, and not only ruined the day but – which was worse – acted as if they hadn't even noticed the appalling carnage at Hillsborough a few weeks earlier. With fights having started in a part of the New Stand (as the Arthur Wait stand was still called), a number of others broke through the recently lowered barriers and staged a full-scale pitch invasion, complete with the pathetic parody of combat so beloved of British youth. The cavalry arrived after what seemed like an age and broke up the proceedings with ease, allowing the game to continue. Although the blame mostly goes to a small number of the visiting supporters, there were enough home fans relishing getting involved to make one thoroughly sick and ashamed. The sad truth is that no legislation can prevent the barely concealed macho instincts of the young male from surfacing with the slightest excuse.

With order restored, Ian Wright completed a hat-trick, and Palace's domination of the game was such that they could certainly have won by more than 4–1, but the delay meant that the result from Bradford was known long before the end; a draw meant that Manchester City had finished just a point ahead of Palace, and the disappointed players saw out the bulk of the second half without too much strenuous effort.

Rudi Hedman

At last, after three years of coming so close, Palace had made it to the play-offs, and approached them confident in the knowledge that they had finished a clear third in the table, and simply deserved promotion. With both O'Reilly and

Nebbeling injured, the latest signing – Rudi Hedman – was thrown in at the deep end, and played his part in a decidedly dodgy defence, although it was Jeff Hopkins whose own goal gave Swindon the advantage in the first leg of the semifinal. It was fitting that Bright and Wright should score the two goals in the home leg which won the tie, and put Palace through to the final against Blackburn. One of the worst defensive performances of the season had been in the earlier 5–4 defeat at Ewood Park, and once again Palace were prone to some alarming errors at the back, Blackburn this time winning 3–1; even the to the most optimistic fan, it was now hard to fancy Palace to come back in the second leg. Nevertheless, a capacity crowd of 30,000 turned up at Selhurst Park to give them a final push, and the atmosphere surpassed even that of the Burnley game ten years earlier, with the task apparently that much more difficult and the tension palpable. Steve Coppell had a crucial decision to make, because both of his injured centre backs were now fit again, and his choice of O'Reilly rather than Nebbeling precipitated the latter's angry demand for a transfer. As it turned out, O'Reilly played out of his skin alongside Hopkins, and Palace's triumph was built on a defence that looked safer than it had all season. Alan Pardew had still not been accepted by the crowd despite his undeniable improvement throughout the season, but the pass which he made with the outside of his right foot to set up Ian Wright's first goal was a touch of genius which transformed him overnight into a cult hero. Wright himself reacted instinctively to the half chance to make it 1–0, and Palace were steaming.

In the second half Eddie McGoldrick received the ball and set off on a diagonal run towards the goal, which was something he had been oddly reluctant to try, considering his status as the Coppellite winger of the side. McGoldrick ran out of steam and lost control of the ball as he came inside the penalty area, but defender David Mail bundled him down anyway, and George Courteney pointed without hesitation to the penalty spot for the most peculiar and unnecessary offence I have ever seen. Back in March, Palace had been awarded four penalties in a game against Brighton and only scored one: since then the job had been successfully given to the player now wearing the No.4 shirt, the transfer-listed Dave Madden. Although he was obviously Coppell's fourth choice in midfield behind Thomas, Pennyfather and Pardew, Madden had got better and better since being given his chance, and the crowd really appreciated a player who could consistently make space and time for himself to look up and make long, accurate passes to his colleagues.

Dave Madden

Madden it was, then, who kept his cool to put Palace 2–0 ahead from the spot, levelling the aggregate scores and taking the game to extra time. After another half-hour's play, that scoreline would have been enough for Palace to win, with the away goal counting double, but Ian Wright's simple header near the end from McGoldrick's cross made it 3–0, and put Palace once again back into Division One. That game had many heroes, but the one who deserves particular praise is Perry Suckling. With the score still at 2–0, Blackburn's admirable Simon Garner struck the best shot of the game, a perfect volley from the edge of the box, but Suckling made a first class save to tip it over the bar, and ruin what appeared to be Garner's best chance to make it to where he belonged, in the First Division.

To have missed out on promotion for a fourth time might have been so disheartening for Palace that it could have left the club in crisis, and certainly both Bright and Wright would have been strongly tempted to move on, but the emphatic way that the team overcame both Swindon and Blackburn after being behind was an indication of the quality that they had above all others: their spirit. Coppell had assembled a collection of good and average players, the sum of which was greater than its parts, and nobody could deny that they deserved their chance in the First Division, although most also thought that their stay would be a brief one. To be a Palace fan that day felt wonderful; at 3 o'clock we were more or less resigned to applauding a brave but doomed effort, and by 5.15 we were celebrating with all the passion that had been unspent for the past ten years.

1989-90

The dilemma that Steve Coppell faced as he made his preparations for life at the top was whether he should stay loyal to the players who had earned promotion, or strengthen the team in the areas where it was obviously weak. Taking a dispassionate view, most fans would have agreed that Phil Barber and Alan Pardew – for all their dedication – were not likely to be up to the task, and many also had doubts about the defence, particularly David Burke and Jeff Hopkins. Coppell largely agreed with that assessment, buying Mark Dennis and Andy Gray from Q.P.R. to replace Burke and Pardew, and trusting that Alex Dyer would at last be fit to take over on the left wing from Barber. Curiously, though, he didn't see fit to invest in another centre back, which meant a lack of cover in that position since the departure of Gavin Nebbeling; this proved a big problem once O'Reilly was injured, and forced Geoff Thomas to stand in, with mixed results.

Steve Coppell

The decision to bring Andy Gray back to Selhurst Park was a brave one by Coppell, who knew that it would be seen as eating humble pie, after taking such an apparently principled stand when he sold Gray less than two years before. On top of this was the fact that he cost Palace more than three times what Villa had paid, but Coppell couldn't resist restoring the Gray / Thomas / Bright / Wright combination, and I for one agreed with him wholeheartedly. As it turned out, Gray and Thomas only played three games together in central midfield before Thomas was used first in defence, then wide on the left, after which Gray played the second half of the season on the right wing. Some would say that it was foolhardy of Coppell to give Mark Dennis another chance to resurrect his career, but we were never given much opportunity to judge whether or not he had become a reformed character, injury keeping him out of the side for all but nine mid-season games.

The season started with an unattractive fixture away to Q.P.R., and although Palace played reasonably well they were beaten fair and square by Trevor Francis' team, the main disappointment being the failure to score. The next game was at home to Manchester United in midweek, Ian Wright's well struck late goal after Alex Dyer's flick on earning Palace a draw against a United side already being touted as title contenders after their impressive victory over the champions Arsenal. Palace in fact played much better in their third game, at home to Coventry, but were taught a lesson in how to kill a game stone dead by their defensive opponents, whose 1–0 win was completely undeserved.

The prognosis, then, was worrying; three games played, one goal scored, and only one point. Luckily, their next opponents –Wimbledon – were absolutely awful, and perhaps the ease of the 2–0 victory deceived the players into thinking rather more of themselves than was warranted, and was certainly no sort of preparation for the devastation to come at Anfield, just two days later. According to Steve Coppell, Palace created more chances that night than they had in any game so far, and Geoff Thomas even missed a penalty, but it seemed that whenever Liverpool came forward they scored a goal, which happened nine times. My knowledge of the game is all second hand, because I haven't yet been able to bring myself to watch the rush-released video of the game, but the consensus seems to be that many other teams have played worse at Anfield and got away with losing 3–0 or 4–0. If Liverpool's performance will go down in history, then so will the behaviour of Palace's travelling fans that night, who took their team's humiliation with humour and a strange sort of pride. The best joke was the chant: 'You only sing when your winning', directed at the empty Kop end after the stadium had been cleared of Liverpudlians, and although Coppell said that 'This will haunt us for the rest of our lives', the fans who were there made sure that they would look back on that night with affection.

Up to that point the defence had looked competent enough, but now Coppell was under intense pressure to make improvements, with poor Perry Suckling bearing the brunt of the criticism, unfairly in the view of many. With few alternatives available to him in defence, Coppell had little choice but to name an unchanged side for the next game, and they showed extraordinary character to bounce back in the way that they did, pushing Southampton all the way to earn a 1–1 draw. That result was overlooked by Palace's critics, who had now written them off as certain to be relegated at the end of the season, but the players confounded everyone with their next two results – victories over Nottingham Forest and Everton – which pushed them into the top half of the table. Those two games saw them playing with a confidence and

discipline that nobody would have believed possible a couple of weeks earlier, and they maintained their impetus against Millwall, coming back from Hopkins' farcical own goal to win 4–3, with Bright and Wright scoring two goals each and looking at their buoyant best.

This surge of good form reached a peak in their next game, when they met Nottingham Forest in the third round of the League Cup, having narrowly negotiated the previous round over two dramatic legs against Leicester. Palace completely outplayed Forest – the eventual winners of the trophy – but just couldn't get the goal they deserved, which is why it was so hard to believe that they could have lost the replay as heavily as they did, by 5–0. Having defended his goalkeeper until now, Coppell had to concede that Suckling's loss of confidence was permeating the entire defence, and when he let in three more goals just three days later, it was the final straw. Suckling was replaced by Brian Parkin for the next game, ostensibly with a hand injury, and then Palace finally got the man they had been thinking about for a long time, the first million-pound goalkeeper, Nigel Martyn. Palace fans were deeply divided about Martyn at first, many thinking that a million pounds could be better spent in other areas, and believing that the popular Suckling had been unfairly treated. Such misgivings were reinforced when Martyn let eight goals past him in his first three league games, barely managing a save of any note. Perhaps the worst performance of the season came at home to Q.P.R., when the superannuated midfielders Peter Reid and Ray Wilkins were given as much time and space as they could wish for, and the recent, belated dismissal of Trevor Francis as manager inspired them to a decisive 3–0 win.

Now down once again to 18th. position, prospects again looked bleak, when Coppell finally made the signing that everyone had been clamouring for, that of a good centre half. Andy Thorn was the player needed to firm up the defence, and he immediately looked the part in his first game, away to Manchester United. Playing five at the back for the first time, Palace didn't gain many friends, but they did register their first away win of the season against all the odds, and this proved to be a turning-point, after which Palace always managed to keep themselves just clear of the relegation places. There were some more bad results – in particular at Arsenal and Everton – but also some convincing victories over Southampton, Spurs and Aston Villa, and survival was comfortably secured with three games still to be played. In fact, were it not for Manchester City's last minute equaliser in the final game of the season, after Niall Quinn had clearly controlled the ball with his hand, Palace would have finished the season in 12th. place in Division One – their highest ever.

John Salako

If there had been no more to Palace's season than that, it would still have been just cause for celebration, bearing in mind the low

expectations at the outset: but of course this was also the year that Crystal Palace reached the FA Cup final, for the first time in their history. For the record, let us also remember that for the second year running Palace reached the last four of the Full Members / Simod /Zenith Data Systems Cup, cruising past Luton, Charlton and – eventually – Swindon, before falling apart against Chelsea, who went on to win the final. The other route to Wembley had been less challenging up to that point, at least on paper, and Palace certainly had the luck of the draw. They entered the FA Cup in the third round, and made heavy weather of despatching Second Division strugglers Portsmouth. Nigel Martyn in the Palace goal was at fault as Guy Whittingham's looped header put Pompey ahead, and it took a cracking volley from Geoff Thomas to put his team back in the game. With time running out, and the match heading for a replay on the South coast, Andy Gray found himself just outside the Portsmouth box with the ball at his feet, and instantly decided to win a penalty. He pushed the ball forward past Mark Chamberlain, who obligingly stuck out a leg for Gray to trip over, slowly pick himself up and thump home the resulting spot kick.

The next round was somewhat easier, as it should have been against an awfully poor Huddersfield defence, and although Ian Wright was missing after breaking his leg in a league game against Liverpool – just as he was about to score – Palace should still have got more than the four they managed, courtesy of Hopkins, Salako, Bright and a messy own goal. Rewarded with another home tie in the fifth round against Fourth Division Rochdale, Palace were nearly thwarted by a series of stunning saves by goalkeeper Paul Welch, who was only beaten by Barber's firm right foot shot from close range. Having hit the winner, Barber reeled away triumphantly towards his chief critics in the New Stand enclosure who had been getting on his back after his recent form, which had been undeniably bad. With only eight teams left in the competition, Palace were once again given nearly the best draw possible against another Fourth Division side, this time away at Cambridge. One always had a feeling that this would be a difficult one, though, and Cambridge played the better football for much of the game; but Palace never panicked and finally won with a scrappy goal, weakly directed into the net by Geoff Thomas's normally redundant right foot.

With due respect to Palace's opponents, few teams can ever have had such an easy passage to the semi-finals, and everyone watched the live draw for the next round praying to be paired with Oldham, or at a pinch Manchester United, but definitely, definitely not Liverpool. We got Liverpool, and we knew that we were in for another onslaught of sneering reminders of the 9–0 scoreline back in September. The more recent league game, however, had offered some small encouragement to the more optimistic among us, because Palace were never overrun, and might even have snatched a draw. With Liverpool 1–0 up in that game, Palace nevertheless came back into it and almost scored when Ian Wright took the ball swiftly past Grobbelaar, only for Barry Venison to save a certain goal with a blocking tackle that, it turned out, broke Wright's leg. He hobbled on for a while, but when McGoldrick was fouled, Coppell took the opportunity to replace him and Pardew with the two substitutes; a rash move, since McGoldrick was also badly injured, and Palace were left with ten men for the last 20 minutes. The final score of 2–0 at least illustrated how far Palace had come since the start of the season, and with Ian Wright having recovered in time for the

Cambridge game, they felt that they would be able to put up a decent fight in the semi-final, even if it was now more improbable than ever that they would be going to Wembley this year. After Ian Wright had broken his leg for a second time, a victim of his own skill in turning wickedly past a Derby defender, any chance of upsetting the champions elect had – according to every expert they could dig up – completely vanished, and the semi-final was now seen as nothing more than Liverpool's chance for a bit of target practice before completing the inevitable double.

Executives of television companies now dictate the fixture list for cup as well as league games, so for the first time both semi-finals were to be played on a Sunday, one at noon and the other at 3.30, for the benefit of the TV audience. The Football Association, determined to prove beyond all doubt their incompetence, scheduled the local derby between Manchester United and Oldham for 3.30 at Maine Road, meaning that the other two sets of fans had to make their way from Liverpool and London to Aston Villa's ground in Birmingham, with orders to arrive by 11 in the morning. I am ashamed to say that I didn't bother going, being convinced that a long journey up would be followed by a longer one home, after a noble 1–0 defeat. My decision was also influenced by memories of the terrible anti-climax of losing the semi-final in 1976, and of course by the fact that I could see the game live on the box anyway.

A room full of us settled down to watch the game hoping for the best and fearing the worst, and were surprised how calm and confident our team looked, in the biggest game of their lives. For the first time all season they were taking their time on the ball and passing it around at the back, in fact doing exactly what Liverpool did when they were sitting on a lead. Coppell's tactic was to contain Liverpool for the first half and then have a go at them later on, and to this end he detailed Pemberton to stick to Barnes, O'Reilly to Rush, and Shaw to Houghton, orders which they carried out to perfection. Then, out of the blue, McMahon gave the ball to Pardew, who gave it straight back, and McMahon's through pass caught O'Reilly coming forward, leaving Rush clear to place a precise shot past Martyn. That goal was all that separated the teams during the first half, but Palace stayed calm, stuck to their plan, and went into the break pleased with having played every bit as well as Liverpool. John Motson, the BBC's most annoying commentator (or most cherished, for some), was watching a different game, and Ray Wilkins didn't have the wit to depart from his prepared script, the gist of which was that Liverpool are majestic: 'Majestic', he proclaimed of their complete control of the game. And Alan Hansen? Well, he was just 'majestic – I can't think of any other word!'. Ironically, the one pundit to look at the game objectively was Terry Venables, whose fair and intelligent comments may have bought him some forgiveness from those who called him Judas, not that he could care less.

As Liverpool kicked off the second half, they were quietly confident of the course of the next 45 minutes, but as John Pemberton quickly intercepted the ball, someone lit his fuse and let him go. He skinned two Liverpool defenders – which you simply don't do – and belted a cross towards the head of Barber. It fell to Salako, whose fierce shot hit Grobbelaar, looped into the air and was blasted into the net by Bright for the equaliser. If we went potty then, we went even pottier when Gary O'Reilly forced the ball in from close range to put Palace – unbelievably – in front, and for a while it looked as though they would

hold on to the 2–1 lead, so well were they playing. Then McMahon equalised after an extremely dubious free kick, and minutes later Liverpool went ahead again, this time following an equally dubious penalty decision, Barnes scoring from the spot. Having regained the lead so emphatically, the natural response was to assume that this time Liverpool would hold on tight, and after the earlier ecstasy we couldn't help but think that now it was all over, gallant though the effort had been. Andy Gray's equalising goal, when it came, epitomised the difference between the two teams that day, with Geoff Thomas twice getting first to the ball and heading it goalward, and then Gray outjumping the besieged Liverpool defenders to head firmly into the net. Palace had put themselves back into the game again by displaying the same sense of purpose and solidarity that had earned promotion the year before, and 90 minutes of pure drama came to a climax with Andy Thorn heading against the bar, when he looked certain to score the winner.

John Pemberton

Another half an hour's play was ahead of us, and logic decreed that Palace's novices could surely not withstand Liverpool's superior fitness, experience and skill in this unknown territory. Certainly the pace slowed, but Palace defended superbly, given strength by Nigel Martyn's assurance in goal, and a replay seemed on the cards until Alan Pardew's late, unforgettable and frankly preposterous winner. The corner played hard to the near post had become the vogue in recent years, and this one looked like an illustration from a coaching manual; Thorn flicked Gray's corner across the box and away from the goalkeeper, and Pardew popped up between two defenders needing only the slightest contact to convert the goal for which that player will always be famous. What had been the most astonishing and exciting game of football in recent memory had been witnessed by millions on television, but those fans who had travelled up to the Midlands were privileged to be a part of the most intense, emotional and unreal day in Palace's history. All I could do at home was scream with joy as the final whistle went, knowing that the team I loved had beaten the nation's finest 4–3, and were in the Cup Final. How good it felt being a Palace fan for the next day and the next few weeks; all sorts of unlikely people offered congratulations as if you had scored the winning goal yourself, and so many said that it was the best game they had ever seen that you couldn't help almost bursting with pride. What made it perfect was that Palace utterly deserved to win, and everyone except that prize bore Jimmy Hill – who preferred to blame Bruce Grobbelaar – recognized the fact. The last word on the semi-final is that the score between Crystal Palace and Liverpool that most people will recall is not 9–0, but 4–3.

Opinion was sharply divided on who Palace would prefer as their opponents at Wembley: the Second Division giant-killers Oldham, a team with a similar spirit to Palace's, or the ragged collection of over-priced individuals known as Manchester United. After United had unconvincingly whinged their way past the Latics, Palace were confident that the cup was theirs for the taking, having already beaten and drawn with United in the league, and finished the season on the same number of points. The big question leading up to the final was whether Ian Wright would be back in time from his second broken leg, and it was only during the final week before the game that he had his first 90-minute run-out in a reserve game. Andy Thorn was in danger of missing out for a while, but made a spectacular recovery from a badly injured heel, and Mark Dennis, Jeff Hopkins, Alex Dyer and Eddie McGoldrick were all fighting to be fit in time. The other talking point was the patently unjust allocation of tickets by the FA, which resulted in Palace having only 14,000 out of 80,000 available seats in the ground, with Manchester United's quota nearly double that. Confusion reigned, with Ron Noades on the one hand laying into the FA, ostensibly on the fans' behalf, and on the other hand making sure that he realised the maximum revenue by allowing those with enough money to effectively buy themselves priority. The arguments about the fairest way of allocating Palace's share of the tickets could go on for ever, but I could see no reasonable opposition to the notion of giving top priority to existing Club members, in recognition of their loyalty.

The town of Croydon was festooned with red and blue, and everywhere you went you would see Palace shirts, thousands of people having paid over £20 for the honour of walking around advertising Virgin Airlines. The prospect of Palace meeting and maybe beating United seemed to excite the rest of the country as well, and it became the most eagerly awaited Cup Final for many, many years. Although United have an amazing number of supporters throughout the world, everyone else was rooting for Palace, and when it came to the day itself we certainly didn't feel like the underdogs the bookmakers claimed we were.

Alan Pardew

The atmosphere at Wembley was simply wonderful, and with no hint of trouble from rival fans it just felt that you were part of a great old-fashioned sporting occasion, with a cloth cap and a rattle. As the players came on to the pitch, the cascade of red and blue balloons from the Palace section made a display of colour that the TV cameras couldn't hope to do justice to, and the club's biggest moment in 85 years had arrived. With Ian Wright on the substitutes' bench, the team who started the game were the same 11 men who had seen off Liverpool, and once again it was clear that Coppell had decided to retain the man-for-man marking system that had been so effective in that game. Richard Shaw stuck closely to Neil Webb, and with John Salako more or less at left back, Mark Bright was left alone up front with support on the wings coming from Barber and Gray. It was no surprise that the first goal should come from a free kick planted high into the penalty area, since

all the experts had latched on to the fact that all four Palace goals in the semi-final had come from such free kicks or corners. Gray feinted, Barber crossed, and O'Reilly's header squeezed away from between him and Pallister and looped over the flapping Jim Leighton into the net. Palace tried desperately to hang on to the lead for the rest of the half, but a clear foul by Bruce on Gray gave possession to United, and the defence stood and watched as Wallace and McClair combined to set up Robson for the headed equaliser, although the decisive touch came from John Pemberton's shin. That mishap aside, Palace had defended well, making at least as many chances as Manchester United, and went in at half-time still feeling confident that they would win.

The second half continued along the same lines until another bit of lax defending by Palace presented a chance to Mark Hughes, who had done little up to that point, but who snapped it up to put United 2–1 ahead. Steve Coppell delayed the inevitable substitution until 20 minutes from the end, but when Ian Wright eventually came on, the effect was devastating. With his very first touch of the game he got away from Phelan's lunge, left Pallister on his backside in the box, and stroked the ball past Leighton for one of the most perfect goals he ever scored in his illustrious and prolific career. The game had swung Palace's way, but with players already dropping with cramp they were just unable to press home their advantage in normal time, although Gray came extremely close with a right foot shot on the turn, and another half an hour of a classic Cup Final was needed.

The game was barely two minutes into extra time when Geoff Thomas chipped an exquisite ball through to Salako, who wheeled away from Phelan and swung the ball across the face of the goal, catching Jim Leighton once again in two minds and groping thin air. Ian Wright timed his run impeccably and launched himself into the air to punch the ball home with his right foot and put Palace 3–2 ahead. It was a simple goal, but brilliantly executed, and it felt for all the world like the winner until just seven minutes from the end, when Mark Hughes again levelled the scores. United had come back into it with their best football of the whole game, and always looked like scoring, but the goal when it came was a slightly soft one: O'Reilly's momentary lapse of concentration allowed Hughes into a scoring position from where he just managed to squeeze the ball agonisingly between the defender and the goalkeeper. The final score of 3–3 left the fans not knowing what to do with themselves, unable to celebrate or drown their sorrows, and knowing that they had to go through the whole exhausting process in a replay; after such an afternoon, the appropriate response was to sing: 'We're proud of you'.

Not too many people really wanted a replay, but of course Ron Noades was one who relished the prospect, Palace having a much bigger allocation of tickets to sell due to the absence from the second game of all the freeloaders and corporate shindiggers. Nevertheless, the arrangements for selling tickets were a complete shambles, with nobody having a clue what was going on even as the queues were forming on the Sunday morning. The most shameful profit-making enterprise was the club's telephone ticket information service, which required you to pay an excessive amount to find out information which most other forms of entertainment provided via the box-office, or even on a free telephone number. Even this, at 25 pence a minute, was unforgivably giving out the wrong information all

Sunday morning, but after all the hard luck stories from the first game, this time it appeared that everyone who wanted a ticket was able to get one.

Ultimately, though, the replay turned out to be a major let-down, and while nobody could honestly claim that Palace deserved to win, the same can certainly be said for Manchester United, and it was undeniably a bad game. The Palace players were heavily criticised for their physical approach to the match, but I sincerely believe that this was not a deliberate tactical ploy by Coppell, rather an ill-advised reaction by individual players to United's similar style in the first game. Players such as Wallace, Hughes and especially Robson, not only relied on systematic foul play as part of their game, but had the gall to appear outraged if they were penalised for it. Robson's reputation for intimidating referees into letting him get away with murder was a feature of his game for many years, but reached a peak as his effectiveness as a player diminished, yet he still retained his image as a world-class player despite scant supporting evidence.

This ugly attitude to the game typified the United team throughout the 1989–90 season, but it was Palace who bore all the brickbats, having taken United on at their own game and lost. To my mind, Coppell's great error was in keeping Ian Wright back as substitute for the replay; the game was there to be won and a more positive approach by Palace may well have won the Cup, but Coppell stuck to the tactics of containment and Palace never looked very dangerous up front, although they were denied a clear penalty. The winning goal was a good one: Neil Webb's found his left back Lee Martin in space, having got away from Andy Gray, and he hit the shot extremely well, but United should be no prouder of their performance than Palace, who actually had the more chances. Perhaps the decisive factor was Alex Ferguson's brave and difficult decision to drop his good friend Jim Leighton from the team, and bring in the on-loan goalkeeper Les Sealey, whose safe handling significantly settled the United defence.

It was a very sad night – not because Palace lost, but because they played badly – but fortunately the memory of that poor game faded fast. The images that will remain are those of the red and blue balloons and ribbons, the singing, the feeling of togetherness and – dare I say it – community, that are rarely experienced and which are almost becoming unique to the game of football, at least in this country. The semi-final victory over Liverpool and the drawn final were two of the greatest days ever, and what was important to the fans was not really the final outcome, but the fact that they were there, and part of it.

'WE'RE PROUD OF YOU'

'When Geoff goes up to lift the Zenith Cup, we'll be there, we'll be there...'

The disappointment of missing out on the FA Cup might have been devastating, but Steve Coppell was fortunate that Palace's achievements back in the First Division still hadn't been fully acknowledged, and that their progress in the Cup was seen by many as just a tale of plucky underdogs. Consequently, he was able to keep hold of talent such as Wright, Bright, Thomas and Gray, since not too many believed them capable of developing into players worthy of playing at the highest level. He also made two superb signings in Eric Young, now reunited with Andy Thorn from the days of Wimbledon's Crazy Gang, and Charlton's captain, right back John Humphrey. Another former Don, winger Glyn Hodges, was also signed during the summer, but it was the two new defenders who made all the difference in what was to turn out to be Palace's best ever season. The defensive unit of Nigel Martyn, Humphrey, Thorn, Young and Richard Shaw was rarely disrupted throughout the whole season, and this gave Palace the sort of stability that Terry Venables had created a decade earlier with Burridge, Hinshelwood, Cannon, Gilbert and Sansom.

Young scored on his debut on Luton's plastic pitch, and although an away draw seemed a pretty humdrum start to the season, the next game was a cracking 2–1 defeat of Chelsea, Andy Gray scoring an early penalty then getting sent off with Dennis Wise, and Ian Wright floating a peach of a winner over Dave Beasant. That game on a hot August night attracted a decent crowd of over 27,000, and was the first time that the front of the Arthur Wait stand was all seated, but home attendances continued to be generally poor, a fact bemoaned by Steve Coppell later in the season. As autumn edged in, Palace went ten games without defeat, and it wasn't until they met Manchester United at the beginning of November that they lost in the league, by which time they were sitting fourth in the table. The high point, though, was a 3–0 victory at Norwich which saw Palace end the day in second position, after putting on a thoroughly convincing display of fluid, attacking football with John Salako really looking the part, and despite missing the injured Mark Bright.

John Humphrey

The impetus continued in the League Cup, when Wright and Bright both scored hat-tricks during an 8–0 pasting of Southend, and after such a fine start to the season, there was a gradually dawning realisation that Palace had some genuinely good players. Eric Young and Glyn Hodges were already part of the Wales setup, but England were starting to show interest in Nigel Martyn, Ian Wright and – controversially for some – Geoff Thomas, and the trio were chosen for the England B squad by new manager Graham Taylor. Although Taylor hadn't yet been cast as a complete incompetent by the press, he had been stuck with the 'route one' label from his days at Watford, and although he had since won promotion and then second place in the league with Aston Villa, this counted for nothing to some of the lazier and more supercilious of the press corps. Otherwise decent football writers such as David Lacey chose to pour similar scorn on Coppell's Palace, deriding the long ball as an affront to cultured souls such as he, the guardian of some pure and mythical version of the game. Throughout the season, it seemed that nobody could accept that Palace were the third best team that year, behind Arsenal and Liverpool, yet when they beat Liverpool 1–0 at the end of December, it was an accurate marker of just how far Palace had progressed since that 9–0 hammering just over a year earlier. Coppell was the first to admit that their game was robust, even simple, but it required a high level of discipline throughout the team, and this was the year that it all came together and gave the fans a team to be really proud of. If winning the ball and getting it quickly forward to strikers of the calibre of Bright and Wright proved irksome to some, it marked out Steve Coppell as a most astute manager, although he had to grow a pretty thick skin at the time.

Coppell read the riot act to his players after they scraped past Orient and then lost to Southampton in the League Cup, despite playing a full strength side – this was the days before the League Cup was seen as an irritant – but Palace continued to make quiet progress in the Full Members (Zenith Data Systems) Cup, which was eventually to lead them to Wembley once again. Winter set in with a vengeance during January, and the dream of returning to claim the FA Cup was over before it had begun after an epic third round tie against Nottingham Forest. A goalless draw at Selhurst Park forced a replay at the City Ground, but torrential rain meant a wasted journey for fans and players alike, as the game was called

off only an hour before kick-off. The tie eventually took place the following week, in thickening fog, and was notable for John Salako's equaliser in the final minute, to force another replay. A misplaced back pass by Forest's youngster Roy Keane led to Crossley's wayward clearance falling to Salako, who lifted it delightfully over the keeper from fully 40 yards; according to Keane, he returned to the dressing room and a fist in the face from Brian Clough. A week later, another trip to Nottingham for the second replay ended with the home side winning 3–0, and then a few days later the teams met once again in the league, again at The City Ground, and this time Eric Young popped up with a headed goal to win the game for Palace.

Andy Thorn

This consolidated Palace's position in the table, third behind Liverpool and Arsenal, and with a little gap opening up to Leeds and Manchester United. Although the league form became patchy from then on, and despite losing 4–0 at Highbury and 3–0 at Anfield, Palace were well enough placed to start thinking realistically about the prospect of a place in Europe the following season, which third place might ensure. More pressing, though, was the matter of the ZDS Cup, known to many as the Mickey Mouse Cup. Part of the reason that the competition was treated as such a joke was that it was dreamt up by the universally loathed Chelsea chairman Ken Bates and our own Ron Noades in the wake of the European ban on English clubs, following the Heysel atrocity in 1985, although the biggest clubs didn't bother to enter in any case. Nevertheless, it was designed to bring in some gate money and offer a chance of winning some sort of trophy to perpetual under-achievers such as Chelsea, Manchester City and Everton, without them having the inconvenience of getting past the likes of Liverpool and Arsenal.

Richard Shaw

The route to the final was mundane, victories against Bristol Rovers, Brighton and Luton leading to a two-legged semi-final against Norwich notable for the first start in the team for the promising Gareth Southgate. Although the crowds thus far had been quite meagre, the atmosphere at Wembley, with over 50,000 turning out for the final against Everton, was extraordinary, lacking the overwhelming tension and trepidation of a year earlier. Was I the only one who thought it was one of the club's greatest

days, and were the rest of you singing just to humour me? On that day it felt like we were one of the best teams in the country, and beating Everton so soundly seemed to confirm that view, although it remained a closely guarded secret throughout the rest of the country. It was a glorious distillation of the style of play that had brought Palace such success all season, with Geoff Thomas showing all his leadership qualities in midfield and scoring the first with a diving header, the defence holding firm throughout, and Ian Wright nicking two goals in typical fashion. Even John Salako bagged himself a rare header. Again, Palace were accused of being too physical, and indeed Everton's Martin Keown took it upon himself to exact revenge on Eric Young in a league game two weeks later, for which he was rightly sent off. However the game was seen by neutrals, it was a great feeling as a Palace fan to see my team dominate a hard fought Cup Final, and shout my heart out when Geoff Thomas lifted a trophy at Wembley. Give me that; I may never experience it again.

Here we were then, in the spring of 1991, among the top sides in England, with Ian Wright having represented his country on a freezing Wembley night against Cameroon, with Thomas and Martyn pressing for places in the full squad, and with our European place almost assured. Steve Coppell had built a side to challenge the best, and the only way was up. Arsenal had sealed the title already, and Liverpool were sitting second in the table, despite Kenny Dalglish inexplicably resigning as manager, but the second European spot was ours. Liverpool had been held responsible for the Heysel disaster in which 39 people died and which led to an indefinite European ban on English clubs, and a further three year ban on top for Liverpool themselves: with UEFA having voted to allow English clubs back into competitions in 1990, Liverpool were due to wait until until 1993 before there was any possibility of them qualifying. Unaccountably, disgracefully, the FA then colluded with UEFA to overturn the original decision, and allow Liverpool back two years early, so destroying Palace's first ever opportunity to compete in Europe. Many other teams had been denied a European place since 1985, but to have that prize snatched away so late in the day was an absolute outrage, and proved catastrophic for the club and the fans. As director Geoff Geraghty wrote in the final programme of the season: 'The whole thing stinks! I can't think of another body of incompetent, senile, decrepit old fogeys who sit in judgement on our national game anywhere in the world.'

1991–92

The question is not whether Ron Noades was a racist – those close to him testified emphatically in his defence, and his wife Novello publicly sported a t-shirt proclaiming that 'my husband is not a racist' – but whether his words could be construed as such. Let's see: 'One of the problems with black players is I don't think too many can read the game... You get an awful lot with great pace, great athletes, love to play with the ball in front of them, but when it's behind, it's chaos... The black players at this club lend the side a lot of skill and flair, but you also need white players in there to balance things up and give the team some brains and some common sense.' Oh, dear.

Paul Bodin

Ron Noades was nothing if not blunt, so it should have been obvious that for him to take part in a TV programme about black footballers becoming managers, and to allow himself to be filmed speaking his mind was going to be a huge mistake. Noades protested that he was stitched up by Channel 4 and Garth Crooks, the presenter of the programme 'Great Britain Limited', and that his comments were all taken out of context, but I must say that as I watched the show I was cringing with embarrassment. Palace's recent success owed a massive amount to black players; not just Wright and Bright, but Andy Gray, Eric Young, John Salako, and Richard Shaw were first team regulars, and perhaps that was why I was so shocked to hear these absurd statements from Noades. It could have gone no further than us shaking our heads and just praying that he would shut up, but the press made a meal of it and reported that Noades' comments had caused turmoil among the players. Whatever the truth, it felt at the time as though this must have played a part in Ian Wright's departure to Arsenal only weeks later, although from this distance I suspect that his decision to leave Palace had more to do with us having been robbed of our rightful place in Europe.

The season started well enough, with a couple of new faces, but with the core of the successful team of the previous year intact. Wright and Bright were still together up front, Thomas and Gray in midfield, Salako and McGoldrick on the wings, and new signing Lee Sinnott filling in for Eric Young alongside Andy Thorn, as Young had still not recovered from Martin Keown's assault the previous April. Coppell started to fiddle with the defence, sometimes using McGoldrick as a sweeper in a five-man back line, and utilising Sinnott in a variety of positions, none of which he particularly shone in. After a defeat at Manchester City in their first game, Palace won three on the trot and things were looking good until a heavy defeat at home to Arsenal shortly after Noades' ill-advised outpourings. Injuries to Richard Shaw and Geoff Thomas were disruptive enough, but the news that Ian Wright was heading to Highbury came out of the blue, and seemed to surprise Coppell as much as anyone. He was moved to write a letter to fans explaining that 'Ian had been unsettled for some time and I had tried very hard to put my finger on exactly what was wrong. It did become obvious to me that Ian wanted to move to further his career and he expressed the desire to go to only one club which was Arsenal. Ian had a clause in his contract that stated, "should a club come in for him who could offer him European football he would be free to leave us for that club." Had we turned the bid down, we would have had a situation where a player was not happy with us and would not have given us 100% effort and commitment.'

Marco Gabbiadini

The £2.5million fee seemed at the time an absolute steal, but what really hurt was that Wright's desire to move confirmed that, however great the strides Palace had made over the past couple of years, we were destined never to be seen as a truly big club, and that was the moment that the rot set in. From Wright's point of view, he did absolutely the right thing, and went on to be top scorer that season in Division One, top scorer for Arsenal for six successive seasons, and break Cliff Bastin's club goal scoring record. It remains a mystery to me why Wright never really clicked for England, and why Graham Taylor chose to take Alan Smith and Nigel Clough to Sweden

for Euro 92, but leave Wright at home. I feel privileged to have followed Ian Wright from his first appearance as a substitute against Huddersfield in 1985, through his alchemical partnership with Mark Bright, and countless wonderful goals including in the Division Two play-off final, the FA Cup final and the ZDS final – yes, I still cling on to that as a great memory. I was never lucky enough to see Johnny Byrne play, but he was the only player before Wright to be spoken of with the same reverence, and I doubted that I would ever see a finer footballer at Selhurst Park, but you never know when another rough diamond might turn up.

If anyone thought that Mark Bright would flounder without his erstwhile partner he proved them wrong, proceeding to score in eight consecutive games and complete the season as the only ever-present player, but Coppell had an immediate problem of how to fill Ian Wright's boots up front. John Salako had been used to good effect as a striker on occasions, as well as in goal after Nigel Martyn was sent off against Wimbledon, and was in the form of his life. After a splendid performance on the wing for England against Germany, he was looking assured of a good many caps for his country, and it was a massive blow when he was badly injured in a game against Leeds in October, after he fell awkwardly and a defender landed on his left knee. As expected, Salako was out for the rest of the season, and coming so soon after Wright's exit, this was a massive setback for Coppell. Rather than take a chance on giving young Stan Collymore a run in the side, as he was more than a little green, the manager splashed out a reported £1.8 million for Marco Gabbiadini from Sunderland, a player who had scored freely for the Black Cats in the Third and Second Divisions, but who had so far flopped in Division

One. As paltry as the fee for Wright had appeared, the sum paid for Gabbiadini seemed ridiculously inflated, but most of Steve Coppell's signings to date had turned out to be well judged, so there was a feeling of optimism among fans that he might have landed a bit of a coup.

David Whyte

At the time it was rumoured that Palace had been looking at a few strikers, including Southampton's burgeoning Alan Shearer, and even now it's painful to think what might have been. Not only was Gabbiadini not a patch on Ian Wright, he wasn't a patch on the Gabbiadini that had hit the headlines a couple of seasons earlier, and Steve Coppell later admitted that he had signed him based on his past reputation, and hadn't seen him play. The high point of his Palace career was hitting the winner in a 2–1 victory over Liverpool at Anfield, but despite the odd goal he never looked at home in a Palace shirt, and was offloaded only four months later to Derby, at a huge loss. There was talk in the press of bust-ups in the dressing room, and certainly Andy Gray left soon afterwards, but it was hard to disagree with the damning verdict of Assistant Manager Alan Smith that Gabbiadini was 'incredibly average'.

Gray himself had managed half a game in an England shirt, and increasingly gave the impression that he felt he had outgrown Selhurst Park, which didn't endear him to the fans or the manager. Coppell commented that 'it is a bit tiresome when you come in every morning and there is one person who really is a cloud over everyone else's training', and made it clear that his time was up. Gray's move to Spurs marked the start of his decline from the top level, and it was hard not to smile to oneself when hearing that his next port of call was Marbella. Another player to fall foul of Coppell was Paul Bodin, who by rights should have benefitted from Richard Shaw's absence through injury for most of the season, but the manager preferred the unremarkable Lee Sinnott at left back, and eventually sold Bodin back to Swindon at a loss, remarking that 'he is basically a failed First Division footballer – if he is a good player he will prove his point with Swindon and throw the ball back in my face in a few years' time', which seemed uncharacteristically unkind.

John Salako's injury gave Simon Rodger the chance to make his debut, but he in turn was injured, so Coppell leafed through the Rothman's Yearbook looking for left-footed players, and came up with the name of Paul Mortimer, who had only been at Aston Villa for a few months, having signed from Charlton. He took up the offer of an early return to London, but Mortimer was also blighted by injuries so Rodger eventually settled into the side, making a name for himself as a hardworking, energetic and reliable player, who I always thought of as somewhere between Geoff Thomas and Phil Barber. Gareth Southgate also started to cement his place in the side, and there were occasional starts for other youth team graduates Simon Osborn, David Whyte, Dean Gordon and Jamie Moralee. For the last couple of months of the season, Mark Bright's partner up front was Chris Coleman, a young Welshman bought from Swansea as a full back, who did a decent job of putting himself about and causing defenders a few problems in the air. There were a few good results to come, notably a 1–0 defeat of Liverpool, completing the double, and prompting the ever sensitive Graeme Souness to whinge 'I feel as if I've been mugged.'

As the season wore on, Palace slowly slipped from a high point of fifth in the table to end up very comfortably in tenth place, and it seems strange now to remember that this was a disappointment after doing so well the year before, because, after all, it still represents the second best season in Palace's history. More than the loss of Wright and Gray, more than the succession of bad transfer deals, what troubled me most as a Palace fan that season was the constant sniping from sections of the media, who continued to denigrate Palace as 'bully boys', which must have started to erode the players' confidence, and which was typified by the general reaction to Geoff Thomas's inclusion in the England team. Even now, he is remembered more for a single wayward shot against France than for the fact that England were unbeaten in the nine games that he played, and that is simply down to the view that he played for an inferior club, who had no right rubbing shoulders with the elite. If Graham Taylor had taken Geoff Thomas and Ian Wright to Sweden for that summer's European Championship, rather than Carlton Palmer and Alan Smith, we might never have heard of 'Swedes 2 Turnips 1'. Did he not like that!

'This penalty will give Palace the three crucial points. Why is Southgate taking it?'

Maybe Coppell himself had by now got a little bored with Palace's customary direct style, and certainly the public seemed to be turned off, with attendances slipping and fans voicing regular criticism of the manager. He spoke before the season started of the need for more subtlety, and of how predictable they had become. Perhaps he had already decided to ring the changes, but the talk was of John Salako returning from ten months out injured to be Mark Bright's new strike partner. As it turned out, Salako was introduced on the wing to ease his way back in, and Coppell persisted with Chris Coleman for a few games, starting a sequence of four draws with the season's opener against Blackburn. Kenny Dalglish's team had invested big money, including bringing in 22-year-old Alan Shearer, and we were immediately reminded of what we had missed out on when he scored two top class goals, although our own Gareth Southgate scored a long-range corker himself from midfield.

Palace's own early transfer dealings were decidedly underwhelming, non-league players Stuart Massey and Martyn O'Connor arriving along with Wigan defender Darren Patterson, and Rudi Hedman and Perry Suckling moving on. Eddie McGoldrick had been holding out for a move, but eventually signed a new contract, and speculation about Geoff Thomas going to either Arsenal or Blackburn came to nothing, although it did appear to noticeably unsettle the skipper. Having spoken about the need for a new partner for Bright, someone who could score double figures, September saw the arrival of a striker who turned out to be Coppell's best signing for several years. Chris Armstrong arrived from Millwall

for a million pound fee, but only started twice alongside Mark Bright before Bright himself was sold out of the blue to Sheffield Wednesday. Bright later described how he knew nothing about Wednesday's interest until Coppell told him: 'Trevor Francis has tried to buy you two or three times, I think the time might be right for you to move.' There were rumblings that Steve Coppell was trying to modify Palace's game, and move away from the long ball, and the player who came from Wednesday as part of the deal was Paul Williams, a very different type of forward to Bright.

George Ndah

It wasn't until late September that Palace recorded a victory, Armstrong scoring twice away to Everton, and the first home win didn't come until early December, against Sheffield United. Luck seemed to have deserted Palace, and there were so many games where they threw away a lead, and ended up drawing games which they could have won, memorably the game at Ipswich when Gareth Southgate smacked a penalty against the post in the last minute. Four years later I watched horrified as Gareth grabbed the ball in the Euro '96 semi-final and stepped up to take that crucial penalty...

The one bright spot was John Salako's return to form, and as well as hitting a wonderful goal to put Southampton out of the League Cup, he was recalled for the England squad to face Norway in a World Cup qualifier. He made the bench for that game, but that was to be his last appearance at Wembley, as bad luck struck again, and he was forced to return to the States for further surgery, which meant him missing another season, and led some to doubt whether he would ever recover.

November ended badly, with a 5–0 humiliation at Anfield, and there wasn't much to be optimistic about when Palace returned three days later to face Liverpool again in the League Cup. Chris Armstrong was cup-tied, Paul Williams – yet to score a goal – was injured, and Coppell decided to start with the untried Bobby Bowry and George Ndah, with Grant Watts on the bench. McGoldrick reverted to sweeper and Coleman returned up front, heading the goal that meant a replay at Selhurst Park, and prompting yet another petulant whine from Graeme Souness, despite Liverpool equalising through the softest of penalties. As the Evening Standard put it: 'Souness' ill-timed, ill-tempered and ill-informed outburst was perhaps just a smokescreen to cover Liverpool's shortcomings.' Suddenly, Palace's season came to life, and December saw a run of five straight league wins which lifted them from the doldrums to fifteenth in the table, and there was that thrilling League Cup replay against Liverpool. Again, Bowry started in midfield with Osborn, and Grant Watts marked his first start with a headed goal to put Palace ahead before Liverpool drew level with another penalty. Shocking defending by Steve Nicol let in Andy Thorn to head the winner, and Palace progressed to face Chelsea in the quarter-final. Steve Coppell even won a Manager of the Month award, unimaginable just a few weeks earlier.

With Lee Sinnott and Paul Mortimer being placed on the transfer list, and Collymore shipped out to Southend, the squad was looking rather stretched, but again the youngsters played their part in defeating Chelsea, to send Palace into the League Cup semi-final. On a filthy January night, both Grant Watts and George Ndah scored in the 3–1 victory, but it was Chris Coleman's goal which lingers in the memory. The pitch was a quagmire around both penalty areas, and when Frank Sinclair poked a back pass towards Kevin Hitchcock in goal, Coleman was alert enough to spot that the ball had ground to a halt in the mud, and pounced on it before the stranded keeper. Even as he wheeled away in celebration, the ball seemed to take an age to dribble into the goal, before coming to rest exhausted just over the line.

Chris Coleman

That single moment turned out to be the high point of the season, as Palace continued to struggle with injuries to Thomas, Southgate and Williams, and failed to get in any new players of note. Despite Armstrong shining, and scoring fifteen times, goals continued to prove hard to come by, and the ever-present Eddie McGoldrick was second-highest league scorer with eight, pretty good for someone playing almost every position except as a striker. Arsenal beat Palace in both legs of the League Cup semi-final, Hartlepool dumped Palace out of the FA Cup, and the season trudged towards its conclusion with the familiar story of tight games ending in draws, each dropped point seeing Palace slide closer to the danger area and relegation.

Oldham wouldn't win 4–3 at Southampton! Of course they did, and what a miserable anti-climax it was to what had been a pretty glum season all round. It didn't take Steve Coppell too long to decide that he'd had enough, and after almost nine years at the club, he swiftly and quietly resigned.

Paul Williams

With three games to go, captain Geoff Thomas wrote in the programme that 'Our fate is in our own hands and, assuming we get four points from our remaining three games, we shall remain in the Premier League even if our rivals win all their outstanding matches.' Sadly, Geoff had his sums wrong. The players did a lap of honour after beating Ipswich, and then a goalless draw at Manchester City meant that Palace went into the final game at Arsenal three points clear of relegation, and with better goal difference than Oldham, with Middlesbrough and Forest already down. Surely Ian Wright wouldn't score against us, surely Arsenal wouldn't win 3–0, surely

1993-94

'That's Armstrong's first hat-trick for Palace, and I doubt if it's his last.'

With Steve Coppell gone, the time seemed right for Geoff Thomas to move on, to Wolves, and who could blame Eddie McGoldrick for jumping at the chance to join Ian Wright at Arsenal? Thomas had suffered a frustrating season all round, unsettled by transfer talk, disrupted by injury and loss of form, and we were all ready for a bit of a change. It would have been no surprise to see the likes of Young, Thorn, and especially Nigel Martyn leave the club, especially since Martyn seemed in pole position to become England's regular keeper. It was great news that all three chose to stay, along with John Humphrey, and with Salako due to return once again from his long rehabilitation and Chris Armstrong already having shown real quality, there was at least good reason to be more optimistic about the coming season. That was tempered somewhat by the fact that no new players arrived during the summer, so there was a nagging feeling that the emerging younger players such as Southgate, Rodger, Osborne and Bowry would be carrying the weight of too much expectation.

Of perhaps more concern was that chairman Ron Noades had decided not to look elsewhere for a new manager, but gave Coppell's assistant Alan Smith his chance. Smith had been at the club since 1982 with responsibility for youth development, which had seen the emergence of John Salako and Richard Shaw, and had looked after the reserves before ending up as Steve Coppell's right hand man. Given the revisionism that swiftly followed Coppell's resignation, the appointment of Smith could have smacked of 'same shit, different shovel', but before the season began both Noades and Smith went to great lengths to assure the fans that

they would be playing a new style, which Smith liked to call 'pass and move'.

Chris Armstrong

We'd heard much the previous season about Palace trying to change their style, but the criticism of Coppell was that he was by inclination too negative, and was too ready to revert to Palace's customary long ball approach when things weren't going well. I never saw it that way, and always felt that he was simply being pragmatic. He adapted his team according to what he thought was needed at any given point in a game, and was desperately unfortunate that it didn't pay off at the very end of what had been a really difficult season on and off the pitch. Ron Noades never came across as a 'hands-off' proprietor, and expressed his views in some detail: 'I personally did not enjoy the last two seasons... I felt that we were getting more and more introspective and more fearful of the opposition as each week went by... I don't want to see our best attacking players used at home to defend against the other team's full backs and I don't want to see us playing sweeper systems at home against the likes of Everton and Coventry when I think we should be attacking them and winning matches.' Smith was also explicit in outlining his vision to the fans: 'I ask you for your continued support and encouragement to play the open, flowing football that I believe will earn us promotion. I, Steve Harrison and David Kemp have introduced a style of play you will enjoy.' Fine words butter no parsnips, thought the sceptics among us, but we were wrong, and very happy to be so wrong.

Things didn't start too well, with only a point and no goals from the first two games, but Smith stuck to his guns and suddenly everything just fell into place. Nottingham Forest came to Selhurst parading their new £2.2million signing Stan Collymore, who had sloped off to Southend from Palace less than a year previously, but with Paul Williams looking much happier alongside Armstrong, and Southgate working well with Shaw in midfield, Palace embarked on a glorious run of six wins and two draws, playing throughout with real panache. The mood was typified by the home game against Portsmouth, which ranks as one my favourites of all time, not just because of the 5–1 scoreline, but because the team were playing with exactly the kind of open flowing style we had been promised.

Chris Armstrong's luscious hat-trick wasn't even the highlight, that honour going to Gareth Southgate's stunning solo goal, one which for me brought back memories of John 'Yogi Bear' Hughes against Sheffield United many years ago. Southgate had started out at Palace as a defender, playing at right back and centre back, but during this vintage season he came into his own as a midfielder of rare quality. He got in a tackle wide on the left, deep inside his own half, dinked it past the challenger, then strode unchecked over the half way line into a great chasm where the Pompey midfield should have been. He might have thought about laying it off, but went for goal himself and without breaking stride

lashed the ball past the keeper from well outside the area. That goal was the making of him as he grew in confidence to become a key player in the Number 4 shirt, taking over the captain's armband with distinction after Andy Thorn's injury in November and scoring a host of similarly swashbuckling goals throughout the season.

Damian Matthew

Williams had a spell up front, clearly relishing Palace's new brand of passing football, and David Whyte showed glimpses of real flair, which meant Chris Coleman settling into his proper defensive role, but without doubt the star turn was Chris Armstrong. His gait looked a little awkward, but with the ball at his feet he had an instinctive ability to outpace the last man and get his shot on target from any distance. He was terrific in the air as well, getting on the end of Rodger and Salako's crosses rather than having to fight for the ball hoofed from the back; I was moved to sport a t-shirt with a picture of Armstrong celebrating, and the caption 'Ian who?'

With Dean Gordon coming in at left back, Coleman switching to the centre alongside Young, and Humphrey and Shaw fighting it out for the right back spot, the defensive unit became tighter as the season progressed, and by Christmas Palace were top of the division, where they were to stay for the rest of the season. John Salako marked his long-awaited return from injury with a hat-trick against Stoke, and Simon Rodger was establishing himself down the left, but cracks were starting to appear, and there were still a couple of perceived weaknesses which Alan Smith needed to address to make sure the team didn't slip up in their quest to get back into the Premier League.

Dean Gordon

In midfield, the youngsters Osborne, Bowry and Ricky Newman all succumbed to injury at various points, and Smith filled the gap very effectively with Damien Matthew from Chelsea who did a good job down the right and looked a cut above, particularly in terms of physical presence. The real coup, though, was the loan signing of Paul Stewart, the former Spurs and England striker who had fallen out with Graeme Souness – a recommendation in itself – and slipped down the pecking order at Liverpool behind Ian Rush, Robbie Fowler and Nigel Clough (yes, really). Stewart immediately added that bit of aggression and power that neither the

nimble Williams nor Whyte could offer, and although not prolific, he got through an awful lot of work up front, on and off the ball, which allowed Armstrong to continue to flourish.

This was a good season for 'concentrating on the league', and before going out of the League Cup to Everton after a replay, and to Wolves in the FA Cup, there was the small matter of the newly reconstituted Anglo-Italian Cup (now that the Full Members' Cup had died a death, mourned by few). I had been there at Selhurst Park in 1971 to see Luigi Riva play for Cagliari, and Bobby Tambling score the winner for Palace. I didn't make it to the San Siro to see Tambling's two goals sink Inter Milan, but this time, at last, I was determined that I would make it to a game in Europe. The furthest we got was Woolwich, where Palace lost to Charlton before beating Millwall at home, and Europe would have to wait. I've heard that Brescia isn't up to much in any case.

Ricky Newman

Another great success in this Championship season was local boy Dean Gordon, possibly the most one-footed player I've ever watched, but by Jiminy, what a left foot!

He thumped home a couple of unstoppable penalties, but most memorably cannoned in a spectacular late equaliser against Derby to help Palace to their second nine-game unbeaten run of the season. From that moment, every time he advanced down the left to within range, we would expect another belter, and he'd generally pop up with one or two for each of the next four seasons. Gordon, Coleman, Southgate, Rodger and Armstrong all grew up very quickly that year, and Palace coasted to the title with a run of six straight wins putting them seven points clear of runners-up Forest before an anti-climactic home defeat to Watford, but the jubilant celebrations reflected a season in the starkest possible contrast to a year earlier, one which – as Alan Smith had pledged – was ultimately a sheer joy to witness.

'I think that maybe it's like a dream for some people sometimes, to kick these kinds of people. So I did it for them. So they are happy.'

That was Eric Cantona in 2011, still talking total tosh sixteen years after the event.

There had been plenty going on under the surface as Palace won promotion the previous season, but as long as results had been going well, not too much was made of it. Alan Smith had seen fit to have a purge of his unwieldy squad, though why John Humphrey was sent on loan for a while to Reading remained a mystery. Among the players not making the cut for the new campaign were Paul Mortimer and Lee Sinnott, and in a characteristically poor bit of business for Palace, Charlton took David Whyte and some cash in return for Darren Pitcher. What was blindingly obvious was that we needed a new striker, not a new right back, nor a superannuated Ray 'Butch' Wilkins ambling around the midfield. Perhaps he could have done a job for Palace, who he had been so dismissive of as a TV pundit covering the FA Cup Final in 1990, but we never found out since he broke his foot in the very first game and never played for Palace again. Alan Smith had wanted to keep Paul Stewart, but couldn't agree terms with Liverpool, so was left with the same problem that he had identified before Stewart arrived, that of finding a worthy partner for Chris Armstrong. It was certain to be much tougher for Armstrong in the Premier League, and if money was to be spent to keep Palace up, the priority had to be a strong target man. Everyone said so, and everyone kept saying so after the new man was revealed: not the Swedish World Cup star Kennet Anderson, whose signature was supposedly in the bag, but Armstrong's best mate from Wrexham, latterly making a few waves at Stockport, Andy Preece. By all accounts Preece was on holiday with

Armstrong when he got the call, and the word was that he'd been signed as a sop to Armstrong, who was being courted for big money by Everton. That lack of real investment at the start of such a crucial season, whatever the reasoning, will always be cited as Noades' biggest error, and that is not just with the benefit of hindsight. I'm sure that it wasn't just every single fan who thought that, but Alan Smith as well.

Bruce Dyer

Bruce Dyer, a teenage prodigy from Watford, had signed towards the end of the promotion season for over a million pounds, but was still very raw, so Preece lined up alongside Armstrong, with Pitcher and Wilkins replacing Humphrey and Matthew respectively for the first game, at home to Liverpool. What an unmitigated disaster, Pitcher making an impression only by giving the ball away for Liverpool's third of six goals, Preece taken to hospital with a back injury, and Wilkins leaving the ground that afternoon on crutches. Looking for some crumb of comfort, at least Chris Armstrong scored Palace's solitary goal, but it was to be his last in the league until November, some thirteen games later. We were in for a very long, hard season, but this turned out to be perhaps the least predictable year I can recall. The next six games resulted in four draws, with the defence paradoxically improving with the inclusion of Darren Patterson, but nevertheless there was very little expectation that the season's first victory would come at Highbury, of all places. Naturally, Ian Wright scored for the Gunners, but John Salako's brace secured a famous, and rare, triumph over Arsenal, to the massive delight of the brave souls who had dared to return to North London after that miserable relegation day two years earlier. Two more narrow defeats followed, but then a run of four straight wins left Palace in 10th place, a massive achievement following that first day debacle.

Yet still goals were at a premium, and as Palace went on an unprecedented run of nine league games without scoring, it was clear that Armstrong was becoming a shadow of the player he had been. Salako, Preece and Dyer all had spells up front, and none of them provided the answer, but there was at least some good news in the League Cup, an impressive 4–1 defeat of Villa setting up a quarter-final against Manchester City, which saw a rare start for the almost forgotten George Ndah, as City were dispatched 4–0.

That City game was one of the two home games I missed that season, as I was working evenings for a while, and the other one came just a fortnight later against Manchester United, but at least I was able to listen to full commentary on the radio as United were welcomed to South London. It turned out to be one of the most infamous nights in Selhurst Park's history, and although I would normally have been way over the other side of the ground, in my commentary box in the back corner of the Arthur Wait stand, I still feel that I missed out somehow. I must even confess

that in the aftermath, whenever I discussed the Cantona 'Kung Fu' incident with neutrals, I would never actually say that I had witnessed it first hand, but equally would never volunteer the fact that I hadn't. United were pressing Blackburn for the title and the undisputed star of the show was 'King Eric' Cantona. He had been voted PFA Player of the Year as United won the title in 1994, but was as arrogant as he was talented, a short fuse helping him collect a fair few red cards already.

Andy Preece

Strutting around as usual, posing with his artfully upturned collar, he took exception to the fact that Richard Shaw had the temerity to man-mark him out of the game, and as a long clearance sailed over his head he aimed a petulant and spiteful kick at the Palace defender. The referee had no hesitation in showing the red card, and even Alex Ferguson in the away dugout appeared stoical, uncharacteristically unmoved to rant and rave at the decision. Cantona started to walk, paused, looked around as if to seek support from somewhere, and then accepting his fate with apparent dignity walked a little too theatrically along the touchline towards the exit. Naturally, the Palace fans closest to him were highly delighted, jeering as they would any opposition player sent off, but perhaps enjoying it even more given Cantona's notoriety, which he relished. Whatever insults were directed at the Frenchman, he suddenly reverted to type, and decided to pick a fight with someone in the crowd, attempting a leap over the advertising hoarding, and a flying kick to the fan's chest. He made some contact before falling in a clumsy heap and then picked himself up to land a blow with his fist before being dragged away down the tunnel. Listening on the radio, it sounded as if he had hurdled the barrier and gone into the crowd for a fight, but the pictures show that it was less dramatic than that, and more cowardly. Nevertheless, it was an outrageously childish reaction, and the ban that ensued would have been just as deserved had an anonymous lower league player committed the same criminal act of violence. A jail sentence was commuted to community service, on the grounds of provocation, viz: 'they called me names'.

racism, or swearing, or general abuse, but the FA, in a rare moment of wisdom, extended Cantona's ban to nine months. Cantona's famously enigmatic press conference shortly afterwards drew this priceless comment from his erstwhile team mate Gordon Strachan: 'If a Frenchman goes on about seagulls, trawlers and sardines, he's called a philosopher. I'd just be called a short Scottish bum talking crap.'

Ray Houghton

Darren Pitcher

The Manchester publicity machine, loyally supported by the more slavish sections of the media, tried to turn Cantona's thuggery into some kind of noble stance against

Cantona's later reinvention of the incident as his personal crusade against hooliganism was pathetic, and unworthy of him. It is widely believed that United have some of the worst hooligans in the country following them and in the aftermath of the Cantona incident a group of Palace fans travelling to Villa Park for the FA Cup semi-final were reportedly ambushed, leading to the death of one of their number, Paul Nixon, from multiple injuries. Cantona can't be held responsible, but perhaps he could consider not appearing quite so nauseatingly pleased with himself when recounting that infamous night.

The semi-final itself went to a replay after Palace had led twice and had chances to win it, and it was a measure of how far the shine had been taken off Palace's season that a disappointing replay, which United won 2–0, attracted fewer than 18,000 paying customers. Despite the managers calling for calm in the aftermath of Nixon's death, Roy Keane was playing, so that was never going to happen. Palace's own would-be hard man Darren Pitcher made his mark on the Irishman with a tackle that left Keane needing stitches, and when Southgate made a fair tackle in the second half, Keane exacted delayed revenge with a vicious stamp on the prone Palace midfielder. This earned him his first red card in United colours, and provided a handy self-mythologising anecdote for his autobiography some years later.

Palace had also lost to Liverpool in the League Cup semi-final and were reeling from yet more controversy when it was revealed that Chris Armstrong had been suspended after testing positive for cannabis and 'sent for counselling'. This exposed the huge rift that had clearly developed between Alan Smith and Ron Noades, when Smith very pointedly called a press conference to neither confirm nor deny the real reason that Armstrong was missing from a cup game against Watford, when Noades wanted the whole thing covered up, as is customary.

Armstrong actually returned a sharper player, but his improvement was helped by the purchase in January of Iain Dowie, exactly the direct, powerful striker that we had needed all season. Like Paul Stewart before him, he didn't score too often, but led the line very effectively, and by April the experienced Ray Houghton had arrived from Aston Villa. Eight points from his first four games seemed to signal that Houghton was the man to save Palace's season, but there was a horrible inevitability about Palace losing five out of the last six games

and being relegated once again. Last time it was on goal difference; this time they finished fourth from bottom, but for the first and last time four teams went down in order to reduce the Premier League to 20 teams. Founder members Palace may have been, but it was beginning to look like they weren't terribly welcome.

1995–96

'It's only a matter of time before the goals start flowing for Gareth Taylor.'

Having parted company with Alan Smith, which in reality had been a long time coming, Ron Noades surprised everyone by bringing back Steve Coppell to the ill-defined role of 'technical director'. Given how disparaging the chairman had been about Coppell after relegation in 1993, this didn't bode too well, and I for one was curious as to why our most successful manager ever would want to work with Noades again, although responsibility for the first team was handed over to Ray Lewington, assisted by Palace old boy Peter Nicholas. After so many breathless and anxious seasons, a bit of mid-table mediocrity would have been welcome, and that was probably all we could hope for in any case, with so many players moving on during the summer. Gareth Southgate secured a well-deserved move to Aston Villa, where he went on to establish himself as a centre back, John Salako was off to Coventry, having fallen out of love with Selhurst Park, and Chris Armstrong went for £4.5 million to Spurs. Eric Young also left, for Wolves, but at least Chris Coleman, Richard Shaw, Iain Dowie and Nigel Martyn were there for the start of the season. By December though, Martyn was the only one still sticking around.

The new players to arrive were on the face of it uninspiring, but Marc Edworthy and David Hopkin slotted straight into the side for a storming 4–3 home win over Barnsley, during which Dowie scored his last two goals for Palace before moving to West Ham, with big Dutchman Jeroen Boere coming in part exchange. The other major signing, Millwall's Andy Roberts, was unfit until October, and with Boere also injured, again Palace had a shortage up front. Although Bruce Dyer was starting

to show his potential as a striker, two more forwards arrived soon after the start of the season: Barnet's 20-year-old Scot Dougie Freedman and the big money signing we had all been desperate for, Gareth Taylor from Bristol Rovers. Having started out as a centre-back, he had become a useful striker due to his height, and it seemed to take an eternity for Palace to finally land their man, the fee reported at the time as £1.25 million. Hopes were high that Palace had unearthed another young talent like Chris Armstrong, but it took Taylor twelve starts before he found the net, and by that time he had become the crowd's favourite scapegoat despite plenty of effort and a big dose of bad luck. He only scored one other goal, against Port Vale in the FA Cup, before being sold at a loss to Sheffield United, a bit of business reminiscent of the Gabbiadini fiasco.

Andy Roberts

Freedman was a horse of a different colour though, and his quality was evident from the very start. The player he was most like in style was the underachieving Paul Williams, but he had the end result to go with the fancy footwork and clever positional sense. It was a great shame that Dowie had already left, for I am certain they would have formed a formidable partnership up front. The only other options for much of the season were Bruce Dyer, a revitalised George Ndah back from a spell on loan at Bournemouth, and the 17-year-old Leon McKenzie, who scored on his debut in the League Cup, was voted man-of-the-match, and went home that night with his prize of a mountain bike.

Marc Edworthy

With so many changes, and with Coleman and Shaw being sold to Blackburn and Coventry respectively as winter drew in, it was no surprise that Palace spent the first half of the season looking nervously down the table, despite some highly enjoyable successes; notably Dougie Freedman's first hat-trick against Eric Young's Wolves, and Dean Gordon's three goals away to West Brom, with two penalties and a rare header. David Hopkin had also impressed wide on the right or in central midfield, and Andy Roberts was starting to look a player of real quality after a delayed start to his Palace career. However, the pattern was of far too many draws, and an inability to get points from what should have been very winnable home games. A case in point was the home fixture against Millwall, when Bobby Bowry, who had moved to the Den

along with Ricky Newman, outshone Andy Roberts, and the Lions won 2–1, which hurt greatly.

Confusingly, Ron Noades decided to bring in a proper manager, although Coppell and Lewington were still in place, but the decision to call for Dave Bassett wasn't universally celebrated. 'Harry' Bassett had pitched up as the new manager at Palace a dozen years earlier, having had strong connections to Noades at Wimbledon, but, famously, he changed his mind after only a few days, and we ended up with Steve Coppell instead. This time Bassett seemed to relish the challenge of doing something with a team in transition, but with some obvious potential and ambition, and nobody can deny that he made a difference.

He managed to offload Gareth Taylor to his former club Sheffield United, and brought two journeymen in the other direction, defender David Tuttle and Australian Carl Veart. The goals started to flow from Freedman, Dyer and Ndah, but more importantly Nigel Martyn's form picked up and the defence started to look more and more secure, with clean sheets becoming the norm. Almost unnoticed, Palace went on a wonderful run of form which meant that by the time of the return match at Millwall at the end of March, they were sitting in third place, and starting to get serious about promotion. A most unlikely scorer that afternoon was defender Kenny Brown, on loan from West Ham, and Ndah's second on the way to a 4–1 win, a weak speculative overhead kick squirming embarrassingly out of Kasey Keller's fingers into the net, was indicative of the fact that luck was going Palace's way. The trio of Scots, Houghton, Freedman and Hopkin, were all in their best form of the season, and although the automatic promotion spot proved beyond them, Palace ended the season in third place, a real achievement for a team in such a constant state of flux, and for Dave Bassett as manager.

Leif Andersen

The play-off semi-final matched Palace with Charlton at the Valley, and the first leg didn't start well when Norwegian defender Leif Andersen made his most memorable contribution in a Palace shirt with an inexplicable diving bullet header at his own keeper. Martyn could only parry it, and Charlton's Shaun Newton followed up to score, but Kenny Brown equalised with a belter before Carl Veart stooped to knock in the winner after George Ndah had attempted another spectacular overhead shot. Ndah was again instrumental in creating the only goal in the second leg for Ray Houghton, and Palace were back at Wembley once again, for the final against Martin O'Neill's Leicester City.

Just queuing for tickets at Selhurst Park the following weekend was an epic struggle itself, and unusually farcical even for Palace, but the sun was shining and there was a real mood of optimism as there was a sense that the fates were with us, and we were heading for a most unlikely promotion party. The game itself was very tense and cagey from

both sides, but Andy Roberts made a rare advance to the edge of the opposition box to score his first ever Palace goal early on, and Leicester came back with a penalty after a clumsy lunge by Marc Edworthy. On balance, Leicester perhaps looked the better side, but the game went to extra time, and for the whole of the added 30 minutes it just seemed inevitable that we would have the excitement of a penalty shootout.

I love the drama of penalties, and if we could have had them at Wembley in 1990 we might have won the FA Cup rather than enduring the trudge back to North West London on a midweek evening for a desperately disappointing replay. This time, with the kind of luck we'd been having in games, I was almost pleased that we didn't score a winner in normal time. With the game about to end, Leicester prepared for the shootout by bringing on the giant substitute goalkeeper, Zeljko Kalac, all six foot seven inches of him, and he took his place in goal in front of the Palace end. This was going to be fun, and that was all I was thinking as Leicester lumped the ball up the far end, Palace failed to clear, and Steve Claridge swung hopefully at the awkwardly bouncing loose ball. With his shin. Martyn never moved, and Claridge, briefly on Palace's books in the 80s, had sealed his place in Foxes' folklore forever to put them back into the Premier League a year after they had come down with Palace. As Martyn stood bemused on his line, he was surely thinking 'maybe it's time to move on…'

1996-97

'...walking along, singing a song, walking in a Dougie wonderland'

After a relatively uncontroversial and placid year, the first for many seasons, it looked like we could expect more of the same, another season of consolidation, or put another way, low expectations. The summer transfer activity certainly pointed that way: Nigel Martyn, after perhaps too many years' loyalty to Palace, moved to Leeds United and was back in the England frame, while Dave Bassett made a move for Sheffield United keeper Simon Tracey, who he knew well. The transfer got as far as Tracey having a medical at Selhurst Park, but after the deal broke down, Ron Noades slated Tracey in public for his 'exorbitant' wage demands, and settled for Tottenham's well regarded reserve keeper Chris Day instead. Jamie Vincent had shown promise at left back following Dean Gordon's injury problems the previous season, but with Vincent moving to Bournemouth, that position was filled by Australian Kevin Muscat, who joined his compatriot Carl Veart in South London. Around the same time, Palace gave a trial to another young Australian centre-back, Tony Popovic, but for now that came to nothing.

Again the fans were calling for a true target man up front, but Dave Bassett persisted with Bruce Dyer to partner Freedman, and Palace made an unremarkable start to the new season. Dyer had shone for the England Under-21s, but despite his undoubted strength and speed, there was something missing from his game at club level, although this was by far his best season for Palace, ending it as top scorer. Dyer's England involvement, and that of Chris Day, together with Houghton's selection for the Republic of Ireland, meant some early disruption to the line-up, and goalkeeper Bobby Mimms came in for

his one and only game for the third match of the season, at Huddersfield. Dougie Freedman got off the mark as Palace drew 1–1, but during that game Darren Pitcher was badly injured, and certain to miss the rest of the season. As it turned out, Pitcher never really recovered despite playing briefly for Orient later on, and tried unsuccessfully to sue Huddersfield for the tackle that ended his career. Players such as Pitcher and Muscat, wholehearted in the team's cause, or savages, depending on your point of view, were never really taken to the bosom of the home fans, and far more to my taste was David Hopkin, a natural leader who combined uncompromising battling qualities, in keeping with his appearance, with great creative flair and an eye for half a chance at goal.

Dave Bassett

The real news concerned speculation that Dave Bassett would take over at Manchester City, following the sacking of Alan Ball as manager. City had been relegated from the Premier League, but came to Selhurst Park in September still parading some big names, Uwe Rosler, Nigel Clough and the great Georgi Kinkladze among them. At the time, the assumption was that Bassett would be certain to take the job offered to him by Francis Lee, but perhaps Palace's superiority that day convinced the manager to stay, despite the idea of having big money to spend at City. Two fine goals from Hopkin and a pretty lucky one from Leif Andersen put Palace in command before Dougie Freedman raced through on goal and was brought down by Kit Symons, denying him the chance to extend the lead to 4–0. That game finished 3–1 and Palace then started scoring for fun, 6–1 against Reading, despite Roberts' red card, another 6–1 against Southend, and seven goals over two legs in the League Cup against Bury. The goals were being shared out by players in all positions, but despite this purple patch there was still a perceived need for a target man, and for a while it appeared that Mark Bright would be returning on loan, before Sheffield Wednesday demanded a cash sale instead. The player who eventually came in was 22-year-old Neil Shipperley, who looked the part, and was Palace's first big, strong – and slightly slow – centre forward since Iain Dowie. He struck up a good partnership with Freedman, and Dougie had by now come to the attention of Scotland manager Craig Brown, who put him on the bench for a World Cup qualifier game against Estonia in Tallinn. Scotland kicked off, but the opposition hadn't arrived because of a dispute about the time of the game, and Freedman played no part as the referee called the game to a halt, the Scots fans singing '...there's only one team in Tallinn'.

The other remarkable story was that Steve Coppell, still Technical Director at Palace, having been talked of as successor to the recently sacked Ray Wilkins at QPR, then accepted the job at Manchester City that Bassett had turned down. It didn't seem right at the time, and Coppell only stayed at Maine Road for just over a month before resigning, bravely facing up to the reality

that he couldn't cope with the pressures of that particular job.

By November, Palace were up to second place in the table, but there were a few rather worrying and unpleasant undercurrents. There had been a mass brawl on the pitch during the home defeat to Swindon, and then again at Norwich, during which game Houghton and Muscat were sent off, and both clubs were later fined by the FA. A home defeat to Sheffield United particularly incensed Dave Bassett, and he made his thoughts crystal clear: 'We were negative, we played without passion, we were lacking in enthusiasm, we looked frightened and quite simply, we bottled it... At the end of the day players wearing our shirts didn't want the ball, didn't pass the ball, and I will even go to the extent of saying that they went hiding.'

Andy Linighan

Things were starting to slip, and the defence was looking shaky despite Dean Gordon returning from injury, but improved with the arrival of former Arsenal centre-back Andy Linighan, signalling the end of Leif Andersen's undistinguished career in England. Reserve goalkeeper Carlo Nash earned rave reviews when he stood in for

Chris Day against QPR, and kept his place in goal, but Palace continued to look as though they didn't really want another go at the play-offs this year.

Neil Shipperley

Having turned down Manchester City earlier in the season, citing his desire to see things through at Palace, Dave Bassett shocked everyone when he suddenly left for Nottingham Forest in February, perhaps echoing the fans' own suspicions that their club was treading water, and heading for another disappointing end to the season. All in all it was looking a bit drab, with functional players like Veart and Tuttle regulars in the side, and a whole host of clubs lurking, ready to replace Palace in the top six. Even when there was yet another unexpected twist, Steve Coppell being reappointed as caretaker manager, it felt as if he was a stopgap to see out the season quietly. As late as mid-April, Coppell's side were down to ninth position, albeit with a game or two in hand, but somehow – following a dismal 3–0 defeat at Sheffield United – three wins from four games and a loss of nerve by Port Vale meant that Palace scraped into the play-offs in sixth place, with a game to spare. Curiously, Dougie Freedman had lost his place in the starting

eleven, but came back for the final home game against Port Vale, and pointlessly got himself sent off for punching an opponent, meaning that he would miss the Wembley final should Palace get that far. It was completely out of character for Freedman, but seemed to fit with the theme of Palace's indiscipline throughout the season.

A year before, the semi-final against Charlton had seemed almost an entitlement, but this time it felt nervy from the start, the first leg against Wolves coming at home, where Palace had largely struggled. Furthermore, Geoff Thomas and Simon Osborn were in the Wolves side, and we had come to expect ex-players to score against Palace as a matter of course. Neil Shipperley's headed goal was the difference between the two sides until two minutes from the end, when substitute Dougie Freedman scored a sublime volleyed chip from distance to double the lead. Wolves immediately hit back through Jamie Smith for 2–1, which would have been a very fragile lead to take to the return leg, but once again Freedman scored the coolest of goals in the dying seconds, among the most important he would score for Palace, and the last for some while. Wolves did win the second leg 2–1, but never had the advantage after David Hopkin's magnificently emphatic equaliser, and we had yet another date at Wembley, this time on a sweltering hot day against Sheffield United.

Perhaps because of the glorious sunshine, the day felt more joyous from the very start than the Leicester game had a year earlier, and as tightly fought as the game was Palace always had the edge, although goal chances for either side were scarce. The five man defence, with Edworthy outstanding as sweeper, dealt with what little the Blades offered, but still the game seemed to be heading towards extra time, with the heat draining the players' energy. The clock was just ticking around to 90 minutes when David Hopkin picked up a loose clearance outside the opposition box, with virtually every other player between him and the goal. It was fitting that he should curl the ball so exquisitely past Simon Tracey in goal from distance, and it capped a superb season for Hopkin during which he had scored a fair few similar goals, taken over the captaincy, forced his way into the Scotland squad and into the thoughts of various acquisitive Premiership clubs. Delirium followed, although it was hard not to feel for the Sheffield fans having to suffer the same fate as we had against Leicester. Steve Coppell, although generous in acknowledging the part that Dave Bassett had played, had won promotion again in what had been a very difficult year for him, although in his usual downbeat way he admitted to slightly dreading what was ahead.

David Hopkin

'This penalty from Zohar to give Palace their first home win of the season...'

Lombardo, Zohar, Padovano, Brolin, Curcic, Goldberg... How do I start to make sense of this insane season? With Lombardo, I suppose. The fans had bitter memories of Palace's previous short-lived stay in the Premier League, and it was generally accepted that they came straight down because Ron Noades wouldn't invest big money to strengthen the side. Hence when a new director, Mark Goldberg, joined the board and pledged money to help seal Palace's place in the elite, Noades let him have his head, and went along with the audacious signing of Juventus and Italy star Attilio Lombardo, affectionately known as 'Popeye', and soon to be renamed 'The Bald Eagle'. This was beyond anything we had known before at Palace, and was by far the most exciting signing in our history. Although Lombardo was just past his prime in Serie A, he still oozed quality, and it almost didn't matter that we had lost our talisman, and arguably our best player, David Hopkin, who had jumped ship to Leeds United. The transfer news just kept coming; Paul Warhurst from Blackburn, Watford keeper Kevin Miller, Icelandic defender Hermann Hreiðarsson, unknown Scot Jamie Fullarton, and even Ray Wilkins returning as a coach.

Ray Houghton had worked his socks off in the First Division, but wouldn't have had the legs for a tough season at the top level, so he moved to Reading. Nevertheless, it looked a decent Palace side that faced Everton at Goodison to open the season. It looked even better after Lombardo and Dyer scored in a 2–1 victory, with stalwarts Dean Gordon and Simon Rodger in the line up alongside new skipper Roberts, and Warhurst coming in as a striker ahead of Shipperley and Freedman. Dyer had enjoyed his best season yet during the promotion run, so kept his place up front, with high expectations. Palace were also on the trail of another overseas player, Israel's Itzik Zohar, who eventually came with a reputation as a dead-ball specialist.

Attilio Lombardo

A patchy first couple of months of the season saw Palace at least holding their own in the middle reaches of the table, with Lombardo the undoubted star and a wonderful influence on the players around him, but injuries started to play a part when David Tuttle limped off during a win against Wimbledon, the away leg of the Selhurst Park double-header.

Neil Shipperley forced his way back into the side after 'losing weight and adjusting his lifestyle', but Dougie Freedman found himself down the pecking order once again, and was never given a real chance to have a go in the Premiership, which ranks as the first of Steve Coppell's many errors of judgement during the season. Kevin Muscat had also become something of a fringe player, with Fullarton preferred, and he and Freedman went to Wolves in a swap deal for right back Jamie Smith. I would have said that was the worst transfer business of the season, were it not for the £2 million paid for Wolves defender Neil Emblen, who returned to Molineux a few months later at a big loss. By late November George Ndah had gone to Swindon in search of first team football, and another expensive and slightly over the hill Juventus player arrived, the hugely disappointing Michele Padovano. Padovano made his debut at White Hart Lane, and Palace deservedly won 1–0, giving them their fifth away win of the season, and the best away record in the Premiership. The flip side, though, was that they could not win a home game for love nor money, and once Lombardo was injured, they began to slide slowly down the table, eventually going into free-fall with a run of eight straight defeats as they went into 1998.

Hermann Hreiðarsson

With constant speculation about Mark Goldberg's plans to take over the club, Ron Noades revealed the terms of the sale. Goldberg was to pay £3 million pounds up front, which Noades claimed would be used to fund the Padovano deal, and Noades would give him until February 25th to come up with the rest of the £30 million asking price. Meanwhile, Goldberg appeared to be calling the shots regarding

the comings and goings of players, and enticed the unhappy and unfit Swedish international Tomas Brolin, who had been a massive failure at Leeds. Brolin turned up almost out of nowhere to make a start against Everton, and put in his one decent performance in a Palace shirt to win a contract for the remainder of the season, during which time his contribution was minimal. Naturally, Palace lost against Everton to maintain their dreadful home record, but the hoodoo could have been broken in the previous game at Selhurst, on Boxing Day against Southampton. With the score at 1–1, Itzik Zohar came on as a substitute for Shipperley, and was no great shakes, wandering around as he had done on his previous few unremarkable appearances. When Bruce Dyer was brought down in the box, Zohar made a show of grabbing the ball ahead of Dyer and insisted on taking the penalty. Let us be charitable and assume that Steve Coppell's account – that Dyer had hurt his ankle – is accurate, but let us also remember that Dean Gordon was on the pitch, a veteran taker of unstoppable penalties by this time. Zohar shot feebly, the keeper saved it, we didn't win, and that was the last we saw of the £1.2million Israeli.

Paul Warhurst

Marcus Bent

Both Lombardo and Padovano had flown home to Italy over the Christmas period and both Warhurst and Shipperley were out for lengthy periods as Palace tumbled towards relegation, with a wretched home defeat to Wimbledon perhaps the nadir. All the while, Goldberg's attempted takeover rumbled on and on, with more players coming and going. Andy Roberts, who had admittedly had a poor season, switched to Wimbledon, and Carl Veart and Welsh defender Gareth Davis had become surplus to requirements, but in came Valérien Ismaël, Marcus Bent, Patrizio Billio, Matt Jansen, and finally Sasa Curcic. Ismaël was Palace's most expensive signing, at £2.75 million, but frankly we would have been better off with a fit Tuttle. Billio came and went within a few weeks, but Jansen was to prove the find of the season. He reportedly turned down interest from Manchester United to come to Palace from Carlisle, and scored a wonderful individual goal against Villa. However, it was already clear to everyone that Coppell, whether because of the boardroom shenanigans, interference from his masters, or his own inability to stick to a plan, had lost it.

As if Palace hadn't already become a laughing stock, it became common knowledge that Goldberg was lining up Terry Venables to take over following relegation, as well as attempting to get Paul Gascoigne in on loan, but in the meantime he put Lombardo in charge of team affairs with Brolin acting as interpreter, since Popeye's English was minimal. As Ron Noades tells it, this was done behind his back while he was on holiday, but the deed was done and Steve Coppell reverted to Director of Football. Lombardo's great achievement was to finally win a home game, against Derby, but once relegation was assured he reverted to his playing role, and the final embarrassment for the fans came when Ron Noades picked the team for the final three games. Of all the recent relegations, this one was the worst, an abject season with no excuses, and mayhem entirely of Palace's own making. Horrible luck with injuries had played a part, for sure, but a series of dreadfully misjudged and highly expensive purchases had been their undoing, and the season's top scorer, Neil Shipperley, had managed a measly seven goals. Nevertheless, for some, there was a lot to look forward to; Goldberg would be investing fortunes, perhaps Lombardo was even staying, and Venables was coming back. For me, there wasn't a lot to look forward to; Venables was coming back.

1998–99

'Palace was my first club as a manager and now I think it could be my last.'

Let's be fair to Venables. Let's put aside the way he left Palace and took half the team with him to QPR in 1980; let's put aside his sacking as Chief Executive of Tottenham and the parlous mess he left at Portsmouth; let's even put aside his ban from being a company director after the Department of Trade & Industry described his conduct in business as 'such as to make him unfit to be concerned in any way with the management of a company'. We must put all that aside in order to understand what on earth Mark Goldberg was thinking when inviting such an unctuous spiv to lead up his 'Five Year Plan' for Crystal Palace, a plan which was to culminate in Palace becoming 'a major force in Europe'. Clearly, Goldberg had been taken in – as have so many before and since – by the myth of Venables' tactical brilliance on the pitch. Nobody believed this more than Venables himself, and with a compliant press corps in his back pocket, he was able to sidestep the inconvenient truths about his record of relative failure over the years with his reputation intact. Goldberg was blinded by the idea of landing someone apparently at the very top of his profession, and it seemed that money was no object. It was reported later that it cost Goldberg £135,000 even to enter into discussions with Venables, and that was just the beginning of what proved an extremely costly series of mistakes by the new owner.

Surprisingly, given Goldberg's grand plans, as the new season approached there appeared to be a remarkable level of continuity, with Steve Coppell staying as Director of Football, star players such as Lombardo, Curcic and Matt Jansen pledging themselves to the cause despite interest from Premiership clubs, and stalwarts like Simon Rodger, Bruce Dyer and Neil Shipperley still on the scene. However, in the background there was feverish activity, and Venables was explicit in his desire to build a large squad of players, with early transfers in for Dean Austin, Fraser Digby, Nicky Rizzo and David Amsalem. Also trumpeted were two other new arrivals, stars of the Argentina under-21s, Pablo Rodrigues and Cristian Ledesma. Dean Gordon did well to earn himself a Premiership contract at Middlesbrough, and poor Carlo Nash, who never got a look in once Kevin Miller arrived, started to rebuild his career at Stockport.

Sasa Curcic

For Palace's first venture into European competition since the Anglo-Italian Tournament, they had entered the Intertoto Cup as England's sole representative, which might have offered a route to the UEFA Cup. Despite no enthusiasm from the new management, and with Terry Fenwick in charge whilst Venables completed his media commitments, a large crowd turned out to see Palace lose the first game against Turkey's Samsunspor, delaying the kick off because the club had severely underestimated the level of interest. Some then even travelled to the Black Sea port of Samsun for the away leg, to see Palace lose again in scorching heat, with the players not even acknowledging the effort that the fans had made to support them. Given the number of new signings, it was a little surprising to see so many youth team players taking part, such as Tony Folan, Steve Thomson, Hayden Mullins and striker Clinton Morrison, who had made a great impact and scored a last minute winner on his debut at the fag end of the previous season.

That brief flirtation with European glory out of the way, there was great anticipation ahead of the opening fixture against Bolton, but it was surprisingly familiar line-up that drew 2–2, with Austin and Mullins the only newcomers to the first team. It only took a couple of weeks for the cracks to start appearing, beginning with Marc Edworthy's departure to Coventry after he had been frozen out of the team. Still more players were arriving, among them Australian Craig Foster from Venables' previous club Portsmouth, two Chinese players, Fan Zhiyi and Sun Jihai, and a third Argentinian, Walter del Rio, instead of Rodrigues and Ledesma, who had mysteriously disappeared back to South America without kicking a ball for Palace. Early results were mediocre to poor, but a portent of the troubles ahead came when Neil Shipperley was unexpectedly sold to Dave Bassett's Nottingham Forest. The loss of Shipperley prompted Venables to reveal that 'I did not want the player to go. However, Mark Goldberg had explained to me the temporary financial position which at the present time is making things very difficult for everybody including Mark himself. There is no problem between Mark and myself, in fact we get on very well together...' The cracks were widening by mid-September, and when the promising Herman Hreiðarsson left just as

unexpectedly, the revolving door just kept on spinning: in came Matt Svensson, Craig Moore, Lee Bradbury and Gordan Petric, out went Bruce Dyer, Valérien Ismaël, Michele Padovano, and Paul Warhurst. It wasn't November yet, but Venables had already used 27 outfield players in the first 13 games of the season, and Palace had stayed resolutely at the tail end of the division.

Mathias Svensson

There were some positives to take from the first third of the season, not least the potential of Fan Zhiyi and Sun Jihai before departing to the Asian Games for over a month, and Matt Jansen was continuing to show that he was destined for greater things, but Curcic started to fade from view, and newcomers such as Amsalem, Rizzo, Foster and Bradbury were massively disappointing. In stark contrast to the previous season, a run of six straight home wins balanced out the shocking away form, and the fans perhaps started to believe that Venables was getting it right, although Palace were still in no danger of troubling the top half of the table. As the year drew to a close, the media continued to focus on financial problems at Palace, with Ron Noades suing Goldberg, and on rumours that Curcic and Jansen wanted to leave, but in the programme for the QPR game just before Christmas, Goldberg was quick to pour scorn on such talk, and reaffirm that everything was hunky dory: 'Behind the scenes my staff have been through the infrastructure, finances and all operations of the club, and are bringing everything into line with the five year plan I set in place last summer. In terms of football, I am proud to have assembled one of the strongest management teams in the country, and a squad who, over the five years, will take this club to heights it has never experienced before.' What a fantasist Goldberg turned out to be; that was to be Jansen's final home game for Palace, and by mid-January both he and Venables had gone, along with Attilio Lombardo.

However bad we all thought things had become, they turned out to be much worse, and with each passing week the truth began to reveal itself. The departure of Venables and his coaching staff, as well as that of Lombardo, was meant to save on wages, and the fee for Jansen was reported to be over £4 million, yet soon it became clear that players and other staff weren't being paid, and the club somehow found itself in huge debt.

Steve Coppell once again stepped in as manager, and by early March Goldberg had no choice but to take the club into voluntary administration. The administrators quickly established that Palace's debts amounted to £22 million, with a cash flow shortage of an astonishing £500,000 a month, and soon any player who could be sold or sent on loan was out of the door. Lee Bradbury, David Tuttle, Jamie Fullarton, Andy Linighan and Jamie Smith all left within days of each other, as did Sasa Curcic, sadly. Curcic had been a huge favourite with the fans, and could turn a game with a flash of brilliance,

or famously with a theatrical dive which won a penalty against Watford, but Steve Coppell was candid – as candid as he could be – about the reason that he wasn't being selected for much of the season: that he couldn't be bothered to train or play in the reserves, so was never really fit. The last we saw of Sasa at Selhurst Park was when he carried a placard around the pitch protesting against the NATO bombing of Belgrade, where his family and that of Gordan Petric still lived, and of all the players who came and went over those bizarre two seasons at the end of the 90's, Curcic was the one who I would have loved to have seen much more of, along with Lombardo.

Matt Jansen

It wasn't only the players who didn't know if and when they would be paid, and on April Fools' Day 1999, 46 members of staff were made redundant, many after years of service to the club. A few days later, the programme for the home game against Sunderland carried another page of upbeat twaddle from Goldberg, interviewed by the Publications Manager Pete King who, by then, had also found himself out of a job as a direct result of Goldberg's ineptitude. King's view of Goldberg is hard to argue with: 'As far as I'm concerned the worst thing ever to happen in the history of Palace was Goldberg. Until he is out of the picture, Crystal Palace will go nowhere and achieve nothing.'

Gordan Petric

With such a massive haemorrhaging of players, and after a run of eight games without a win, the task of keeping Palace from relegation should have been impossible, as Coppell was forced to rely on a growing number of youth team players, some of whom had hardly been heard of before. Leon MacKenzie, David Woozley, Andrew Martin, Andy Frampton, Sagi Burton, Wayne Carlisle, Gareth Graham and Stephen Evans were among those who played their part, and although none of them went on to long Palace careers, they all deserve our everlasting gratitude for saving Palace in those dark days. Somehow the team were galvanised to grind out unlikely results, typified by a 1–0 win at Norwich which sealed the previously unpopular Dean Austin's place in Palace folklore for his winning header in a game which some thought may have been Palace's last before extinction. A run of ten games unbeaten sent Palace as high as ninth in the table, safe from relegation with a handful of games left, and the real finds of the season

had been Hayden Mullins and Clinton Morrison, who ended up as top scorer just a year after making his debut, and who didn't cost a bean.

So who was to blame for the whole disaster? Certainly, Goldberg demonstrated monumental stupidity for getting into bed with Venables, Tel did what comes naturally in wanting a share of what he thought were Goldberg's millions, and Ron Noades stood back and let the whole thing happen in the first place, spotting early on how a fool and his money are soon parted. Who's to blame? The whole shabby, venal bunch.

1999–2000

'Maybe we can keep that Ashley Cole...'

Far from being a quiet summer, Palace's dire straits were as newsworthy as ever, as details emerged of the money owed to creditors, including Ron Noades and Terry Venables, as well as to players and other football clubs, including Strasbourg and Juventus. The lid was lifted on the extortionate contract, new house and car secured by Venables, as well as the amounts squandered on some very ordinary players, and it became ever clearer that Goldberg had really never come close to being able to secure the funds that he claimed in order to buy the club. The original firm of administrators had withdrawn, to be replaced by Simon Paterson, and there was much talk of a number of rival consortia bidding to become the new owners. One of these groups was apparently linked to Ron Noades, who had spent the past year running Brentford, and who still effectively owned Selhurst Park, but in pole position appeared to be a 'City consortium', which turned out to be a front for Goldberg himself. Fortunately, Goldberg was by now facing personal bankruptcy, and the bid came to nothing, yet somehow Paterson was able to convince the Football League that Palace would be able to fulfil the fixtures for the season ahead, and by the start of the season Mark Goldberg had been forced to resign as chairman, to be replaced by long-standing director Peter Morley.

Goldberg's departure was greeted with delight by the fans, who had shown their solidarity by organising a comedy night at the Fairfield Halls to raise funds for those made redundant. 'Glad All Over' featured acts from celebrity fans Kevin Day, Jo Brand, Sean Hughes and the wonderful Eddie Izzard, as well as the sympathetic Hammers fan Phil Jupitus, with auctions of items donated by several ex-players,

including Geoff Thomas and Nigel Martyn, raising over £15,000. Further proof of the determination of fans to get involved in rescuing their beloved club was the launch of what was to become the Crystal Palace Supporters' Trust, which succeeded in raising over £1million in loans, with a view to becoming part of any potential rescue package, and giving the fans a presence on the board. The Trust were lucky enough to have the full support of Steve Coppell, and the response of the fans gave us all a great collective hope that the club would somehow survive.

Hayden Mullins

There wasn't a lot to be upbeat about on the pitch, though, and before the season had even started, a lucrative tour of China was soured somewhat by the news that Sun Jihai wouldn't be coming back to South London. Clearly no new players could be bought, so the squad started the season with a very threadbare look to it. It was hard to make a convincing case for the season to be anything but a dour battle against relegation, with so many young players in the team. With Kevin Miller having gone, and David Tuttle being sold after the first game, there was very little experience to fall back on. However, a thrilling 3–2 victory at Barnsley raised hopes temporarily, before a dreadful 7–1 mauling by Huddersfield confirmed what a long season this was going to become. Coppell picked his men up, though, and with the commitment of players like Simon Rodger, Andy Linighan and Fan Zhiyi, allied to at least some finesse from Hayden Mullins and Clinton Morrison, results began to improve, with again some terrific results at home. A 4–0 defeat of Portsmouth, Lee Bradbury's last Palace game before returning to Pompey, and a 3–0 win over QPR stood out, and despite losing Morrison for some months, Matt Svensson returned from injury to put together a good run of games for once, scoring freely and showing a bit of quality as well as power.

Simon Rodger

A couple of months into the season Steve Coppell started to busy himself in the loan market, and we saw glimpses of the Venezuelan, Fernando De Ornelas, and the Brazilian, Fumaca, both quickly forgotten, before Terry Phelan arrived from Manchester City. Phelan had been part of Wimbledon's famous cup-winning side in 1988, along with Eric Young and Andy Thorn, and had been close to signing for Palace at one point. His presence at left

back gave the defence a bit more guile, but as Phelan's loan period ran out, Svensson decided to move to Charlton, Simon Rodger suffered another injury and results dipped again, with relegation remaining a distinct possibility. Come March, though, Coppell brought in two more loan players who played a big part in the scrap for survival, Chelsea's Finnish striker Mikael Forssell and left back Ashley Cole from Chelsea. Forssell had come to England with a big reputation, and was very much being groomed for the future by Chelsea, but Ashley Cole hadn't yet got near the Arsenal first team, and was unheard of. As soon as he came to Palace, Cole's control, speed and ability to take the ball forward marked him out as a young player of real quality, and I wasn't alone among Palace fans in remarking that he would play for England one day, and wishing we could keep him.

Craig Foster

In a season that unsurprisingly lacked too much excitement, the quality of Forssell and Cole was some antidote to the continuing anxiety about the club's continued existence, and as the season wore on there was a very real concern among fans that various mystery buyers had evaporated. We heard of an elusive figure called Gerry Lim, which we started to suspect was a pseudonym for Noades or Goldberg, but despite positive noises from the administrator, nothing seemed to materialise, and it started to look as if any deal may have been dependent on Palace avoiding relegation.

Clinton Morrison

A poor run of six games, with only two points to show for them, left Palace going into the penultimate game of the season still in danger. Matt Jansen returned to his old stamping ground with a first half goal for Blackburn which left the Palace fans in a state of shock, and which he chose not to celebrate. Palace fought back in the second half against a Blackburn side whose season was well and truly over, and Ashley Cole marked a great performance with his one and only goal for Palace, a clever chip from just inside a crowded penalty area to equalise. Clinton Morrison then rounded off another excellent season for him with a headed winner, ensuring Palace's unlikely survival with a game remaining. Jansen confirmed his enduring reputation as one of the good guys of football when he stayed on the pitch to congratulate his former team mates after the final whistle. The season

ended with a 2–1 victory at Tranmere, the goals fittingly coming from Morrison and Mullins, perhaps the club's two best players by now, and the final table showed Palace in 15th place, a startling eight points clear of relegation. Although there had been a few glimpses of flair, this had been a season of knuckling down and digging deep. Players such as Dean Austin, Andy Linighan, Wayne Carlisle, David Woozley, Steve Thompson, Craig Foster and Andrew Martin will never be counted among the most talented footballers in Palace's history, but there is no doubt that, with Steve Coppell's expert guidance, they had performed something close to a miracle.

'Once he's properly fit, I'm sure Ruddock will show us his quality...'

Administrator Simon Paterson's quest to find a buyer for the club had dragged on for almost a year when it emerged that the enigmatic Mr Lim was indeed a real person, and that he had been trying to buy the club, but had then reached an agreement to sell it straight away to Simon Jordan, a name that had not previously been widely touted. Jordan was another self-made millionaire with claims to being a lifelong Palace fan, who had made his fortune when selling his mobile phone business, and, in all honesty, the fans were just relieved that the club had been saved from going into liquidation, which had seemed highly possible. Never mind that he looked just the sort of person you would want to avoid doing any kind of business with; at least he wasn't Goldberg. His whole demeanour smacked of arrogance and vanity, and perhaps it was no surprise that he and Steve Coppell didn't see eye to eye from the start, and concluded that they couldn't work together. The premise for Coppell's shock departure before the summer had ended was a string of bad results in the pre-season friendlies, and losing 6–0 to Millwall was the final straw, but it isn't hard to see why the humble, intelligent and honest Coppell felt that there was an insurmountable clash of personalities.

With all the signs suggesting that Jordan was looking for a yes-man to come in as manager, it was a real surprise when he announced the appointment of Alan Smith, who Ron Noades had sacked following relegation five years earlier. The thinking was sound: Smith had won promotion to the Premiership in his first season as manager, and had a good reputation for working with young players, which was still the core of the Palace squad. Although

he had been dismissed as manager at Wycombe Wanderers, Smith had spent a couple of years in charge of Fulham's youth academy, and above all was perceived as the anti-Noades candidate, having fallen out with him in style during the relegation season. Perhaps Simon Jordan wanted to curry favour with the large number of fans who still felt bitter about Noades' part in Palace's descent into near oblivion, or perhaps he really had considered several strong candidates and concluded that Alan Smith was the best man for the job. Either way, it was obvious that he wasn't getting his yes-man, and I was probably in a fairly small minority in anticipating that Smith would do a great job.

Simon Jordan

Despite the Supporters' Trust having had a part to play in bringing Gerry Lim and Jordan together in the first place, the new owner decided that he didn't want them buying a stake in the club or being represented at Board level, which set the sidewinding tone for Jordan's reign, so the Trust decided to offer to repay everyone who had lent money to help save their club. Jordan had been offered a golden opportunity to build real bridges with the fans, and to get them on his side, but from the very start that never really happened, and although grateful that he came along when he did, from then on the supporters never felt any real warmth towards him.

With Ashley Cole having played himself into Arsenal's first team reckoning with his performances at Selhurst Park, he was clearly out of reach, but Palace did pick up two other young Arsenal reserves in Tommy Black and Julian Gray, as well as goalkeeper Stuart Taylor on loan for the start of the season. A new left back was a priority, and the position was filled by Middlesbrough's Craig Harrison, but the two headline signings for the start of the new campaign were Jamie Pollock and Neil Ruddock. Pollock had been an impressively skilful player for Middlesbrough in past encounters with Palace, but already his best days were well behind him at the age of 26, and he was renowned for scoring a wonderful own goal for Manchester City which had consigned them to relegation. If Pollock looked unfit and overweight, that was nothing compared to Ruddock, who revelled in his reputation as a villain, and who had long since conceded defeat in the battle against the bulge.

Very little went right early on for Smith although games were being lost only narrowly; there were signs of promise from Black and Gray, and Morrison's first goal of the season, a cool finish in the first minute to defeat Barnsley, seemed to signal better times ahead. Instead, a sequence of six defeats on the spin culminated in a home defeat at the hands of Grimsby, which prompted ever louder calls for Alan Smith to be given the boot, and following which Simon Jordan was moved to storm into the dressing room to bawl out the players. Smith pointed the finger at the players in no uncertain terms: 'I think the players really need to look at themselves. I had all 16 of them in the dressing room for one-and-a-half hours and only four of them had anything to say and two of them are on loan, that says it all. Someone said that they were giving their all but if that is their best I'd hate to see what their worst is… If these attitudes don't change, it will be anarchy and you'll have the lunatics running the asylum… I feel like Michael Caine in Zulu. A pistol in my hand, 16,000 coming over the hill trying to claim my head… I can't shoot all of them so I might as well shoot the three fellas nearest me who are causing all of the problems. I think our players live in cloud cuckoo land… The bottom line is "have we got any balls?" and the answer is "no we haven't".' Morrison and Mullins, Palace's most consistent players the previous year, were placed on the transfer list with Jamie Smith, and it looked like the season was heading for disaster.

Neil Ruddock

Perhaps it was Alan Smith's rant that did the trick, or perhaps it was the surprise and welcome return of Dougie Freedman, who had been frozen out by David Platt at Nottingham Forest, and the arrival of Steve Staunton on loan, but Palace immediately embarked on their best run of results for some time, remaining unbeaten in eleven league and cup games. Freedman and Clinton Morrison immediately struck a rich vein of goals and new Latvian signing Andrejs Rubins hit a cracking goal from distance in the 3–0 League Cup win over Leicester. A 2–1 victory over Sunderland, with a brilliant effort from Morrison, sent Palace into the League Cup semi-final, the first time Palace had enjoyed any cup success of note for six barren years. The semi-final pitted Palace against Liverpool over two legs, and the home leg on a Wednesday night in January proved well worth the wait, with Rubins scoring another stunner with his left foot, and Palace winning 2–1 in front of a near capacity crowd. Clinton Morrison was quick to offer his analysis of Liverpool's shortcomings: 'Heskey missed a few and Owen missed a few. On a better day they would have put them away. But I was thinking, I wish I had some of the chances they had. I would have put at least two of them away.' A few days later, Freedman was ecstatic to contribute one of Palace's three goals which beat Nottingham Forest at the City Ground, but Liverpool demolished Palace 5–0 in the second leg of the League Cup game, with Morrison's humiliating air shot in front of the Kop perhaps just deserts. With two thirds of the season gone Palace had climbed to what seemed a fairly acceptable mid-table position.

By now both Pollock and Ruddock had proved themselves unfit for the first team, in every sense, and various new loanees were tried, none of whom caught the eye as Palace started to tumble downwards, and towards Division Two. Matthew Upson, Amir Karic and Ricardo Fuller came and went before Palace finally made two proper signings to try and rescue their season, the Finnish international Aki Riihilahti, and the return of another former hero, Freedman's fellow Scot David Hopkin. In truth, neither made a huge impact at

first, and couldn't halt the slide, so that with two games remaining, the relegation that had seemed unthinkable was looking almost certain. Simon Jordan belatedly sacked Alan Smith and replaced him with Steve Kember for the final two games, but although it seemed a pointless gesture, plenty of us ventured down to Portsmouth for the midweek evening game, knowing that nothing less than victory would suffice, against a Pompey team also fighting for survival.

Wayne Carlisle

Kember made a couple of bold changes to the side, bringing in Wayne Carlisle for Craig Harrison, and starting Steve Thomson and American defender Greg Berhalter, but crucially he chose to use Clinton Morrison in deep role behind Freedman and Forssell, which worked an absolute treat. The team played with a self-belief which we hadn't seen for a while, and during the first half we were treated to goals from Forssell, Riihilahti and a trademark individual effort from Freedman, leaving us exhilarated at half time, with the score at 3–1. We hadn't had a great view of those goals from the far end of the ground, but Dougie made up for it with a casual header from Morrison's cross bang in front of us in the away end, and with the game ending 4–2, we knew that a victory at Stockport on the last day of the season would at least give Palace a mathematical chance of staying up.

Steve Kember

The permutations at the bottom of the table were complex, with Palace, Portsmouth and Huddersfield all endangered, but what was clear was that we had to beat Stockport, who were already safe. I had a prior arrangement which meant that I had to drive from London to Devon on that Saturday afternoon, so I timed the journey to coincide with the radio commentary for the last two hours. The tension throughout wasn't conducive to safe driving, and I listened anxiously as Palace failed to score the goal they needed. The game wore on and I found myself arriving at my destination ahead of time, with five minutes of the match left. I parked up in a narrow street in a Devon village, to listen glumly on the radio to my beloved team's demise. I had parked just yards from the birthplace of John Lee, later to be known as John 'Babbacombe' Lee, and later still as 'The Man They Couldn't Hang'. Sentenced to death for murder, Lee went to the gallows, but the trap failed three times, and he was spared.

Three minutes remained when David Hopkin bundled the ball away from defence with more than a hint of handball and lumped it up to Morrison with his back to the defence. Dougie took the ball off Clinton's toes and headed for the box. A little feint to the left, a jink to the right, and he placed it perfectly past the keeper for the winner. The trapdoor could still have opened for Palace, as there was an agonising wait for the final whistle at Huddersfield, who would have sent Palace down if they had equalised against Birmingham, but luck was smiling on us that day. The TV footage of Steve Kember's reaction to the goal tells you all you need to know about his love for Crystal Palace, and in that sublime moment Dougie Freedman joined him in the pantheon of genuine Palace legends.

'*Steve Bruce is happy here and the chances of him ever going to St Andrews are a million-to-one against.*'

Whether it had been a stroke of genius, or simply great good luck on Simon Jordan's part to turn to Steve Kember, it had done the trick, and the players had responded magnificently. The question was, should Kember be given the job permanently, or indeed would he want it? Kember's place in the hearts of older Palace fans was already secure. He had been an outstanding young player for Palace in the promotion team of 1969, skippered the side in the old First Division before leaving for Chelsea, and had returned as the key player in Terry Venables' young promotion team of 1979. Ron Noades had given him a brief spell as manager in the gloom of the mid-eighties, between Dario Gradi and Alan Mullery, and he later returned to Selhurst Park as a coach during Alan Smith's first reign. Quite properly, Jordan told Kember that he had a 'job for life' at Palace, which although not technically in the chairman's gift, was a gesture born of both gratitude and respect for the man. However, perhaps mindful of the mistake he had made in bringing back Alan Smith, Jordan decided to look elsewhere for a new manager, and very swiftly unveiled Steve Bruce, with Kember staying on as his assistant. Bruce had been in the Manchester United team that had eventually beaten Palace in the 1990 FA Cup final, and had already had short spells as manager at Sheffield United, Huddersfield, where he was sacked, and Wigan, who he had only joined seven weeks earlier.

Bruce had fallen out with Huddersfield, the chairman writing in a programme that he had 'made a mistake by believing that a great footballer would make a great football manager'. Nevertheless, at Wigan he had

impressed the chairman Dave Whelan, who wanted to keep Bruce until Jordan made him 'an offer he couldn't refuse'. It was good that Jordan had acted decisively, and Bruce appeared to have an aura that convinced the sceptics that he was someone going places as a manager. He looked the sort of person who could certainly stand up to Jordan, and would share his evident ambition for the club, so on balance, despite Bruce's long association with Manchester United, it appeared to be a pretty good appointment.

Steve Bruce

The summer transfer targets failed to stir much excitement, and included Coventry's Australian striker John Aloisi, Middlesbrough's Andy Campbell, and Arjan Van De Zeeuw of Wigan, but none of these materialised. The only new faces turned out to be American international Jovan Kirovski and Australian Tony Popovic, followed soon after by Bradford City goalkeeper Matt Clarke. All in all, it was a pretty stable side that started the season, with Freedman and Morrison continuing their potent partnership up front and Fan Zhiyi and Dean Austin still at the back, and in the first game they came from 2–0 behind to beat Rotherham 3–2, Jamie

Smith scoring a rare goal. Fan Zhiyi also started the second game, an early rematch with Stockport, and all went very smoothly in the 4–1 win, but that proved to be Fan's last game for Palace. There had been disquiet for some time about the time that Fan spent captaining his country, and once again he was needed for China's World Cup qualifying games, which necessitated some changes to the defence, and gave Bruce the opportunity to assess Popovic, Austin and Craig Harrison, as well as trying Matt Clarke in Kolinko's place. Three defeats followed, with eleven goals conceded, and after Steve Vickers arrived on loan from Middlesbrough, Bruce concluded that he could do without Fan, who, in his words 'had let the club down after indicating when he signed his new contract that he would not be travelling to China'. Yes, that was Steve Bruce, in his own words, taking the moral high ground on honouring contracts. Fan eventually ended up at Dundee United after helping China to qualify for the World Cup finals for the first time in their history, and Palace were left with a very big hole in their defence, which was never really plugged for the rest of the season.

Nevertheless, Bruce appeared to know what he was doing, and made good use of what players he had. Julian Gray started to excel down the left, Riihilahti continued to improve and become a fixture in midfield, and newcomer Jovan Kirovski added a bit of style alongside him. But most of all, it was the form of Dougie Freedman and Clinton Morrison that sent Palace up and up the table, with a run of seven straight wins, including a 5–0 demolition of Grimsby – sweet revenge for the woeful home defeat a year earlier – a joyous 4–1 win over Sheffield Wednesday, and 4–0 against Wimbledon. The reward for the two strikers came as they were called up for their respective countries. Dougie

finally made his Scotland debut against Latvia, even scoring against his team mate Kolinko in goal, and South London boy Clinton Morrison was in the lucky position of having a grandmother from Dublin, so became an Irishman, and later went on to win 36 caps, scoring 9 goals.

Tommy Black

All was going extremely well, better than most people expected, and it looked as if Jordan had chosen his new manager very wisely. In mid-October, Trevor Francis left as manager of Birmingham, and there were mischievous rumours linking Bruce with the vacant job, but Jordan quickly scotched them: 'Steve is happy here and the chances of him ever going to St Andrews are a million-to-one against. Steve has a three-year contract and there is no get-out clause.' A 1–0 victory over Wolves saw Palace leapfrog them to take top position, but the Birmingham rumours wouldn't go away, and eventually Bruce tendered his resignation, although apparently there had been no official approach from Birmingham. Palace were all over the papers again, and Simon Jordan took out an injunction forcing Bruce to work his nine months' notice on 'gardening leave', putting Steve Kember back in charge of the team, along with

Terry Bullivant. Although compensation was eventually agreed with Birmingham, there was no doubt that, whatever Bruce's underlying reasons for leaving, Jordan had won the public relations war and claimed the moral high ground. His war of words with the then Birmingham owners has been fantastically entertaining over the years, and he has made great play of the fact that their wealth was accrued through pornography: 'If I see another David Gold interview on the poor East End Jewish boy done good I'll impale myself on one of his dildos.'

final, but as a manager his record had been no more than humdrum. He was sacked by Sheffield Wednesday before a spell at Birmingham characterised by consistently failing to win promotion out of Division One via the play-offs. It was hardly one to get the pulse racing, and there was a slight suspicion that Jordan was keen to get one over on Birmingham, who had given up on Francis so recently.

Tony Popovic

Alex Kolinko

With the matter finally settled, and Bruce's reputation as Judas sealed, Palace's form dipped a little, but hope was restored when a new manager arrived to oversee a fine 2–1 victory over Manchester City. Trevor Francis was to be the fifth manager to serve under Jordan in his 18 months at the club so far, if one counts Steve Coppell, and the sincere hope was that he would get it right this time. Francis had been a fabulous player for Birmingham, which led to Brian Clough signing him for Nottingham Forest, famously becoming Britain's first £1 million player. For Forest he scored the winning goal in the European Cup

All too predictably, results continued to be patchy, and Palace settled into a zone familiar to Trevor Francis, on the fringes of the play-off positions, while trying to strengthen the defence with Christian Edwards, on loan, followed by permanent signings Kit Symons, Curtis Fleming and Danny Granville. None were especially bad players, but all fitted the mould of decent enough Division One journeymen, and the fans were kind of getting the point, that this was the limit of the club's ambition. What was needed was a big money signing, someone to make the headlines, and revitalise a season that was heading nowhere. £2.4million was big money, and Ade Akinbiyi certainly attracted headlines, but none of them good. Peter Taylor had made Akinbiyi Leicester's record signing when paying an astonishing £5.5million, and by any standards he had failed at Filbert Street, being cited as the main reason that Taylor was later sacked. He came to Palace with the nickname of Akinbadbuy already given to him by Leicester fans and the press, and never showed the slightest glimpse of casting it off. Akinbiyi only scored twice before the season ended, and I actually saw his one home goal that year, a tap in against Preston giving him the chance at last to display his celebrated torso. I shall add it to that other treasured memory, Marco Gabbiadini's goal against Notts County ten years earlier.

Finishing just in the top half of Division One was actually a pretty good achievement considering how recently the club had nearly gone out of business, and how close they had been to relegation, but it just felt a little disappointing after the season had promised so much under Steve Bruce, and it was also quite disconcerting to finish a season without the usual drama and trauma of relegation or promotion that we were accustomed to. There had been a lot to enjoy, not least Freedman and Morrison scoring 42 League goals between them, fine seasons for Julian Gray and Hayden Mullins, and an outstanding one for Aki Riihilahti, but was Trevor Francis the forceful and charismatic leader we needed to become promotion contenders next season? I didn't think so, but Simon Jordan must have done.

2002-03

'Who needs Andy Johnson when we've got Tommy Black?'

Sometimes a new player will come into a team and make an instant impression, for good or bad, and sometimes they need more time to settle in and find their feet before flourishing. Of the four new signings that lined up for the opening game against Preston, it was the imposing centre-half Darren Powell who looked the best. Finding a decent partner for Popovic had been a huge problem for Trevor Francis, but Powell looked the part from the off, scored a goal on his debut, and was very soon being likened by fans to the mighty Eric Young. Danny Butterfield also looked comfortable at Division One level, having signed from Grimsby, and Shaun Derry had arrived to beef up the midfield. There was another new starter, a short bald bloke called Andy Johnson, who was stretchered off with a suspected broken neck. Johnson had arrived as the makeweight in a deal that took Clinton Morrison to Birmingham for £4.5 million during the summer, which was an offer that Simon Jordan couldn't resist after Steve Bruce had irritatingly won promotion to the Premiership. Morrison was at his peak, and it was an ideal chance for him to play at the top level, but Johnson's move in the other direction seemed to confirm that Palace were at a point where they were prepared to take cast-offs from a team like Birmingham.

As the team made a stuttering start, so did Johnson, and before long Francis had signed Dele Adebola for a bit of power up front, since Akinbiyi was likely to be out injured for several months. Johnson's first goal for Palace was tapped home from a yard against Plymouth in the League Cup, but despite his endeavour and evident pace, he didn't look the ideal partner for Freedman, and looked possibly better when played on the right wing. His speed

and tenacity won a penalty for Freedman to score against Wolves, but for the first couple of months he was substituted more often than not, and I had certainly made my mind up about him. From what I had seen, pace was his only real asset, but he was too small to be an effective striker, and more to the point, didn't seem to know where the goal was. The season was beginning to pan out in a very predictable way for a Trevor Francis side, and apart from a 7–0 stroll past Cheltenham in the League Cup, the expectation for most games was yet another draw. The biggest drama was in the home draw against Bradford, when Francis was sent from the dugout after punching his own substitute keeper Kolinko, who he said was smirking after the opposition scored. The 'away' fixture against ground sharers Wimbledon was meant to be the last before they moved to set up shop in Milton Keynes, and Andy Johnson finally got off the mark in the league with another tap-in, but the result was, again, a draw.

Danny Butterfield

There are a few opposition teams that it is very important to beat, whereas others you can take or leave. For me, it's nice if we beat Aston Villa, but not essential, whereas a result against Wolves is vital. We've beaten Liverpool a few times, and it's always fun, but Everton are more satisfying. Charlton? Not really, but Millwall, absolutely. There's a logic to the long standing local rivalry with Millwall, if not to the others, but I've not met a Palace fan who doesn't get a very special feeling whenever we face Brighton. Although a relatively new phenomenon, dating back to Alan Mullery's days there in the 70's, the rivalry has become real and enduring, but the game against Brighton in October 2002 was special for a number of reasons. First of all, this was the first time in over a decade that the two sides had been in the same division, and with Brighton already stranded at the bottom of the table after losing eleven games in a row, it looked like being the last for a while. Secondly, it was a chance for the crowd to welcome back Simon Rodger, whose epic career at Palace had been terminated by Trevor Francis, and who had just signed for Brighton. But most of all, Brighton's manager that day was Steve Coppell, still worshipped by all at Selhurst Park, who gave him a rousing and emotional reception. With all of that, the most probable result was an uneventful draw, but this was to be the day that Andrew Johnson was reborn as AJ, a brand new Palace hero. He scored a toe-poke for 1–0 and a diving header for 2–0, then burst through into the box to win a penalty which Dougie put away for the third. Another powerful run into the box drew a foul from the defender, a red card, and another penalty which this time AJ claimed for his hat-trick. Julian Gray's splendid individual goal made it 5–0. Just so everyone is clear, that's Crystal Palace 5, Brighton and Hove Albion 0.

If AJ had disappeared from the first team after that game, he would still have been lauded forever, but the hat-trick transformed him, and with a new-found confidence he scored a second hat-trick only three days later, at Walsall. A stunning left-footed volley, a header, then a low right-footed shot to win the game 4–3 was followed by a goal at Ipswich and two against Coventry, which made it 10 goals in 5 games. I've never been so happy to be proved wrong about a player who I'd dismissed as pretty ordinary. I still didn't think much of Adebola, though, or Shaun Derry, for that matter.

Wayne Routledge

Things were surely moving in the right direction, with Julian Gray impressing on the wing, young Wayne Routledge contributing some outstanding cameos, and Kolinko regaining his place in goal once again from Matt Clarke, but when Freedman was injured in November, and Johnson the following month, there was a worry about where the goals would come from. Adebola chipped in with a couple, but the revelation was Tommy Black, in and out of the side under Francis, and starting to look out of condition and surplus to requirements. His little spree of 9 goals in 8 games earned him a renewed contract, and saw Palace at last thinking seriously about the play-offs come the New Year.

However, the season's only remaining drama was confined to the FA Cup, with Palace drawn against Liverpool in the fourth round. Every few years Palace face Liverpool in one cup or another, and the ties are never dull, this being no exception. It was by no means a vintage Liverpool team at the time under Gerard Houllier, and although they were still in the upper reaches of the Premiership, they had a beatable look about them, which gave Palace confidence, along with AJ's recent return from injury. Both sides had chances to win, but the game finished goalless, the main incident being a serious injury to Chris Kirkland, which halted what was developing into a highly promising career as Liverpool's goalkeeper. It came after a burst of speed into the box from Dele Adebola, showing a rare change of pace to round a defender, but the Palace striker was utterly blameless for the collision which caused Kirkland's injury. Approaching the replay, it was difficult not to think back to the 5–0 drubbing at Anfield under Alan Smith, but this time Palace defended stoutly, and Julian Gray was the star of the show. A precise and powerful volley from Gray for the first goal was followed by an own goal from Gray's cross to win the tie at Anfield. What made the victory even sweeter was that Palace had achieved it with only ten men after Dougie Freedman was sent off for retaliation with 20 minutes remaining. The prize was a home tie in the fifth round against Leeds United.

When they came to Selhurst Park for the cup game, Leeds were a Premiership team just starting to deteriorate and head towards the relegation zone, and their manager was coming under increasing pressure. Indeed he was sacked a month after the Palace game, but for now Terry Venables knew that his welcome back to South London would be less than friendly. The boos for Venables before the game contrasted with the reception given to Steve Coppell earlier that season, and gave a pretty fair idea of their respective places in the hearts of Palace fans. How fitting that Venables should be witness to daylight robbery, as Tommy Black's shot to give Palace the lead was not only handled by Michael Duberry, but was clearly over the line. Well over, massively over, obviously over the line to anyone with eyes. 'Goal!' said the players. 'Goal!' said the crowd. 'No!' said the ref and linesman. 'Thank you very much' said Venables, as Leeds won 2–1, and Palace's season dwindled to nothing.

Shaun Derry

For the first time since I'd been going to Selhurst Park, I found myself losing interest a little. Palace continued to win a couple, lose a couple and draw a few, but something about Trevor Francis just made me switch off for a time. I have no recollection of the on-loan striker Noel Whelan scoring three goals, nor of David Hunt's two appearances. I barely recall Trevor Francis being sacked and Steve Kember taking charge for the rest of the season, and I vaguely remember a feeling of dread when Bryan Robson was touted as manager. There is something in the recesses of my memory, though, which proves that I was there: 'that Ben Watson looks a good player.'

bouncebackability, *n. chiefly sport: The capacity to recover quickly or fully from a setback, bad situation, etc.*

The collapse of ITV Digital in 2002, and the loss of £180million still owed to the clubs outside the Premiership, was starting to have the impact that many predicted and a dozen or more clubs had followed Palace's example and gone into some form of administration. One of these was Wimbledon, who under chairman Charles Koppel planned to move to Milton Keynes and set up as MK Dons, which was disgracefully sanctioned by the Football League. Having shared Selhurst Park since 1991, Wimbledon had planned to move to a hockey stadium in Milton Keynes until their new ground was finished, but as this was delayed, they were forced to start the season still sharing with Palace. In lieu of rent owed, Palace took back Neil Shipperley, who had still been playing and scoring regularly for the Dons, although when he appeared again in a Palace shirt he looked badly out of condition, bringing back memories of Jamie Pollock, who Simon Jordan claimed to have sacked for being overweight. Palace were starting to tighten their belts as well, and high earners Ade Akinbiyi and Danny Granville were transfer-listed, with a likelihood that Hayden Mullins and Julian Gray would be on their way to bigger clubs. Gray had by now become highly unpopular with the fans, who picked up the clues in Jordan's reference to 'big-time Charlies' at the club. Mullins' attitude however was unimpeachable, despite him running down his contract in the hope of a move.

In fact, Gray's planned deals with Leeds, Charlton and Blackburn fell through, because none thought that he was worth the fee that Palace wanted and he eventually went on loan to Cardiff.

Granville didn't attract too much interest, and Akinbiyi proved very hard to shift until Stoke took him off Palace's hands for nothing, to Kember's great relief. One sad but inevitable departure was that of Alex Kolinko, now in dispute with Palace over claims of money owed, and Dele Adebola was released after an unremarkable year of effort but no great inspiration. Following a bitty season of injuries and loss of form, Aki Riihilahti's midfield place was threatened with the arrival of Michael Hughes, who had been kicking his heels for a year after a contract dispute between West Ham and Wimbledon.

Michael Hughes

Without too much fanfare, Steve Kember was kept on as manager, this time without the 'caretaker' label, and vowed to get Palace playing the passing game, playing to the strengths of Freedman rather than the likes of Akinbiyi and Adebola. With that in mind, the decision to bring back Shipperley perhaps seemed an odd one, but it seemed to work. Dougie scored a hat-trick on the first day as Palace came from behind to beat Burnley, despite both Routledge and Derry being sent off. Two more wins followed and Kember had made a dream start to his latest stint in the hot seat, winning over some of the sceptics who, despite loving Kember for his devotion to Palace over the years, had misgivings about his credentials as a manager, and above all were desperate for him not to fail. From top of the table after three games, four games after that the doubts were starting to surface, with five players already sent off, and home defeats at the hands of Sheffield United ('Warnock can't help being a prat', said Kember afterwards) and Bradford City. Mullins finally got his move, not to a big club as expected, but to West Ham, and really, who could blame him? Slowly but surely, it all started to go a bit Trevor Francis, and by mid-October Palace were already sliding down into the bottom half of the table when they faced Ipswich in a midweek home game. When Andy Johnson and Dougie Freedman score three between them, you don't expect to get beaten, but Ipswich scored a late goal to win the game 4–3, a neat chip after dreadful defending, coming from the boot of big Ipswich striker Shefki Kuqi.

Iain Dowie

'Jordan Out' was becoming a pretty regular chant by now, but it was Steve Kember who was starting to fear for his job, as his team tumbled towards the relegation places. The Palace team that lined up against Wigan for a Saturday lunchtime televised game was one that should have been pushing for promotion from what was a quite ordinary Division One, but I could hardly believe what was unfolding on the screen as I supped my pint in a South London pub. Derry, Riihilahti, Freedman, Johnson, Butterfield, all good players, at times terrific players, plus Danny Granville returning from the wilderness, all played abysmally as Wigan strolled to 5–0. It was the single most depressing and shambolic performance I could remember in all my time as a fan, and I had seen plenty of pretty poor games in those years. This was a new kind of bad, a display that made you start to wonder what the point of it all was. Utterly clueless, shapeless, purposeless, hopeless. By Monday, Steve Kember was told that his time was up, but the truth was that if the players wearing Palace shirts had shown a fraction of the spirit and passion that Kember did as a player, they wouldn't have found themselves in such a parlous state.

With Kit Symons as caretaker manager, the team pulled themselves together and appeared to recover from the trauma of Wigan, but after losing at home to Crewe, a performance that nearly matched that at Wigan for sheer incompetence, it was inevitable that a new manager would replace him. In what seemed like the last act of a desperate man, he recalled Julian Gray to the side, who the fans thought they seen the back of, and Palace promptly won the next two games. By now Iain Dowie had been lined up to take over a job that was thought of as a poisoned chalice, with Jordan having earned a reputation as a trigger-happy chairman. Dowie had only spent a few months at Palace as a player back in 1995, but he had made himself popular with his wholehearted efforts, and that was just what was needed to drag Palace out of the bottom three. The Boxing Day defeat at home to Millwall turned out to be the one really bad result for the remainder of the season, and as 2004 got going, the transformation was palpable. Andy Johnson hit a purple patch, Julian Gray rediscovered his form on the wing, although not enough to get the crowd off his back, and Riihilahti and Hughes both found their best form as Palace stalked their way up the table. Mark Hudson came in to stiffen the defence, and a sequence of five victories, starting with a 5–1 win at Watford, and ending with a 6–3 scoreline against Stoke, pushed them to the fringes of the play-off places. Stoke were at the time the only side with better recent form than Palace, and beating them so comprehensively was evidence of the confidence that Dowie had instilled in his squad, who had looked defeated in every sense just two months earlier.

Mikele Leigertwood

The key to Palace's turnaround was the new training regime introduced by Dowie's sidekick, part fitness coach, part motivational evangelist John Harbin, who famously got the players boxing, and based his philosophy on the poem by boxer James Corbett, 'One More Round'. As well as

palpably improving the players' fitness and stamina – even Shipperley started to look slightly trimmer – they started working together as a team with real self-belief. For the first time in years, it was a delight to see Palace making news, and not just in the sports pages. Dowie had coined the word 'bouncebackability', which became a minor cultural phenomenon, leading to bouncebackability merchandise, knowing use of the word in other fields, and a petition to have the word included in the Oxford English Dictionary which was ultimately successful. More importantly, it summed up the attitude that was now prevalent throughout the club, on and off the field.

The final two new faces to add to what had become a quite settled side were promising defender Mikele Leigertwood, picked up from the cash-strapped Wimbledon, and keeper Nico Vaesen on loan, Palace's fourth goalie of the season after Matt Clarke, Cédric Berthelin and Thomas Myhre. Still it seemed unlikely that Palace could climb all the way from the bottom three to the top six, and having been offered a week's holiday in Spain at the end of May, I was faced with a big decision knowing that the date clashed with the play-off final. I did all the calculations meticulously, and concluded that it would take a miracle for Palace to be involved, and was pretty happy that I'd made the right decision to book the flights.

A nervy 1–0 win against Walsall in the final home game, with a dodgy penalty decision for Palace, and Johnson's spot kick saved before he followed up to score, meant that a point was needed at Coventry on the final day to seal sixth spot. The game was lost, and with it the play-off place, until West Ham's late equaliser against Wigan which pushed Paul Jewell's side out of the top six and Palace back in, literally at the last minute. If that result had panned out differently, it would still have been an incredible feat for Iain Dowie to have Palace so close, but now there was a real possibility of something even more dramatic. After a couple of frankly turgid years, we now had a huge and meaningful game to look forward to, and the two-legged semi-final against Sunderland didn't disappoint. A goalless first half was followed by a breathless second half, Palace coming from behind to win 3–2, with a late winner from AJ, making it 32 for the season. The second leg three days later was going Sunderland's way when they went 2–0 up by half time, and with 90 minutes gone they still had the lead at 4–3 on aggregate before substitute Darren Powell, who had missed most of the season, headed a goal in injury time to force another 30 minutes. Palace finished with only ten men after a red card for Gray, and finally the game went to penalties. At last we could enjoy the kind of drama that we had been robbed of at Wembley in 1996, and what high drama it was. After Oster hit the post for Sunderland, Palace's Johnson, Freedman, Shipperley and Popovic all scored, leaving Derry to seal it. His shot was saved, and in sudden death Jason McAteer missed to nearly the biggest cheer of the night (in my pub, at least), then Routledge missed, then Jeff Whitley missed, leaving Michael Hughes to step up, cool as you like, and put Palace through to the final. After the tedium of the past two seasons, that moment felt like we had won promotion already, but there was more to do.

With Wembley demolished, the final was to be held in Cardiff, and by all accounts getting there was a complete nightmare, but I had my own travel problems. That was the very day I was flying to Spain for a holiday, and uppermost in my mind were the logistics of getting from the airport to the apartment, and then quickly finding out if there was a bar anywhere showing the game. Dragging a weary family with me, the very first place I tried had a framed aerial photograph of Selhurst Park on the wall, and a passionate Eagle as the owner. Some days things just fall into place, and everything is right with the world, and so it was in Cardiff, as West Ham barely turned up for the game, allowing Neil Shipperley's tap in to send Palace once again back to the Premiership. By my count this was my seventh promotion as a Palace fan, and by far the most sensational of them all, because after that 5–0 defeat by Wigan in November, it wasn't just unlikely, it was actually impossible.

Andy Johnson

'Fight one more round. When your feet are so tired that you have to shuffle back to the centre of the ring, fight one more round. When your arms are so tired that you can hardly lift your hands to come on guard, fight one more round. When your nose is bleeding and your eyes are black and you are so tired that you wish that your opponent would crack you one on the jaw and put you to sleep, fight one more round – remembering that the man who always fights one more round is never whipped.'
'Gentleman' Jim Corbett

'What on earth is Speroni doing trying to dribble the ball out?'

When Division One transmuted into the Premier League in 1992, Palace were briefly founder members, but each attempt to break back in since then had been short-lived. Promotions in '94 and '97, quickly followed by the misery of relegation, had convinced some that perhaps it would be better if we didn't put ourselves through that again. Maybe we should accept our lot as a middling club in the comfort zone of the second tier, by now rebranded as the Championship. I don't hold with that for a moment, and to my mind it's never a season too soon to go up. I've grown up with the expectation of a rapid cycle of promotion and relegation, and the few seasons without the promise or threat of either have felt rather pointless. When Arsenal were winning everything under Arsene Wenger, I honestly thought how very dull it must be to follow a team like that, and to expect victory week after week. Any Palace fan will know how far from our own experience that attitude is, and nor do we covet that kind of success. It would be nice to win something now and again, admittedly.

Perhaps Simon Jordan felt a sense of dread at having got Palace to where he wanted, because he started to declare that he was disillusioned with football, and was looking for a way out. He continued that theme wearily for a further six years, and although his stance at the time against the greed of agents seemed admirable, the result was that Palace missed out on signing Tim Cahill, who turned out to be a magnificent player in the Premiership for Everton. Whilst Iain Dowie was committing himself to a further four years, speculation grew about who might relieve Jordan of his tiresome burden, and of course the name of Ron Noades loomed large, although Jordan's

response was: 'So long as I've got breath in my body, I won't sell this club back to Ron Noades.' A firm moral stance then, against the man who still owned Selhurst Park, and who many blamed for cynically taking Mark Goldberg's imaginary millions. Not such a firm moral stance, though, when it was rumoured that Libya's Colonel Gaddafi was interested: 'If it's beneficial to the club, it will be considered. If Gaddafi's money was able to progress Palace and allow them to compete at the top of the tree and be a successful football club, then one would have to take that into consideration.' It was nonsense, of course, but Jordan's newly acquired 'PR Guru' and prime bottom feeder Max Clifford should have tipped him off that there is indeed such a thing as bad publicity.

Emmerson Boyce

Money was tight, with the windfall of Premiership money barely covering trading losses and liabilities, so Iain Dowie's plans to strengthen to side were hamstrung. Two new goalkeepers arrived, Julián Speroni and Gábor Király, defenders Emmerson Boyce and Fitz Hall, and with Shipperley injured and Julian Gray gone to join Steve Bruce at Birmingham, Palace started the season with a new centre forward, Hungarian

Sándor Torghelle, and Finnish winger Joonas Kolkka. None cost very much, and none were a great improvement on the players who had scraped up from Division One. How disheartening it must have been for Derry, Shipperley, Butterfield, Powell and Freedman to find themselves out of the first team, but the reserves did at least have a splendid season. A little more tantalising was the signing of Iván Kaviedes, an Ecuadorean 'icon', we were assured, and then two fringe players on loan from Inter Milan, Nicola Ventola and Gonzalo Sorondo. We still hadn't heard of any of them, and we waited to see whether any of them turned out to be the new Lombardo or the new Padovano.

Sándor Torghelle

With points certain to be precious, a draw in the first game at Norwich was welcome, but Palace's entire season turned on one moment in the first home game, against Everton. This was on the face of it a fairly moderate Everton side, who had flirted with relegation the previous season, and it was Palace who looked the better side, taking the lead early on through Mark Hudson's header. At 1–0, the home side continued to dominate and could have scored two or three, but then Julián Speroni, in the Palace goal as first choice ahead of Király, tried

to dribble a back pass out of his area, lost the ball to Kevin Campbell, then panicked and brought down the veteran striker for a penalty. As confidence drained from Palace, Everton's grew, and a game that Palace were looking like winning slipped away from them, with Marcus Bent's goal for 3–1 being particularly galling. Bent had been popular during his time at Palace, but had been inexplicably neglected by Terry Venables before leaving for Port Vale, and in a way it was gratifying, if painful, to see how far he had come since then. Speroni's confidence was shot to pieces after that howler, and soon Király came into the team, staying put for nearly three years.

Tommy Black was another player who found himself sidelined, and at one point both and he and Dougie Freedman were about to sign for Leeds, until Freedman declared that he wanted to stay and fight for his place in the team, and take his number of goals past 100. Sándor Torghelle quickly dropped out of the reckoning up front, and one would have expected Freedman to renew his partnership with AJ, which had looked exceptional at times, but instead Iain Dowie decided to switch to a formation with five in midfield and Johnson on his own up front. This did have an effect in the short term, with Johnson continuing to score freely, but it meant that Palace were becoming a little one dimensional, with no Plan B. However, when Arsenal came to Selhurst Park at the beginning of November, things seemed to be falling into place, and Aki Riihilahti rounded off a barnstorming performance with the equaliser in a game that Palace deserved to win.

That game was to be the highlight of the first half of the season, though, and Palace failed to win in the course of the next ten games, finding themselves in the bottom three by Christmas. Routledge had started to alienate himself from the fans by making it clear that he wanted a move to a bigger club, despite growing up at Palace; Kaviedes had disappeared having 'failed to settle', and Greek international Vassilis Lakis had taken over from Kolkka on the left, but it felt as if Dowie was running out of ideas. Johnson continued to score regularly, including a spell of nine goals in as many games, and was finally selected to play out of position on the right wing for England, but if he wasn't scoring nobody else was. Freedman's return to the team coincided with a surprising 3–0 victory over Spurs, but on the whole Dowie's team selection became erratic, Popovic dropped from the side, young Tom Soares being preferred to Ben Watson, and Wayne Andrews on the bench emphasising the thinness of Palace's squad. For a team in trouble, to let the January transfer window pass by without adding to the squad was distressing and, sure enough, Palace were by now firmly entrenched in the bottom four.

Palace's famed bouncebackability made an appearance with a satisfying 1–0 victory over Liverpool, and the battling spirit shown by players like Hughes and Riihilahti announced that once again Palace would respond to Dowie's urgings to fight one more round. Draws against Newcastle and Southampton, both attritional slugging matches, set up the final day of the season, a game at Charlton which Palace needed to win to stay up. That penultimate game against the Saints would turn out to be Sorondo's last for Palace as he was sent off after a punch up with Peter Crouch, with Graham le Saux provoking a mass brawl, and featured a rare appearance for Nicola Ventola as substitute. This was only Ventola's third appearance all season, and the tidy goal that he scored turned out to be the only goal of the entire campaign for

a striker other than AJ. It appeared to have won a reprieve for Palace, but Southampton equalised in injury time, keeping their own hopes alive, and on the last day relegation came down to any three out of four.

Joonas Kolkka

Needing three points against Charlton at the Valley, Iain Dowie picked Ben Watson ahead of Riihilahti, and restored Butterfield to the defence, but in a surprisingly open game, Palace found themselves a goal behind at half time. Cometh the hour, cometh the Doug, and as soon as Freedman came off the bench the game swung Palace's way. Freedman scored a beautifully judged chip, then won a penalty, put away by Johnson, to surely save his team from relegation once again. Watching from distance on the big screen at Selhurst Park, I couldn't see precisely what was going on, although what I could make out seemed to suggest safety with just eight minutes to go, before a poorly defended free kick into the box gave Charlton their second, and sent Palace out of the Premiership yet again, to the glee of the locals.

This relegation felt different somehow to the others. Palace certainly weren't a shambles, like in 1998, nor could they point to terrible bad luck, as in 1995. Instead, we had to accept that we were just that little bit off being good enough, and could just as well have finished mid-table as bottom, but simply hadn't strengthened the squad sufficiently to bridge the gap between the top two divisions. Ventola might have been the striker we needed, but he was injured for most of his time at the club, and despite efforts to sign Tim Cahill and Dean Ashton – either of whom could well have kept Palace up – those deals came to nothing. Iain Dowie had to struggle on with what he had, and the team that finished the season wasn't noticeably better than the one that had won promotion at Cardiff a year earlier.

'100 years of Passion and Pride'

So went the strapline for Palace's centenary year, and it was a good season to reflect on what that meant, to us as fans, and to players. As footballers have become increasingly mercenary, so the laughable hypocrisy of kissing the shirt to curry favour has become more and more prevalent, and increasingly nauseating. Mercifully, we haven't seen too much of it at Selhurst Park, although a few instances stand out, and you want to believe that players like Lombardo share your undying love for the club they probably hadn't heard of until a few months ago. When Sasa Curcic declared: 'I will only leave this club if they carry me out in a dead box', it gave us something to cling on to in that bleak season. There are a few players, though, who renew your faith that there is still the concept of loyalty, and a genuine bond with the fans, and despite relegation for Palace there was a true sense of unity. I believed Aki Riihilahti when he wrote, just the day after relegation against Charlton: 'I'd have done anything for us to stay up. It is painful and I've been crying a lot since yesterday. I put everything into it and still it wasn't enough.' I believed him every time he celebrated a goal; when he kissed the badge with a furious defiance as relegation drew inexorably closer, he meant it, and had earned the right to display his passion. Dougie Freedman had showed us what Crystal Palace meant to him when he refused to leave, and pledged to fight for his place in the team, despite being ill-used by both Trevor Francis and Iain Dowie.

Andy Johnson, though, had shown himself to be a class act in the Premiership, was in the England squad, and had done his level best for Palace, so after he put in a transfer request, it was only a question of which team could afford him. However it was that Dowie and Simon Jordan eventually persuaded him to stay, whilst he was being courted by Spurs and Everton during the summer, it was a massive boost to the fans, and a guarantee, surely, of another promotion season ahead. Gábor Király had also impressed a number of clubs, but chose to stay, although the foreign legion of Lakis, Sorondo, Ventola and Torghelle all sloped off, to be followed soon after by Joonas Kolkka. Apart from Sorondo, none left a huge gap, but the most significant departure was that of Wayne Routledge, who had outgrown the club who had looked after him as a boy, given him his debut aged 16, and turned him into a Premiership footballer, electing instead to sign for Spurs reserves. His direct replacement was Jobi McAnuff, a proper winger who had grown up at Wimbledon with Mikele Leigertwood, and who had developed into a good Championship player with Cardiff. Iain Dowie replaced Sorondo with Darren Ward from Millwall, and with the need still for an old fashioned centre forward in his own image, rescued Jon Macken from Manchester City, where he had slowly declined after they had paid £5.5million for him a couple of years earlier.

Gábor Király

Another club in the market for Andy Johnson was Birmingham, who had realised what an error they had made in letting him go as part of the Clinton Morrison deal, and their chairman David Gold continued his spat with Jordan when he reiterated the idea that AJ needed to be playing in the Premiership to keep his England place. Morrison was by now out of favour with Steve Bruce at Birmingham, and appeared to be heading to Norwich until Palace came up with the wonderful idea of bringing him back to play alongside Johnson. Morrison declared himself Palace through and through, and made the move. Never go back, they say. It worked for Dougie Freedman when he came home to Selhurst Park, but not for David Hopkin, who returned as a shadow of the player he had been. Steve Kember had two successful spells to bookmark his career, and later on Peter Nicholas, Andy Gray and Neil Shipperley were all welcomed back, but what would we be getting with Clinton Morrison? A more mature and thoughtful player, desperate to give his all for club who nurtured him, or someone disenchanted by slipping down the hierarchy at Birmingham?

Gonzalo Sorondo

Macken was already labouring up front against Stoke when Clinton came on as substitute for his first game back, and combined with AJ for Johnson's second goal of the game, and naturally much badge-kissing followed. In the next game, he started up front alongside AJ, and they both scored, and the same happened in the game after that. This was looking a masterstroke by Dowie, and Macken soon found himself struggling to get in the team, but when Johnson faced several weeks out with a knee injury, we were treated once again to the double act of Freedman and Morrison from four years earlier. For a spell the two of them clicked and Freedman was back to his best, scoring six goals in five games, moving Palace towards the top end of the table, and taking in yet another League Cup tie against Liverpool. The idea of beating Liverpool in a knockout game was by now becoming commonplace, and goals from Marco Reich and Freedman won the game for Palace, although the outstanding player on the night was the forgotten man, Julián Speroni, who had kept clean sheets in the two previous rounds, with Király rested, and showed what a spectacular shot stopper he could be. Freedman's 100th goal finally came in the 3–2 victory at Brighton, avenging their 1–0 win at Selhurst Park just a month earlier, and although Palace were a little below where they had expected to be approaching Christmas, an unprecedented winning streak of four wins in eight days over the holidays put them back in the running for the play-offs.

It already seemed, though, that Steve Coppell's Reading and Sheffield United were running away with the automatic promotion places, so the season became a steady jog to stay in the top six for several teams, rather than a sprint to the finish. The latter part of the season was characterised by the good form of McAnuff, both wide and in front of goal, the indifferent form of Morrison, and the welcome return of Aki Riihilahti from injury. Some questioned whether Aki would win back his place with Soares and Watson preferred, alongside the evergreen Michael Hughes, but in his few remaining appearances he reminded everyone what a valuable all-round asset he was, getting forward to score a couple despite his reputation as a destroyer. By the time the home game with Watford came around, the top of the table had more or less sorted itself out and both sides were already thinking ahead half a dozen games to the play-offs. Palace ran out pretty comfortable 3–1 winners, whilst Dowie experimented in a few positions; Popovic made a rare start in defence, and Riihilahti dropped to the bench. We didn't realise at the time, but this was to be the last time that Aki pulled on a Palace shirt, and he didn't even get on the pitch. The following few games saw starts for Reich, Macken and Butterfield, who had all become fringe players, but none of made the cut for the vital first leg of the play-off semi-final, where Palace were to face Watford once again.

Darren Ward

Here we were again, not going up as champions, as Simon Jordan had confidently

promised, but scraping through to fight one more round, which looked a formality against a Watford team that had looked anything but stiff opposition a few weeks earlier. The question was whether we would prefer Preston or Leeds in the final, but on the day Palace showed no pride, no desire, and capitulated 3–0, which was almost embarrassing. A 0–0 draw at Vicarage Road was remarkable only for a huge punch-up after Fitz Hall tried to wrestle the ball from Watford's time-wasting manager, but that was more passion than anyone in the team had shown all season, a season that ended in disappointment and a little sadness, as it was to be the last we would see not only of Iain Dowie's victory punch to the Holmesdale end, but of Andy Johnson's burger-munching goal celebration, and of the great Aki Riihilahti.

'I pictured myself in Cardiff, on the podium celebrating in the sea of red and blue another promotion for the club I've been privileged to play for over five years. In that moment of complete fulfilment I could have even sang along my tone deaf version of Glad All Over. Victorious moment, a mutual thank you – have a good summer! That would have been my perfect ending for this season. Instead my great years in Crystal Palace might have ended to a disappointing result, on a grey evening sitting behind the dugout at Vicarage Road kicking a seat in front in despair. Small injuries and a failed promotion campaign leaves a bitter taste to what has been done over the years. You don't want to be remembered as bit of a sick note after you've played 180 games for the club. Or that you didn't achieve the widely expected promotion after the club was almost relegated from the same league when you joined. In the history of sports, though, you are always as good as your last game.'

Aki Riihilahti, 16 May 2006

2006-07

'Peter Taylor will get Palace playing exciting, attacking football in his own image...'

Only two people really know what was said in a long and difficult telephone conversation between Simon Jordan and Iain Dowie, and as they have since settled out of court, it will stay that way. The outcome was that less than a fortnight after the 2005–06 season ended, the news broke that Dowie was leaving Crystal Palace 'by mutual consent'. In Simon Jordan's version, he suggested that Andy Johnson, Fitz Hall, Ben Watson and Tom Soares should be sold. Dowie disagreed. Jordan suggested sitting down and watching a video of the Watford game together 'so that I could better understand his viewpoint and how he saw the game'. Dowie's response, according to Jordan, was 'under no circumstances am I going to watch matches with you, if you want to manage, do your coaching badges.' Crucially, again according to Jordan's version, Dowie said that he wanted to leave to be nearer his family, who lived in Bolton, and as a result Jordan waived a contracted £1 million compensation payment. One thing the two men did agree on, when both were cross-examined in court, was that each had grown to dislike the other quite some time ago, and both knew it.

The press conference that confirmed Dowie's departure had been preceded by a rumour that Dowie was going to take over at Charlton, who had just removed their highly successful manager Alan Curbishley, but according to Jordan, he had assurances from Dowie that he wouldn't be going to the Valley under any circumstances. Within a week, Charlton confirmed that Dowie was to take the manager's job, but Jordan had a coup lined up for their press conference, trying to get a writ served on Dowie, accusing him of misrepresentation, and making sure that the camera crews present

were tipped off. This was characteristic of Jordan's showboating style, and whatever the truth of the matter, at the time I knew whose word I would be inclined to trust out of the two of them. I thought that Dowie had done wonders at Palace, and that Jordan should have done all he could to keep him there, but the relationship had clearly run its course.

Peter Taylor

After a very public bidding war involving Bolton and Wigan, Andy Johnson wisely chose to move to Everton, and Palace happily pocketed £8.6million, easily the most ever received for a Palace player. Unusually for a player so crucial to their team, there was nothing but good will from the fans as AJ left, as not only was it obvious that he could have gone much sooner, but everyone recognised his complete commitment to Palace's cause whenever he pulled on the shirt, unlike other recent departees such as Julian Gray and Wayne Routledge. Palace also got decent fees from Wigan for Fitz Hall and Emmerson Boyce, both of whom had done enough during Palace's Premiership season to earn a move to another side likely to struggle at the top level, but Sheffield United signed Mikele Leigertwood on the cheap, meaning that three of Palace's most able defenders had gone within weeks of each other.

Shefki Kuqi

The curious thing about Jordan's latest quest for a new manager was that he was assisted by Bob Dowie, brother of Iain, who had remained in his rather mysterious role of Director of Football. Among candidates considered were Luton's Mike Newell, and remarkably – again – Graeme Souness, but in luring Peter Taylor from Hull, Jordan divided opinion like never before. There was no question that Taylor had been a fabulous player for Palace under Malcolm Allison, and had been instrumental in getting Palace to their first ever FA Cup semi-final in 1976. He was immensely popular, a true winger who could get past players and put in killer crosses from either side, and he did a mean Norman Wisdom impression to boot. As a manager, though, the jury was still out. Taylor had done well at Gillingham, Brighton and Hull, earning promotion from the lower leagues with each. He also had a good reputation for his work with the England under-21s, even taking charge of the full England team as caretaker manager for one game. Most people, though, remembered that he had failed at Leicester City, and he was destined to forever be associated with his star signing, the woeful Ade Akinbiyi. There were those who had wanted Taylor as manager for years, hoping that he would bring some of the flamboyance he showed as a player, and perhaps some of the glamour of the Allison years, when Palace plummeted from the first to the third division, but the crowds kept coming. Others were worried that, if and when he fell out with Jordan and was fired, it would overshadow the memories of those happier times. Sometimes you just don't want to know that your heroes are fallible human beings like you, but there it was, and perhaps Peter Taylor had found his destiny, to guide the Eagles to glory and become a legend.

With what should have been a considerable sum of money to spend, he set about bringing in new faces, and the hope was that he would already have a list of promising young talent in his back pocket as a result of his England job and could attract them to Palace to join the likes of Watson, Soares and Borrowdale. We could be looking at something like Venables' young guns of 1979 here. Leon Cort – 14 caps for England under-21s – came from Hull, and looked a good centre back, perhaps a fair replacement for Fitz Hall. Next in was the young goalkeeper Scott Flinders from Barnsley, who had played for the England under-20s. Here we go, who's next? Charlie Sheringham, 18-year-old son of England's Teddy Sheringham. Looking good. James Scowcroft, aged 30? Well, maybe he can do a job up front. Carl Fletcher, a bit of Premiership experience with West Ham, OK, I suppose. Matt Lawrence... didn't he play alongside Darren Ward when Millwall got to the FA Cup final a couple of years back, but isn't he knocking on a bit? And Mark Kennedy... he used to be quite good, I seem to recall.

In all honesty, it was beginning to look like Peter Taylor was putting together a side to stay in the Championship rather than take it by storm, but the first three games confounded that theory. Three straight wins sent Palace to the summit; Scowcroft and Cort both scored goals and looked good, Mark Kennedy could hit a dead ball better than the consistently disappointing Ben Watson, and Morrison and Freedman both got off the mark for the season. However, it was soon apparent that Taylor really didn't rate one of the great strike partnerships in Palace history, and with Jon Macken ditched, Torghelle finally gone, and not even Wayne Andrews on the bench to come on and run around a bit, the search was on for a big-name, big-money striker. David Nugent, Izale Mcleod and Freddy Eastwood were all on the radar, but eventually the transfer window closed with the big news that Shefki Kuqi had been signed for £2.5million, and the rather smaller news of Peter Taylor's son-in-law Stuart Green arriving from Hull. Kuqi had been a fine player at Ipswich, taking the eye with his goal celebration which involved diving through the air to land outstretched on his belly, and had spent time in the Premiership at Blackburn, although with less impact. Nevertheless, here was a seasoned international, a team mate of Aki Riihilahti in the Finland side, and someone who had a proven record in the Championship. It seemed a lot of money, but we had got over £8 million for AJ, after all.

It didn't take long for Palace's early season sparkle to die away, just as it didn't take long for everyone to realise that Kuqi was mostly a waste of a perfectly good XXL shirt, but there was a seemingly happy distraction when Simon Jordan smugly announced that he had secretly bought the freehold of Selhurst Park from Ron Noades, under the guise of another company: 'I bought Selhurst Park through a structure that was set up over the last two weeks and I'm not so sure that Ron is aware of who he has sold it to, but he's sold it to me.' This sounded like wonderful news, as it meant that Palace could now get on with developing the ground in the way they wanted, or at the very least fixing the toilets. Whatever the mendacious voices inside Jordan's head were telling him, this turned out not to be true.

Carl Fletcher

By the end of October, and after an appalling run of results, the calls for Peter Taylor to be sacked were ringing out loud and clear, but the first to walk the plank was Bob Dowie, whose role and influence over the manager was unclear from the start. There was much speculation about the nature of the underlying problems, but problems there most certainly were. Taylor had no idea of his best side, swapping Granville and Borrowdale, Ward and Hudson, Fletcher and Michael Hughes, and even Marco Reich got a bit of a look in, but most strangely, he dropped Király, first of all trying Scott Flinders, then the on-loan Iain Turner, with all the while Julián Speroni sitting idly on the bench. It could have been curtains for the manager after Simon Jordan gave him his own personal vote of confidence, but from nowhere results started to pick up, and Kuqi and Freedman briefly started to look like a useful strike partnership, notably in the 3–0 home win over QPR, which bought Taylor some time, perhaps enough time to make some meaningful signings in the January transfer window.

general improvement in performances, it was increasingly unlikely that the last couple of months would offer anything other than paddling in mid-table, and so it proved, but there were just enough green shoots for Taylor to be given more time, with promise of a better season to come. Overall, though, of Peter Taylor's signings, Cort had been the best and Fletcher had worked as hard as he could, but he had completely failed to build what could really be called a team. The fans hadn't enjoyed the manager's largely negative approach, surely a symptom of Taylor's fear of the sack more than of his natural instincts, and there had been little to get hot under the collar about. Some players underachieved, notably Watson and Soares, and some just weren't good enough. Was Taylor a bad manager, were they bad players, or was it just bad luck? Honestly, a bit of all three, but this was a season to be forgotten, reminiscent of the time under Trevor Francis, and in every sense the club had gone backwards.

Matt Lawrence

Taylor had fallen out with so many players at various times – Morrison, McAnuff, Ward, Király, Morrison and Hughes amongst them – and so many had lost their form, that radical changes were needed, but the only new faces were Paul Ifill and Dave Martin, wingers both. Ifill was another Millwall old boy who had lost his way a bit at Sheffield United under Neil Warnock, and Martin was catching the eye at non-league Dartford, but in reality it wasn't wingers we needed, and although Ifill made a decent start, helping Palace to a seven-game unbeaten run, neither signing was what was needed to kick start the season.

Ultimately, it was a season that had promised little, and delivered less. As springtime approached, and despite a

'If we can build a team around young Bostock, we can really go places…'

The only thing less likely than Peter Taylor still being in charge would be Jamie Scowcroft scoring a hat-trick, but the first game of the season, away to Southampton, saw both. It was to be the pinnacle of Taylor's Palace career as a manager, and perhaps even Scowcroft's, whose goals the previous season had been carefully rationed. Perhaps Simon Jordan was a changed man and had been stung by criticism that he was too quick to fire managers, but there had been enough improvement, albeit from a very low starting point, for him to have faith that Peter Taylor was starting to get things right. There had been a big clear out of players during the summer, with Watford paying good money for Jobi McAnuff, and Darren Ward, Gary Borrowdale and Danny Granville all moving on, as well as Gábor Király, Michael Hughes and Tommy Black. That's quite a few players to replace, but with nobody willing to take Kuqi off his hands, Jordan was finding cash flow increasingly problematic, and apart from Portuguese defender José Fonte, the pre-season spend was restricted to left back Tony Craig, yet another ordinary Millwall player, and left winger Jeff Hughes from Lincoln City. Remember them?

Following the fine win at Southampton, Palace were dumped out of the League Cup on penalties by Bristol Rovers, with Freedman and Kuqi both missing from the spot. Palace then scraped a point at home against Leicester through Morrison's goal in injury time, moving him on to 99 goals for the club. Three defeats later, though, and there were already strong rumours that Peter Taylor was going to be replaced as manager by Neil Warnock, which Simon Jordan denied. Taylor had lost patience with Kuqi, who went to Fulham on loan, and still

couldn't see that Dougie Freedman was his only hope of salvation, so he went into the loan market and signed up Paul Dickov and Besian Idrizaj. The young Dickov had been one of the scorers in Arsenal's 3–0 victory that sent Palace out of the Premiership under Steve Coppell, and had gone on to earn a reputation as a combative forward for a number of clubs, while Idrizaj was a promising young Austrian striker on Liverpool's books, and came to Selhurst Park on a season-long loan. Neither made much impact, neither scored, and neither was able to save the manager's bacon.

Clint Hill

Quite why it took Simon Jordan so long to put Peter Taylor out of our misery, I'm not sure, but the reaction to the news could only ever be a shrug, a tilt of the head and a few kind words: 'it's for the best.' Coppell, Smith, Bruce, Kember, Francis, Dowie, Taylor, all managers since Jordan's takeover in 2000, all sacked by Jordan, apart from Sir Steve who sacked himself, yet for some reason Neil Warnock wanted the job. Frequently described as the Marmite manager – you either love him or hate him – more often you either hate him because he's the opposition's manager, or hate him despite him being yours. Without question,

Warnock knew the business of managing struggling football teams inside out, and it came as no surprise to find that a man so wilfully controversial and outspoken counted Simon Jordan as a close personal friend. Underneath it all, Warnock's penchant for winding up fans, players and officials was sharply calculating, but he loved nothing more than upsetting people, which at times was hilarious, at other times tedious. Most recently, he had been in charge of a Sheffield United side relegated from the Premiership on the last day, and felt the injustice of West Ham's survival at their expense very deeply after they were fined for playing Carlos Tevez in breach of regulations but not deducted any points.

After the torpor of Peter Taylor's reign, it didn't really matter what Palace fans thought of Warnock personally, because one way or another things might get interesting at last. It was early enough in the season for the fans to put up with the inevitable period of transition, and indeed Warnock's first win didn't come for seven games, but by then he had started to rip the squad apart and rebuild it in his own image. Out went some of the players perceived as Taylor's men, including Leon Cort, Stuart Green and Mark Kennedy, as well as the new signings Tony Craig and Jeff Hughes, and in came Clint Hill at left back, and somewhat surprisingly, Shaun Derry, who hadn't been a great favourite in his previous spell. The contrast between Leon Cort, considered 'too nice' by Warnock, and without enough scars on his face, and the uncompromising defender Hill, not averse to receiving or dishing out a few scars, was an indication of Warnock's determination to add some grit, and the return of Derry was further confirmation of what we could look forward to. From November through to the middle of January, Warnock galvanised his team to such an extent that

they went unbeaten for fifteen games, and stormed up the table and into the top six. The transformation in some of the players was remarkable. Clinton Morrison, who had generally been moping around under Taylor, found his scoring form again, and Jamie Scowcroft started to look a good foil for Clinton, as well as popping in a few himself, including a memorable long-range strike at Wolves. Danny Butterfield returned to the side, with Matt Lawrence joining Hudson in the centre of defence, and Speroni's form in goal ensured that Király wasn't missed.

Neil Warnock

More surprising was that, with Warnock's reputation for strong, battling teams, he nevertheless started to experiment with some of the more promising young players who strangely hadn't got a look in under Taylor. Victor Moses had been spoken of as a future star for a while, and Warnock eased him in gently, while Sean Scannell made a big impact with his pace and had a good run in the side. Young Lee Hills was given his debut and showed great promise, but for a while all the talk was of John Bostock, also given his debut by Neil Warnock, aged just fifteen. Bostock had been at the club since the age of seven, and had been spoken of as a real prodigy, a future star of English football, destined to captain his country one day. Best of all, his family were true Palace fans, and he intended staying at Palace despite interest already from Arsenal, Chelsea, even Barcelona. He showed tantalising glimpses of his talent in his few cameo appearances, and then he was put away for the winter, until he could sign a professional contract on his sixteenth birthday. When he then signed for Spurs reserves, Jordan was livid with Bostock's stepfather, accusing him of lying to him about wanting to stay, and with the Football League tribunal who set the fee at a paltry £700,000: 'We had a £900,000 offer from Chelsea when he was 14 which we turned down. It's beyond me and it makes me question why I bother with football. I have an academy who have produced a world-class footballer for someone else and got paid two-and-sixpence for it. We weren't unrealistic – we didn't try to be clever and put a value of £5million on the player. We simply said this is what the player is worth, these are the reasons why he is worth it and all we wanted was a fair and equitable outcome.' You had to say, whatever you thought of Jordan's righteous indignation in other areas, that he had a pretty fair point here, and he certainly convinced the Palace faithful that their club had been badly wronged.

Shaun Derry was a revelation under Warnock, twice the player he had been in his first spell at Palace, and his loan deal was made permanent, as was Clint Hill's, and midfielder Neil Danns was signed from Birmingham, although he barely played for another year. With Scowcroft and Morrison hitting a barren patch, to halt the slide down the table Warnock tried a curious experiment, bringing Shefki Kuqi back into the team as a lone striker. The experiment only lasted a couple of games

and once again the crowd was on his back to such an extent that when he was rightly substituted in a home game against Wolves, the fans showed their unanimous delight at him leaving the pitch. We don't have a satisfactory name for the gesture that Kuqi responded with, but in French it is known as the 'bras d'honneur', in Spanish as 'el corte de manga', and in any language the meaning is clear: 'up yours!' Perhaps we should call it the Kuqi in English. Neil Warnock acted swiftly to fine Kuqi and put him on the transfer list, and we were sure that was the last we had seen of the Flying Finn. It turned out that we were wrong, but we were shortly to see the last of Dougie Freedman in a Palace shirt. Freedman had only started three games under Warnock (yet another manager with a blind spot for the most gifted footballer at the club), and reluctantly agreed to go on loan to Leeds for the remainder of the season, where he quickly showed his quality and helped them into the League One play-offs.

Sean Scannell

With Victor Moses and Sean Scannell now becoming established in the side, Warnock continued to do what he does best. He kept Palace in contention for the play-off places, finally ensuring their involvement after a

5–0 rout of Burnley on the final day, with the on-loan Scott Sinclair looking like the player who might give Palace the edge in the scrap for promotion. Their semi-final opponents, Bristol City, had been in the top six all season and in the top two for a while, but looked vulnerable to a Palace side on a late run into the play-offs, much as we had witnessed in Iain Dowie's first season. City always had the edge in the first leg at Selhurst Park and it looked for a while as if Dele Adebola might be the man to win it for the visitors, five years after he had left Palace, but it was a superb long range goal from David Noble that gave City a 2–1 lead to defend at Bristol three days later. Palace didn't make it easy, and took the lead with a Ben Watson header, and then won a penalty which would have put them ahead on aggregate. Everything was set up for Ben Watson, who had grown into a crucial part of Warnock's team, to complete the job, but his shot hit the post and the game swung City's way, winning 2–1 after extra time. It should have felt like a massive let-down, but the atmosphere at Bristol that evening wasn't at all downbeat. Palace had lost fair and square, but hadn't really expected to be contesting the play-offs after the way the season started, and it had seemed like an awful long time since we'd had such enjoyable, competitive games with something at stake. Neil Warnock may be a bastard, but he was our bastard, and with a full season next year he would surely get Palace back into the Premier League.

'Ashley-Paul is goin fulham on Monday. If I pull dis off im on dis ting!!!'

Ashley-Paul Robinson was another promising academy player who had made a few substitute appearances towards the end of Neil Warnock's first season, and had looked a fast, skilful winger, if a little tubby. As a result he had been offered a contract at Palace, but he chose to let the world know that he belonged in the Premier League by announcing a trial at Fulham on his Facebook page, thus ending his Palace career with a few misjudged keystrokes, and clearing his path to the lower reaches of non-league football. As fast as Palace's youth system could produce players fit for first team action, it seemed, they had a battle on their hands to keep them at the club, John Bostock being the most notorious instance. Now Ben Watson wanted a move, and Victor Moses was being courted by Premier League teams, as were Tom Soares and Sean Scannell. Morrison had also rejected a new contract and moved to Coventry, and Dougie Freedman eventually signed for Southend after being told that he wasn't in Warnock's plans for the coming season. Mark Hudson joined Charlton, and even Simon Jordan renewed his efforts to sell the club and get as far away from football as possible.

So without Morrison, Freedman, and probably Watson, and with Scowcroft and Ifill transfer-listed, what were the manager's grand plans to improve on the previous year? Attacking midfielder Nick Carle in for Watson to start with, the Australian international having impressed for Bristol City in the play-off games against Palace. Centre back Paddy McCarthy came from Charlton, which seemed to be a straightforward like-for-like swap with Hudson, but with Kuqi still festering while waiting for someone else to take on his considerable wage bill, extra manpower was needed up front and the only forwards coming in were Luton's Calvin Andrew and non-league player Simon Thomas.

Paddy McCarthy

The opening game, a 0–0 draw with Watford, was a dull affair, as was a 2–1 defeat of Hereford in the League Cup, which featured two other new signings in John Oster and Leandre Griffit. Those two drab performances set the tone for the early part of the season, with all eyes on the transfer window. Stoke City paid a lot of money for Tom Soares, but there were no moves for Moses, Scannell or Watson, and Palace eventually got the centre forward that was so desperately needed to get the season going, Ipswich's Alan Lee. Lee was injured almost immediately, but the season did appear to be improving when Ben Watson returned to the fold against Swansea and played a blinder, scoring directly from a free kick which he had intended as a cross. With Lee absent, Neil Warnock moved quickly to loan another striker, Craig Beattie from West Bromwich Albion, who were by now in the Premier League. Beattie made a huge difference and although he wasn't prolific in front of goal he contributed a lot to an improvement in form that saw Palace move almost unnoticed into the top six by Christmas. Sadly, Beattie was needed back at West Brom, but while he had been there Warnock had unexpectedly given another chance to Kuqi, which smacked of desperation. However, Kuqi confounded everyone by giving total commitment on the pitch, scoring a few excellent goals, and winning over the very fans who he had abused a year earlier. He still wasn't all that good, in truth, but was worth his place on effort alone, and for his continuing comedy value.

Claude Davis

One young player about to make his mark was Nathaniel Clyne, who had gone into the first team almost unheralded, but who immediately looked the business – shades of what we saw of Ashley Cole during his time on loan – but Ben Watson was finally on his way, to Wigan, now managed by Jordan's old adversary Steve Bruce. Watson's departure, followed closely by McCarthy's absence with a dislocated shoulder, signalled a sharp downturn in results, and with no points in January, and only four in February, hopes of promotion started to recede. Alan Lee came into the team, lumbered about to little effect before going out on loan to Norwich, Oster's

early promise tailed off, and Carle and Ifill continued to be huge disappointments. An indication of the financial storm clouds gathering was the decision to let Danny Butterfield go on loan to Charlton, so that Palace could afford to bring in striker Anthony Stokes until the end of the season. It was evident from the lack of new signings, apart from centre back Claude Davis, that money was a big issue despite the earlier sales of Soares and Watson, and the season proved yet again to be a damp squib, made all the harder to accept after flirtation with the play-offs a year earlier. Palace under Neil Warnock had gone back to more or less the mediocre state he had found them in, and it was hard to see a way forward if funds really were that scarce.

By far the best thing about this forgettable season was the playing strip, with Palace reverting to the diagonal red and blue sash for the first time at home since 1986. First introduced in 1976, the sash was evocative of the Malcolm Allison era, of Venables' later 'Team of the Eighties', and of the bleaker years under Dario Gradi, Alan Mullery and, more happily Steve Coppell. Ian Walsh and Dave Swindlehurst scored in the sash when they beat Burnley for promotion in 1979, Jim Cannon when he scored to put the Eagles top of Division One the following season, and Ian Wright made his debut and scored his first Palace goals wearing the sash. It wasn't just nostalgia on the part of us old geezers, though, as the sash had been voted for by the fans who on the whole loved it and wanted to keep it. After a single season, though, commercial considerations and a complete disregard for the views of the fans meant that it was due to be ditched in favour of a generic red and blue striped design supplied off the peg by Nike. The Croydon Advertiser gave voice to some of the fans who were upset by this, and Simon Jordan's petty reaction was to ban the Advertiser from the ground, demonstrating to one and all just how much he had lost the plot.

Alan Lee

The season ended as it had begun, with a goalless draw, at home to Sheffield United during which José Fonte's younger brother Rui, on loan from Arsenal, came on as a substitute. As the Blades still had a shot at automatic promotion, it was good game in front of a large crowd, but Fonte's involvement after his loan period had ended meant that Palace were later deducted one point, although it made no difference to the final position of fifteenth in the table. There had been a few good things to reflect on: the superb form in goal of Julián Speroni, fast becoming a cult figure, the development of Moses, Scannell and Clyne, and Neil Danns starting to look a very good player after a year out injured, but too many players had flopped for the season to be counted as anything but a let-down. In fact Palace were so firmly in fifteenth, their rightful position after a poor season, that had they been awarded ten extra points, or deducted ten points, they still would have been solidly embedded in the hinterland of the Championship.

*'Going down? Are we f***, Minus ten, and we're staying up!'*

Neil Warnock clearly felt that he had unfinished business, with the expectation that he would stay at Palace until Simon Jordan had found a buyer, and then retire to the West Country. The turnover of players continued but Alan Lee remained, Kuqi having finally left, and the ageing striker Stern John was signed for a year along with West Ham's young star Freddie Sears, on loan. That was the strike partnership that started the season against Plymouth, with unknown French youngster Alassane N'Diaye in midfield, Warnock having already hyped him as the new Patrick Vieira. On the bench was another new signing, Darren Ambrose, who had joined from Charlton, and who had helped the Addicks to relegation along with Mark Hudson and Danny Butterfield. Ambrose had shone as a young player at Ipswich, but had never quite made it in the Premier League with Newcastle, and appeared to have a similar career trajectory to Mark Kennedy, whose time at Palace had been inauspicious.

Stern John's first game ended in him being stretchered off with a dislocated elbow, but Alan Lee came on from the bench, scored a goal, and kept his place for most of the season, slowly winning the fans round as he battled away manfully. A midweek Cup tie against Torquay saw Ambrose score his first two goals for Palace, and he retained his place the following Saturday for the trip to old adversaries Bristol City. Freddie Sears got round the back of the defence, and poked the ball past the goalkeeper for his first goal for Palace. Not the cleanest strike, admittedly, but they all count, and Sears lapped up the congratulations as the City defenders walked disconsolately away ready for the restart. The referee, though,

and his assistant, were the only two people who didn't spot that the ball had bounced out after hitting the horizontal support at the back of the net, and awarded a goal kick. The disgrace of it was not that the two officials made such a howler, but that the Bristol City players didn't put them straight. The use of the word 'cheat' by Jordan and Warnock upset the City manager Gary Johnson, but if it looks like a duck...

Stern John

The revelation of the season turned out to be Darren Ambrose, whose quality on the ball and passing ability was better than anything we had seen for a while, and Danns started to come into his own, looking far more effective than either Carle or Oster had been. But the start of the season was overshadowed by a transfer embargo placed on Palace by the Football League over unpaid bonuses and signing-on fees to ex-players, and one started to understand why players such as Ifill, Scowcroft and Oster had appeared disgruntled. Simon Jordan managed to pay off whatever was owed to get the embargo lifted, but then another followed, this time due to money owed to Ipswich for Alan Lee. 'I'm aware of the situation and we will get around it,' said Jordan.

We blinked, and it was as if the past ten years hadn't happened. Perhaps Marx got it the wrong way round when he observed that history repeats itself, first as tragedy, then as farce. Even the most earnest fan would concede that the Goldberg era and ensuing administration was pure farce, never more so than when the legendary Attilio Lombardo was placed in charge of team affairs with so little grasp of English that Tomas Brolin was kept on to act as interpreter (and even got to squeeze into a shirt and play). As bleak as the outcome was, there was nevertheless a feeling that each week would bring some new comic twist to the story, and the heroics of Steve Coppell in securing safety the following season with the most threadbare of squads ensured a happy ending. Indeed, it was during these dark days that we saw some of the great moments in Palace history, Dougie Freedman sealing his legendary status at Stockport, and the formation of the Trust showing the unity of spirit among the fans.

Victor Moses

The difference this time, as Simon Jordan steered the club towards the rocks, was that where Goldberg was clearly a fantasist from the outset, and always destined

for a dramatic fall, there was always the feeling that Jordan just might keep things afloat. Even the most sceptical among us begrudgingly started to accept his talk of a 'legacy'. Even once we had grown weary of his permatanned posturing, and despite a spate of stories about late payments and dates with the Inland Revenue, we chose not to listen to rumblings from the Cassandras among us. Ignoring for the moment the unfathomable double-speak of Jordan's business dealings – a dodgy lease here, a loan shark there – we can reflect on his achievements in terms that we understand and conclude that the Jordan dynasty will ultimately go down as one of failure. The decision to dispense with Coppell – although I prefer to think that was down to Steve trusting his own instincts – was only the first of a series of poor managerial decisions, and while he struck lucky with Iain Dowie, the half season that saw Palace clamber from the wrong end of the table to scrape into the Premiership represented one of the few successes in a decade of mediocrity. There were good times, it's true, but too few; we made the headlines with 'bouncebackability', and the emergence of Andy Johnson as a striker to compare with some of the best made us feel like a serious club for a while. However, these were interludes in an era bracketed by the managerial mundanity of Trevor Francis and Peter Taylor. Neither can Neil Warnock's tenure be viewed as much more than treading water, and by the end of his time he was transformed from 'legend' to 'Judas', neither of which remotely apply to the blameless manager.

The minutiae of Jordan's final meltdown will no doubt emerge one day, and perhaps it will make for a good story, as did the complex boardroom shenanigans of Goldberg and Venables, but a few bare facts already seem apparent. The seeds of Jordan's failure were sown when he brokered the deal to wrest control of Selhurst Park from Ron Noades, which at the time he trumpeted as the key to Palace's future stability. It was absurd for him not to have dealt with the issue when he first got involved, and if he really had been bringing the club and the ground together again it would have been laudable, but it later emerged that the new owners of the Freehold were a property company without Ron's emotional attachment to Palace and whose massive rent increases were hidden from the fans. It turned out that Jordan had no more claim to own the ground than I do, and 'disingenuous' is the politic way of describing his claims at the time. The suspicion remains that the deal was born of nothing more than a personal dislike or mistrust of Noades – understandable, perhaps – but this was an indicator that Jordan's ego was always likely to cloud his commercial judgement. Whoever owned the ground, the expectation was that at last it would be tarted up a bit, if not completely overhauled, but it remained the shabby, utilitarian mess that it has always been. Each corner of Selhurst Park bears the hallmarks of its age; the old main stand is more or less as it was in the twenties and the years have not been kind to it, and Arthur Wait's jerry-built edifice opposite certainly does the job of making visiting fans unwelcome. A trip to the toilets is not to be recommended, except as a reminder of how little thought is given to the comfort of the paying customer.

This disregard for the very people who pay the wages was the common theme throughout Jordan's time, and if the dip in attendances was a factor in Palace's financial downfall, then there is a certain poetic justice. Against a background of commercial underachievement and falling crowds, there were also some disastrously expensive player purchases. We should remind ourselves that Ade Akinbiyi had already earned the nickname Akinbadbuy at Leicester, yet Palace apparently shelled out £2.2million, as well as adding hugely to the wage bill. It was a similar story with the plodding Shefki Kuqi, who at least gave us a bit of slapstick, and a couple of flashy drag-backs in the play-offs for Bristol City convinced Warnock that Nick Carle was worth nigh-on £1million. He was wrong.

José Fonte

The fall, when it came, was sudden and shocking, but we can see now that it should have come as no surprise. Stories of late payment of players' wages were treated with an unconcerned shrug by Jordan and his acolytes, and as fans we just accepted the line that temporary cash flow problems would be sorted out soon enough. The chairman's apologists, some despite their better judgement, had convinced themselves of Jordan's business credentials, and the tone of debate on the BBS and Holmesdale internet forums was far from hysterical. I count myself among those who, although a firm critic of the regime, nevertheless assumed that the club was at least solvent, for which I was grateful. Even when the Inland Revenue's winding-up order was revealed, this was presented as commonplace brinkmanship for businesses owing tax, but what we didn't know at the time was that Jordan had taken out a loan with Agilo, a company whose modus operandi was, in their own words, to 'invest in distressed companies and special situations. The fund's main activities include trading distressed debt and investing in unique, proprietary deals and event-driven situations.' I'm not entirely sure what that means but, by God, the alarm bells should have been ringing out across SE25.

Jordan persisted in trying to paint Agilo as the villains of the piece, and with Michael Portillo on their board, there can be little doubt what kind of operation they were, but the simple fact is that they existed to profit from the misery of troubled companies, and if you invite a venomous snake into your home, don't feign surprise when it bites you. Formal administration was swiftly followed by a mandatory ten-point deduction, and from the fringes of the play-off places, within days Palace faced a struggle against relegation which turned into one of the most epic sagas of the club's 105 years.

The players heard the news as they disembarked at Newcastle airport for a midweek game, and having only suffered three defeats in the twenty games previously, consecutive home defeats to Swansea, Reading and Coventry quickly took the gloss from a fine Cup run – the highlight being Danny Butterfield's unbelievable hat-trick against Wolves – and we realised that this was now a serious business. Moses was withdrawn from the team and sold to Wigan before he could injure himself, Warnock jumped ship to Loftus Road, where he could at least be sure of getting his wages paid, and the Administrator, Brendan Guilfoyle, took a punt on bringing in Paul Hart as the new boss for the remainder of the season, with the very straightforward task of keeping Palace from the drop. The real coup, though, was to bring in Dougie Freedman as his sidekick, and this, more than anything else Guilfoyle could have done, showed a real understanding of the importance of keeping the fans loyal.

Darren Ambrose

As everyone had suspected for months, it all came down to the final day of the season, and a straight shoot-out for survival with Sheffield Wednesday at Hillsborough. The Eagles only needed to draw, and the tense drama of that epic game deserves a chapter of its own, but the joy – and relief – at the final whistle and the 2–2 scoreline ranks alongside Villa Park in 1990. Although Palace always just had the edge, Wednesday would have saved themselves and sent Palace down with just one more goal, but as nail-biting as it was, there was a confidence among the fans and the players that this would be their day, and one of the great days in Palace's history. Players such as Alan Lee, Johnny Ertl, Calvin Andrew, Matt Lawrence, none of them by any means Palace greats, nonetheless found themselves part of a group that demonstrated what it meant to play as a team, to scrap for each other for a common cause, and all were heroic that day, just as much as Ambrose, Derry and the pumped up Clint Hill, shirtless and taking on all comers after the final whistle. Anyone who was at the game will have sung some new songs, but the best one, which we will hopefully never need to revive, was simply 'Going down? Are we f***, Minus ten, and we're staying up!'

Even as the convoy of coaches headed home, we knew that the anxiety was far from over, and that there was hardly a queue of investors foolish enough to secure the club's future. There was speculation about the usual suspects getting involved, and even some unusual ones, such as New York rapper P Diddy and Colonel Gaddafi's footballing son Saadi. By all accounts, it really was touch and go as the deadline approached for Palace to exit administration, and we were hours away from having to find a new team to support, or start our own, as AFC Wimbledon had so successfully. The main sticking point was the ownership of the ground, and maybe I'm delusional, but the positive media coverage of the fans' various heartfelt demonstrations helped to force the hand of the bank, who eventually agreed to sell to CPFC 2010, the consortium of true red-and-blue businessmen who not only bought the club and the ground, but earned an enormous stock of goodwill from the fans which they may need to draw on if times get hard.

'Just 45 minutes into the season, and we're already top of the table. It looks like they got it right with Burley...'

The new owners, CPFC2010, were a group of four Palace-supporting businessmen: Martin Long, Stephen Browett, Steve Parish, and Jeremy Hosking, who came across immediately as sensible, honest and open, and approached the task of keeping Palace alive almost as if they felt it was their duty to look after the club and listen to the fans, whilst being up front about the economic realities. They had pulled off a stunning feat in purchasing the club, together with the Selhurst Park freehold, and had kept their nerve when it looked as if both Clyne and Ambrose would have to be sold, which appeared certain for a while. José Fonte had already gone to Southampton to raise funds as Palace entered administration, and a number of other players had already lined up moves with their contracts having expired. Butterfield, Matt Lawrence and Clint Hill all moved on, together with Derry, but perhaps the most disappointing departure was Johannes Ertl, who had slowly but surely grown into his vital defensive role under Paul Hart, and was starting to look like the kind of player we had missed since Riihilahti's departure. Despite the mass exodus, for the owners to hang on to Ambrose, as well as Neil Danns, Nathaniel Clyne and Julián Speroni, was a major achievement, but the next job was to appoint a new manager.

There was a case for keeping Paul Hart on, and it seemed slightly harsh to discard him after he had achieved his rescue mission, but when George Burley was chosen it seemed quite an imaginative step. Although Burley had failed as Scotland manager, which is built into the job description, he had a good record at club level with Ipswich, Derby

and Southampton, and had a reputation for getting his teams to play a passing game. It was a master stroke to keep Dougie Freedman on as his assistant, although I for one favoured giving Dougie the job straight away; in fact I would probably have made him player manager given the chance.

Owen Garvan

It was clear that Burley had no money for big signings, but he went about rebuilding the squad with defenders David Wright and Adam Barrett, and midfielders Andy Dorman and Owen Garvan. With left back Julian Bennett also arriving on loan, there were quite a lot of new names to get to grips with in the first game, but the one that made an immediate impact was another product of the academy, Wilfried Zaha. Making his first start, as was Kieran Cadogan, Zaha showed some audacious skills that had the crowd almost gasping, and scored the first goal as Palace breezed to a 3–0 lead at half time. That first 45 minutes was almost the peak of George Burley's career, as Palace just about held on to win 3–2, scrambled past Yeovil in the League Cup, then promptly lost the next four games, only scoring one goal in the process. As the influx of loan players gathered pace, three new strikers in the shape of Jonathan Obika, Pablo Couñago, and Everton's James Vaughan made Alan Lee's move to Huddersfield inevitable. Blackburn midfielder Alex Marrow also joined, along with big defender Antony Gardner, but out of the blue Palace made a signing guaranteed to make the headlines, that of retired Dutch star Edgar Davids.

Davids had apparently ended his playing days at Ajax a couple of years earlier, but had been one of the superstars of world football for many years in a career that took in both Milan clubs, Juventus, Barcelona and Spurs, as well as 74 caps for the Netherlands. His image was instantly recognisable as he wore goggles to protect his eyes while playing, and he had a reputation not only as a highly skilled creative player, but as a 'pit bull' in midfield. The question was whether, at the age of 37, he could get back to the fitness required, even at Championship level. The signing seemed uncharacteristic of the new owners' resolutely unflashy approach, and was redolent of Mark Goldberg's time, but Davids was the biggest name at the club since Lombardo, and the prospect was a tantalising one. He must have seriously wondered what he had been thinking when he found himself playing at left back in a team being beaten 3–0 at Scunthorpe.

Of the new strikers, the best by far was James Vaughan, who scored a superb hat-trick against Portsmouth in his second start, but that game apart, the first three months of the season were mostly disappointing and sometimes rank. The first glimpse the home crowd had of Davids was when his awful back pass contributed to QPR's 2–1 victory, and the last was four weeks later when he was in the side beaten 3–0 at home by Swansea to go bottom of Division One. We were getting that sinking feeling with a vengeance, and losing patience with Burley's persistence with a central midfield

of Garvan and Dorman, neither of whom seemed able to get a tackle in or get behind the ball when it mattered. Ambrose could just about get away with that kind of part-time role, as he could turn a game in an instant, but he was out injured for most of the first three months, and Palace simply couldn't afford the luxury of two passengers – make that three passengers when Couñago was on – without a fraction of Ambrose's ability.

November brought a sharp improvement, and Garvan redeemed his reputation with two fabulous strikes against Watford before ruining it again with an idiotic sending-off against Sheffield United for abusing the referee, a game which Palace lost 3–2, but nevertheless showed some long overdue passion. The month ended with a 1–0 victory over Doncaster, notable for being Pablo Couñago's one and only decent game in a Palace shirt, and the signs were that George Burley's job was safe for now, but two points from the next five games soon put paid to that idea. To lose one game to Millwall may be regarded as misfortune, to lose both looks like curtains, and so it was that after a 3–0 defeat at the New Den on New Year's Day, George Burley was sacked after an unremarkable six months in charge. It had been a tall order, for sure, to build a team virtually from scratch, but he didn't seem to be willing to adapt his style to suit the players he had, and never seemed able to make his own luck. The players he had brought in simply weren't right for the job in hand of ensuring survival, and although few Palace fans mourned his passing, fewer still bore any malice.

Dougie Freedman was immediately installed as caretaker manager, but Steve Parish made it clear on behalf of the consortium that they weren't going to be rushed into an appointment, and wanted to take a considered look at all the options. In the meantime, Freedman set about the task of reshaping the team ready for the battle ahead, and got off to a fine start when Steffen Iversen made his debut against Preston, and scored the only goal. When Palace made an early FA Cup exit to Coventry the following week, Freedman acknowledged that he was just keeping the seat warm for a new manager, and it was soon announced that the man Parish had settled on was Bournemouth's bright young manager Eddie Howe. After chewing it over, Howe turned down both Palace and Charlton to stay at Bournemouth, only to accept the job at Burnley a few days later, so Steve Parish turned at once to his second choice, and offered the job to Freedman. It seemed written in the stars that this day would eventually come, but Parish had absolute faith in Freedman's ability, as well as his unquestionable commitment, and Freedman himself had no hesitation in taking on a job already fraught with dangers. Steve Kember and Peter Taylor had proved that, however much the fans might have adored you as a player, they would be unforgiving once things weren't going so well as a manager. The task wasn't to slowly develop a team and make steady progress while learning on the job, it was very simply to save Palace once again from relegation to the third tier, which Dougie had famously already done with his goal at Stockport a full ten years earlier.

George Burley had tried in vain to get his team playing the kind of passing football he advocated, but it wasn't only bad luck that militated against that possibility, although he had his fair share. Freedman took a different approach, and identified that the first job was to keep a clean sheet, so he made that his absolute priority. He had the good fortune of Vaughan returning for another loan spell until the end of the

season, and Scannell back from several months out with a knee injury, but his focus was on repairing what had been a highly porous midfield and defence. Gardner returned at centre back in place of Claude Davis, but his smartest move was to shift David Wright from left back to a defensive midfield position, bringing in a proper left back, Dean Moxey, in the transfer window. With a central midfield of Wright and Alex Marrow, Palace ground out three draws, then a 1–0 victory against Middlesbrough, only conceding a single goal along the way. It wasn't very thrilling, but the players suddenly seemed to know what they were meant to be doing, and responded to Freedman with diligence and discipline, even Ambrose putting in a tackle here and there.

David Wright

There had only been one win all season away from home, and Freedman's side didn't improve on that record, but at home Palace were continuing to churn out results and move steadily towards safety. Wright continued his hard work in midfield, quietly breaking down opposition attacks and getting rid of the ball as quickly as possible, and with Marrow injured, Fulham's South African international

Kagisho Dikgacoi came on loan to do the same job. Freedman also signed another striker, Jermaine Easter, which gave him additional options up front, and with three extremely hard working forwards in Easter, Vaughan and Iversen, the manager was able to largely do without Pablo Couñago, the Spaniard joining Garvan and Dorman in the wilderness.

Neil Danns

The contrast between the results at home and away was startling. Palace had gone an amazing eight home games without conceding a goal after winning a true 'six-pointer' against Sheffield United, Ambrose reminding everyone what spectacular goals he could score, and in in the next home game – a 3–3 draw with Reading – he scored the fastest goal of the season inside 40 seconds. Although a single point left Palace still precariously just clear of relegation, it was one of the most entertaining games for a long while, with superb performances from Vaughan and Danns, a lovely goal from Easter, and even a missed penalty by Ambrose. Despite the huge importance of the two points dropped, it was a measure of what a class act Freedman was as a manager when he said of Ambrose: 'no mistake, he will take the next penalty and

if he misses the next penalty he will take the next one after that, because he is one of the best strikers of the ball at the club and he scores goals.' Sure enough, Ambrose scored his next penalty, and the unbeaten home record had stretched to thirteen games when Scunthorpe came to Selhurst Park for what was looking like the biggest match of the season for both teams. By now Palace had opened up a six point gap to Scunthorpe, who were third from bottom, but Scunthorpe had recently won 4–1 against Neil Warnock's champions-elect QPR, and on their last visit to Palace had won 4–0, so they were never likely to be a pushover. Palace played inexplicably poorly, and Scunthorpe's 2–1 victory meant that we were in for squeaky bum time, or as Ron Noades once delightfully put it, 'bicycle clips time'.

It is always so much more exciting to go into the final handful of games with something at stake, and that has been the norm at Palace for the majority of my many decades as a fan, but this time I felt a little cheated by the quiet, efficient way that the team ground out the points needed for safety. David Wright's return helped them to a point at Doncaster and three against Leeds, and then the final confirmation of safety came way up at Hull. As it turned out, the point won with a late equaliser wasn't needed, but what a way for the unheard of 18-year-old local boy Ibra Sekajja to make his mark with his very first touch of the ball, and what a way to celebrate, with a back flip, that Freedman confessed would have been beyond him. Although the final home game against Forest was rendered meaningless for Palace, and was lost 3–0, the mutual appreciation between the players and the fans during the lap of honour at the end of a tough season was heartfelt, and fully deserved on both sides.

'For F***'s sake, Murray'

Whilst the previous season had been something of a rescue mission by Dougie Freedman, albeit without the epic drama of his past efforts, there was a general feeling abroad that the new season would be one of building slowly, and of 'consolidating'. That is such a deathly word to any football fan, loaded as it is with a subtext of low expectations and lack of ambition, but it was right for both the owners and manager to focus on the reality of the situation that Palace were in. The club had been saved from extinction and from relegation, and recovery would have to be slow and sure in a division full of teams with a great deal more money to throw around. The crowd weren't yet in love with Freedman's managerial style, but he had done the job required, and could now move on up and bring to his team some of the flair and elan that we knew so well from Dougie the player.

The first stage in the process would be to shift out some of George Burley's less successful recruits, and some fringe players, with Adam Barrett and Pablo Couñago joining Claude Davis and Kieran Djilali on the unwanted pile. Andy Dorman and Owen Garvan were still around but clearly surplus, and it was a surprise when Garvan turned down a transfer to Brighton, stating his intention to fight for his place, which seemed futile. The greatest loss, although it had always been on the cards, was that of Neil Danns, tempted by the greater riches of Thai-owned Leicester City, whose wealth was meant to bring guaranteed promotion. Danns had taken a while to really ingrain himself at Palace following an initial long-term injury, but had developed into a real favourite during his last season at the club, and his energy and heart would leave a big hole.

In retrospect, the transfer business going into the new season was masterful, with Kagisho Dikgacoi – known as KG – signed permanently, Gardner eventually returning for another year, and Jonathan Parr and Mile Jedinak arriving with little fanfare. All four were full internationals – although Gardner would never add to his single England cap gained in 2004 – but the most surprising addition to the squad was Brighton's Glenn Murray. Brighton had recently won promotion from League One (as the old Third Division was now called), largely thanks to Murray's 22 goals, and with the impetus that the Sussex club had going into the new season, it seemed curious that Murray should choose to join their great rivals Palace, who were very publicly still strapped for cash. As dismayed as the Brighton fans were that Murray had chosen not to extend his contract, in South London there was excitement that not only had we put one over on them, but that we appeared to have landed a proper centre forward of genuine quality. Murray had worked his way up from the lower leagues via a clutch of clubs in the North-West, as well as a stint in America, but had blossomed during his three seasons on the South Coast, and came to Selhurst apparently in the form of his life.

Anthony Gardner

With Palace having survived the 2010–11 season thanks to solid defensive work throughout the team, the hope was that the time had come to open up with a more positive approach, and after three wins from the first four games, the signs were good. Although at the back it was hard to keep track of who was who, with Ryan McGivern, Peter Ramage, Andrew Davies and Aleksandar Tunchev all signed as short-term defensive cover, at the other end of the pitch games that might previously have been drawn were being turned into victories, and it looked as if the evolution towards a more ambitious style was underway. The most notable game came against Coventry, not only because of the novel experience of coming from behind to win a game at the death, but because it marked the first appearance of another exciting Academy graduate, midfielder Jonathan Williams, who in his brief cameo as a substitute showed no nerves, and great confidence, all at the age of 17. He reminded me straight away of Ben Watson some years earlier, who had similarly looked the part from his very first Palace appearance, and although it took a little while for Williams to earn the nickname 'Joniesta', it was apparent that here was a real footballer.

The scheduled early August League Cup tie against Crawley had been postponed, as the police were preoccupied with what we can still, from this distance, call 'the riots'. Future historians will need to label the events of August 2011 more specifically, but for now the meaning is understood by anyone in the country. Triggered by the fatal shooting of a police suspect in Tottenham, what followed was an explosion of anger and violence which spread first across London and then to other cities, characterised by looting, arson, and voracious media coverage. Commentators variously sought to define what went on as either pure criminality, or as an outpouring of protest from the disenfranchised in a society where the damage done by bankers and politicians was being paid for by those at the bottom. It was certainly a surreally frightening few days, made more worrying because it was so hard to understand clearly either the cause of, or the solution to such a deep and widespread problem. For a while it was as if people had licence to lay waste to their own neighbourhoods and along the way help themselves to whatever worthless consumer goods they could, but one of the iconic images of that week became the pictures of Croydon's House of Reeves furniture store in flames; '...you stupid bastards, you burnt down your town' ran a Brighton chant aimed at Palace fans, and I think that might stick for many years, as it makes a fair point pretty succinctly.

The rearranged Crawley game was the second in what was to become a run of seven floodlit Tuesday night victories in two months, which included fully deserved League Cup victories over Wigan, Middlesbrough and Southampton, but the one that mattered most was the trip to Brighton's brand new stadium in late September, the first 'A23 Derby' between the great rivals for six years. However much one might relish this slightly manufactured enmity, dating back to the era of Mullery and Venables in the '70s, it was hard not to feel some admiration for the way that the erstwhile Dolphins had dragged themselves back from the brink, having been on the verge of relegation from the league, having to sell their ground to pay debts, and being effectively homeless for several years. After a controversial passage through the planning process, despite being plonked on a designated Area of Outstanding Natural Beauty, the new stadium at Falmer was finally readied to herald Brighton's arrival back in the Championship, and by the time

Palace arrived they were yet to lose a league game at their new home. Confidence was high that Glenn Murray's new team would see off his old one with ease, but it was his costly replacement, Craig Mackail-Smith who got on the scoresheet early on to put the Seagulls ahead. However, as the game wore on, Palace kept calm, started playing the better football, and dominated without managing to break through until the last ten minutes. First Wilfried Zaha, whose game had been improving week-on-week, skipped past two or three challengers on the edge of the box before finding the net with a cunning, low cross shot, and then Darren Ambrose gave Palace the lead they merited, with the scrappiest of poor finishes which he somehow bundled in. The 2–1 lead seemed enough as injury time started to tick by, but Glenn Murray had the last word with a long range goal from a very unpromising position, to seal his place in Palace history. Murray had taken a while to get going in a Palace shirt, although we were starting to see glimpses of his quality, but this single goal became symbolic of Palace's superiority over Brighton, and the moment was generously captured and published for the world to see on YouTube by a Brighton fan with a mobile phone and an elegant turn of phrase: 'FFS Murray' went viral in a modest way, spawning a website, t-shirts and a cultish catchphrase.

Buoyed by the result at Falmer, Palace stealthily climbed the table, with some excellent performances against West Ham and Watford in particular, and it seemed that the new signings, notably Jedinak and Parr, were really finding their feet, as was Jonathan Williams, who the crowd had quickly fallen in love with. Williams had been eased in to the side during the cup run, had made his first league start – and a major contribution – in the cauldron of that Brighton game, and was already being talked about as a player to build a team

around, so it was a terrible blow when he broke a leg playing for Wales Under-21s against Armenia. Not only would he miss the bulk of the remainder of the season, he would miss out on the chance to take part in the game that was by now very much on everybody's mind: the League Cup quarter-final, away to Manchester United.

Jonathan Parr

As well as Palace had been doing in the Championship at times, and as well as they had done to reach this stage with a fair few second-string players, it wasn't realistic to expect a result at Old Trafford, but I decided to make the midweek trip up to Manchester on the basis that I had never been there in my life. Each time Palace had played at the 'Theatre of Dreams' – an entirely bogus bit of marketing, dubiously attributed to Bobby Charlton – I had been either too young, too broke, too busy or perhaps too pessimistic to make the effort, and have often cursed myself for missing the 2–1 victory there in 1989 (not long after the 9–0 humiliation at Liverpool). You suddenly find yourself getting on a bit, and things that you had previously assumed you would get around to doing at some point in that wide open plain of the future begin to look like they may never happen. I'm not a fan of the concept of the Bucket List, believing firmly that life is what happens while you're making other plans, but it did strike me that there might not be too many more opportunities to see Palace beat Manchester United, unless the two teams were to find themselves in the same division for a sustained period – a prospect which seemed increasingly unlikely as the gap widened between the big beasts and the also-rans.

It's true that United didn't put out their best side, but that didn't stop them approaching the game with a certain complacency. It's equally true that Dougie Freedman left half of his first team on the bench against a United side starting with nine full internationals, and for once I didn't make a case for us coming away victorious, and I didn't believe that we would. It was enough to get up to Manchester early, have a couple of drinks with a friend in the North, and soak up the pre-match atmosphere outside the ground as I handed out flyers to promote book sales, despite some rather petty stewarding. Apparently, on match days the public highway around Old Trafford becomes the private property of Manchester United PLC, but fortunately the police appeared more sympathetic, if a little confused.

Once inside the ground, which was festooned with banners celebrating Alex Ferguson's 25 years in charge, we settled down to simply enjoy the experience and relish the atmosphere, with an attitude that the game was almost incidental. The noise from the Palace crowd was remarkable, as usual, whilst the famed Stretford End refused to get excited at what would surely be a fairly routine bye to the semi-final. However, the Palace players had other ideas, with Zaha and Scannell rising to the occasion and running freely at the home defence, which grew more nervous as the

game wore on, while in midfield both KG and Stuart O'Keefe, together with the unsung David Wright, looked extremely comfortable, and Palace were by far the better team in the first half. You could say that the Palace back line shackled Berbatov, although you could just as well assume that he hadn't really bothered to turn up, and he was put out of his considerable misery by being substituted at half time. By then, with the game goalless, Zaha's tormenting of Fabio had led to the Brazilian retiring hurt, whilst Palace had lost both Scannell and Moxey to injuries, the latter giving Darren Ambrose a chance to get involved. Ambrose's goal which put the Eagles in front is one worthy of watching time and time again, a devastatingly accurate and powerful long range trademark Ambrose shot which left the keeper clutching fresh air and the Palace end in delirium.

Kagisho Dikgacoi

United drew level within minutes after a clumsy tug by McCarthy gave away a penalty, and although the impetus in the second half had been with the home side up to that point, Palace found a second wind which carried them into extra time, growing in energy and belief as the result they wanted came into view. Fittingly,

Zaha won a free kick on the left, Ambrose took his time and whipped in the ball perfectly for the final substitute Glenn Murray to bundle in the winner via his shoulder from among a ruck of defenders in front of the away end. We went nuts again; there was something about Murray's goal which just felt like it was destined to win the tie, despite wave after wave of United pressure, and so it proved. These are the sort of nights that make it all worthwhile, that make up for all the frustration and tedium of fighting relegation or administration or mediocrity, so very familiar to Palace fans. We'd already had one of those memorable nights at Brighton, but as important as that result had been, to win at Old Trafford, and to fully deserve that victory, had to be the highlight of the season, unless we were to actually win the Cup itself!

As it turned out, the semi-final against Cardiff, over two legs, gave us two more truly epic matches to look back on, between a pair of supremely well-organised teams, and while Palace sneaked the home leg with a headed goal from Anthony Gardner, the same player scored through his own net to send the return leg to penalties. Both games had been so tight and so hard-fought that it seemed a fitting way to decide who would progress to Wembley, although if Paddy McCarthy's rashness hadn't reduced Palace to ten men, it may have been settled in 90 minutes. One of the biggest clichés in the game, and the most inaccurate, is the notion that penalties are 'a lottery', when the very opposite is true; the outcome is entirely in the hands of the players, and chance plays little part. Perhaps there is something random about which way the keeper decides to dive to give himself a sporting chance, but what players should be able to control absolutely is whether they hit the target and test the keeper, and on the night Scannell, Easter and Parr all

froze, seemingly mentally and physically exhausted after what was a thrilling night's football, whichever team you were rooting for. Perhaps Cardiff just edged it overall, and they gave Liverpool a run for their money in the final before themselves losing on penalties, but although the League Cup run ultimately left the team deflated, it had provided some wonderful moments.

It was in the cup run, with the pressure off, that the exhilarating talent of both Jonathan Williams and Wilfried Zaha began to blossom while other young players such as Nathaniel Clyne and Sean Scannell really matured, and hearing 5,000 among the crowd singing 'He's Just Too Good For You' as Zaha ran riot at Old Trafford made the whole season worthwhile. The remainder of the season showed what very short memories football fans often have, as the playoffs remained tantalisingly just out of reach, and the team slipped inexorably back into the middle of the table against a background of whingeing about Dougie Freedman's perceived negativity, drawing comparisons once again with Peter Taylor. I for one was very happy with an incident-free end to a season during which we had started to see a Palace team playing at times with flair, confidence and ambition, and which contained some genuinely exciting prospects for what was sure to be an even better season ahead. In a nutshell, we were solvent, and we won at Old Trafford. That would do for now.

2012-13

'I think I'm halfway there in getting the club the way I want it to be, and I'm not the sort of guy to leave jobs half done.'
Dougie Freedman

'A single lie destroys a whole reputation for integrity.'
Baltazar Gracian.

Love is blind, and in my eyes Freedman could do no wrong. Throughout the turgid latter half of his first full season, when it did become a little hard to defend his apparent enthusiasm for treading water, I maintained that he had a plan, he knew what he was doing, and we just needed to trust in Dougie. Palace were on an upward trajectory, and this would be the season when it all came together, with players like Zaha, Williams and Scannell heading for the Premier League with the team that had nurtured them. Sadly, Nathaniel Clyne chose not to wait that one extra season, and although it was no surprise that he had rejected a new contract, it did seem a little perverse to head for Southampton, when he was most certainly a player destined for the one of the major teams, and for England. There was no ill feeling towards Clyne from the fans, who appreciated that he had always devoted himself to Palace's cause, not least when he could have jumped ship to Wolves during administration, and he had improved each season, setting a good example to any other young stars who might prefer the Bostock way.

I wasn't alone by any means in my uncritical devotion to Dougie, but there was a marked schism between us devotees and a good many others who thought that Freedman didn't know what he was doing. This man, who had spent his life in professional football and was clearly respected by his peers, knew less about the game than the halfwits venting their spleen to anyone who could be bothered to keep up with constant ordure polluting the message boards. That's not to say that any of their opinions were by definition less valid, just because they lacked basic skills in literacy or reasoning, but simply that the level of debate tended to be stuck at playground level. In some quarters there was despair and disbelief at the sale of Darren Ambrose and Sean Scannell, but it seemed to me that they were both good decisions. Ambrose, for all his skill with the ball, was too often a bystander during games, and it wasn't that he was unwilling to track back and put his foot in, it just didn't come naturally to him. Whereas Ambrose had slowly but perceptibly declined, Scannell had never really progressed in the way that we had all hoped, and although he had just had perhaps his best season, it appeared to me that he was destined to disappoint. A greater loss was Anthony Gardner in defence, who couldn't be tempted back for one more year at Selhurst, and Chris Martin's loan from Norwich had ended, leaving big question marks about provision up front, as Jermaine Easter had never looked quite good enough, and Glenn Murray had ultimately had a season somewhere between humdrum and miserable. Younger forwards such as Kwesi Appiah and Antony Pedroza didn't seem to be at the forefront of the manager's thinking, and the signing of Norwich reserve Aaron Wilbraham was a curious one, inviting the suspicion that perhaps all was not right with Murray. A more positive vibe surrounded Joel Ward, who came from Portsmouth as a replacement at right back for Clyne, and Southampton's Aaron Martin came on loan with quite a decent reputation.

It didn't take long for cries of 'Freedman Out' to gather momentum after three straight league defeats, plus a tonking at Preston in the League Cup, left Palace at the bottom of the Championship and certain sections of the fanbase in meltdown. More defenders arrived, with Darcy Blake coming from Cardiff, and Peter Ramage returning permanently, but it was the three signings late in the transfer window that turned the season around so dramatically. With Paddy McCarthy out injured, Damian Delaney was drafted in at centre back, and two less familiar names popped up for us to learn: Yannick Bolasie and André Moritz. Imagine the excitement at discovering that one of them was Brazilian!

Yannick Bolasie

From nowhere, Palace started playing like a team who could leave the rest of the division for dead, and the bare statistic of a run of eleven wins and three draws doesn't do justice to the sheer quality of the football being played. This was unlike anything we had known for many, many years, and if we went a goal or two down, no matter, we were certain to get a few ourselves and go on to win. Delaney made a real difference at the back, Moritz added some swagger, and having Bolasie on the wing was like having two Zahas. Mile Jedinak took the captain's armband and became twice the player we had seen to date, while KG – who many had discounted as overweight and not worth his

place in the side – was transformed into the total 'box-to-box' midfielder, popping up with some important goals, notably the winner at Charlton which was one of true quality, controlling the ball on his chest and volleying it home like an international player should. To cap it all, Glenn Murray became the kind of striker we thought we had stolen from Brighton in the first place, and almost more remarkably, I started to admit that Owen Garvan wasn't bad, sometimes.

It seemed that I was right about Dougie after all, then, although there was some talk that he had been pressured into switching to a more adventurous game by the owners. I have no idea whether that was the case or not, but it was by the by, as Palace now had the players and the confidence to finally get us back into the Premier League. Suddenly Palace were catching the eye in the media, notably Wilfried Zaha, who had cemented his reputation as the Championship's hottest property with more outstanding performances. Anyone studying Zaha's game closely, rather than simply making assumptions, will know that he wasn't just about flair on the ball and eye-catching tricks, but that he worked as hard as anyone defensively, and was never a luxury player. He would have quiet spells, certainly, but almost always they were followed by periods when defenders couldn't get near him. Opposition fans tended to boo Zaha and label him a diver, when in truth he took an awful lot of rough treatment that referees for some reason ignored, and he wouldn't always react in the sanguine manner one might hope. Although it was obvious that Zaha was heading for the top one way or another, Freedman was at pains to point out that he would counsel the youngster not to be dazzled by the bright lights and big money, and that he would put a paternal arm around Wilf and let him know when the time was right. There was even talk of other clubs wanting to poach Freedman himself, first Leicester, then Bolton, but however worried my teenage son was by the paper talk, I was able to reassure him what nonsense that was, as Dougie was Palace to his very bones. It wasn't even necessary, but it was still reassuring to hear him confirm as much, and after all, why would he have the slightest interest in leaving a club heading for promotion for one in the doldrums, even without that powerful emotional bond?

I stopped short of having his poster on the wall, but for me Dougie Freedman represented the very best of football, and perhaps he was just the screen on to which I projected my own image of how things should be. A joy to watch as a player, he knew how much a club means to its supporters, and throughout his career he engaged with fans intelligently and humbly, becoming a local legend along the way, and not simply for his vital goals. He was quick to rally to the cause publicly when Simon Jordan landed the club in administration, and cut short his playing days at Southend to join Paul Hart in the fight against relegation. Even when overlooked at first for the manager's job, he was happy to serve under George Burley, and when he was clearly the Board's second choice to succeed Burley, he swallowed his pride and bore no grudge, taking on the job with pride and determination. Players and managers come and go, and a good many leave behind fond memories, but Dougie was special, and I was ridiculously excited when I went along to a friendly against Dulwich Hamlet and saw him pull on his boots for the last ten minutes, as I had just about given up on my dream of him turning out once again in Palace colours.

I don't believe it was the money that persuaded him to turn his back on us, although who am I to say? I've never even met the bloke, so perhaps he is as venal and grasping as some suggest. Was it a midlife crisis, some kind of existential mental turmoil that made him lose all reason, or perhaps a falling-out with the owners, even something as simple as not feeling loved enough? People think they know the reasons, and maybe someone does, but one day I hope that enough water will have flowed under the bridge for Dougie and I to sit down and talk it all through, without recriminations, in order to reach a better understanding, and maybe closure. For now, though, it's too raw and.. sorry.. I don't think I want to talk about it any more. Except to offer this little Haiku which I wrote at the time, and tweeted on October 23rd 2012:

I looked on Ceefax
It seems the Doog has jogged on
Farewell to them both

While Steve Parish started interviewing prospective managers, and the betting market flip-flopped between Michael Appleton and Karl Robinson, the team set about proving that they didn't really need managing, and carried on playing as they had been, so that when Ian Holloway was finally appointed, he really just had to sit there and enjoy the spectacle as, a couple of wins later, his new side had breezed to the top of the table. After the misery of Freedman's departure, Holloway was the ultimate tonic, and seemed a perfect fit for a club looking to climb out of the Championship in swashbuckling style. Renowned for encouraging an attacking philosophy based on the very simple idea that if you score more goals than the other lot, you'll win, it was hard to find anyone not absolutely delighted to welcome Ollie to Selhurst Park as the man to finish the job so clearly left half done. After five wins in as many games for Ian Holloway, there followed the inevitable blips, but things continued more or less in the same vein until Christmas, by which point Glenn Murray had already scored 20 goals, almost unheard of for a Palace centre forward.

André Moritz

During this magnificent spell, everything just fell right, and plenty of penalties were awarded which might not have been given to a team out of luck. It's not that any of them were bad decisions, just that a good number of them might well have been missed by another referee on another day. Murray even had the luxury of missing a few, and let Owen Garvan take one when he himself was on a hat-trick against Brighton, as goals were coming so easily. On the wings, Bolasie was showing immense strength on the ball and creating all sorts of problems for defenders with his sheer energy, while Zaha deservedly earned himself an England call-up, as his genuine talent was impossible to ignore. There was much debate about whether he would be snapped up in the January transfer window, and while his form did dip slightly for a few games, a below-par Wilf was still streets ahead of anyone else in the division. It was a fabulous bit of business by the club to settle

Zaha's inevitable transfer to Manchester United and keep him on loan to the end of the season, following which he continued to astound, and to give everything for the team.

There hadn't been much movement inwards during January, but one notable transfer target was Peterborough's Palace-supporting George Boyd, aka 'The White Pele'. The Posh chairman went public with the deal before it was done and dusted, which allowed Nottingham Forest to nip in with a better offer at the last moment. Conspiracy theories abounded when that deal fell through due to an 'inconclusive eye test', and Forest's manager left the club a few days later in disgust, but the net result was that the Palace move was scuppered, and Boyd secured a loan to Hull, which turned out to be a great boost to their promotion ambitions under our old friend Steve Bruce. For some, the consolation prize of Ian Holloway's old muckers Kevin Phillips and Steven Dobbie didn't quite make up for the loss of Boyd, but I was delighted that we had Phillips, a player who should have won many more than his eight England caps, and who could always be counted on to pop up with a few goals, even at the age of 39.

As 2013 rumbled on, whenever Palace slipped up, so did their rivals in and around the playoffs, and although Cardiff started to pull away from the pack, second place was still within reach until a calamitous 3–0 defeat at Brighton, followed by a barely credible 4–0 loss at home to Birmingham. In both games Palace played the better football until falling behind, and then crumpled, and it was hard to pinpoint where the problem lay. Once again, games which they dominated, against Blackpool and Barnsley, yielded a single point each, and there were echoes of the early season crisis among some hysterical fans despite

Palace sitting pretty comfortably in fourth spot with only five games to go. What we wouldn't have given for that position after the first couple of weeks of the season! The point at which the blip became a full-blown crisis came at Portman Road, where Palace dominated a poor Ipswich side for most of the first half, until a calamitous lapse of concentration by Julián Speroni just before half time allowed the home team to take the lead. They then promptly scored a second, and Peter Ramage gifted them a third, leaving Palace inexplicably 3–0 down at the interval. Whereas before Christmas even that wouldn't have been irrecoverable, virtually the same team had now been drained of all confidence, and suddenly the play-off place looked under threat, compounded by Brighton leapfrogging Palace into fourth position.

Peter Ramage

What would be worse in the playoffs, losing to Brighton or to Dougie Freedman's Bolton, who had risen stealthily into contention and were now gathering the sort of impetus that could take them back up? A home draw against a similarly stuttering Leicester and a point at Blackburn both offered glimpses of renewed form for Palace, and although the experiment of starting Wilbraham up front alongside Murray was mercifully short-lived, at least the goal drought had ended after five games without finding the net. A dour goalless draw at Millwall and a point apiece suited both sides, as the Lions had plummeted alarmingly since reaching the FA Cup semi-final, and set up a finale at home to a Peterborough side desperate for a win to avoid relegation. When we studied the fixture list earlier in the season this looked like a dream of a final game, as Posh had looked doomed following seven straight defeats at the start of the season, but they had worked wonders to get themselves into the position where this now became a huge game for both teams, and yet another vindication of the worth of the playoff system, invariably sustaining high drama and countless plot twists right to the final kick of a long campaign.

Again, Palace played some good football and had a few clear chances, but when Peterborough took the lead we couldn't help but recall the humiliating collapses against Birmingham, Brighton and Ipswich. A second goal might have meant disaster, and it very nearly came before the massive relief of a penalty for Palace on the brink of half time. It was the right decision by the referee, but it was one of those that Palace had been getting earlier in the season when the luck was going their way, and that could well have been missed or dismissed. The fact that the referee gave it, and that Glenn Murray converted it so emphatically, marked the point at which Palace started to regain the self-belief needed to carry them all the way to Wembley, and perhaps beyond. Another away goal, a good strike that should nevertheless have been dealt with by Speroni, suddenly didn't seem such a big deal, and after a priceless Kevin Phillips equaliser, Peterborough's long, hard season seemed to tell, and it was cruel that a dodgy free kick decision and a scrappy winner by Jedinak in the final minute sent them down. The great news from elsewhere was that Bolton had slipped out of the top six, so that at least that part of the script had to be rewritten, but all thoughts now turned towards the game that nobody wanted: Brighton in the semi-finals.

Jonny Williams

I was genuinely surprised at the level of fear there seemed to be among Palace fans going into the home leg against Brighton, which showed what short memories they had. This was only Brighton, after all, and at any other time in history the prospect of having to get past the Seagulls to get to Wembley would have had us inking the final in our diaries. The recent humiliation at the Falmer was fresh in everyone's minds, but here was the chance to prove that an aberration, and to restore the natural order. It wasn't just the Palace waverers who made Brighton favourites, and there was a decidedly arrogant vibe coming from the South Coast, which can only have been useful as a motivational tool for Ian Holloway. Although not on the same scale, it felt to me a little like the Cup semi-final in 1990, when Palace faced a Liverpool team that had hammered them 9–0, and who apparently just had to turn up on

time to confirm their place at Wembley. On that occasion, I myself was one of the doubters, but this time I was bullish about our chances, as we had come through the nervy last few games relatively intact, and were showing hints of returning to the early season form that had been such a rare joy to witness.

A few doubts started to creep in during the first half at Selhurst, as Gus Poyet's team had the upper hand, and it was with some relief that we got to half time on level terms. Wilfried Zaha had been largely kept in check by Wayne Bridge, and overall Palace were on the back foot for most of the time, which didn't bode well for the prospects of taking some sort of lead into the second leg. The second half was a great improvement, as for some reason Brighton seemed to go into their shell, and allow Palace to play a bit. Zaha switched to the left wing, where he started to cause Calderon problems, and Joniesta began to shine as we knew he could. Suddenly it was Brighton fighting a rearguard action, scrambling efforts off the line and losing possession cheaply, but with the game swinging Palace's way, another spell of pressure in the opposition box saw the ball come towards Glenn Murray in a decent position. With daylight between him and the nearest defender, Murray suddenly collapsed in agony as he twisted to shape up for a shot, and from my position behind the Brighton supporters it was immediately clear that he was in trouble. Brighton players surrounded the referee to complain, and the away fans booed Murray roundly for diving, but it was obvious to all that he hadn't. Sure enough, Murray was stretchered off, and even before any medical bulletins it was pretty clearly the end of his season. Although his replacement Aaron Wilbraham worked valiantly, bolstered by the introduction of Bolasie and Phillips, the goal just wouldn't come and the game finished goalless, which was just about right. What it proved was that there wasn't actually very much between the two sides, and that gave some encouragement for the second leg, but the loss of Murray was bound to cause a huge problem.

I thought it had been a cracking game and a fair result, a thoroughly enjoyable evening all round, until I had the misfortune to become the target of abuse from the away fans filing out of Selhurst Park. Since the away area moved to the Sainsbury's end of the Arthur Wait stand, the commentary box from which I and my colleagues broadcast to Mayday Hospital and to blind fans seated in front of us was surrounded by opposition fans, which did make for a good atmosphere, but also made one feel a little vulnerable. The stewards had long since abandoned the idea of getting fans to sit down, so it was often difficult seeing over them as they stood, but there were few problems, even the likes of Millwall remaining pretty good natured. This time, though, the Brighton fans were the very definition of an ugly crowd, and it was quite depressing to see the anger and hatred being directed at us as we cheerfully packed away our headsets. It did make me wonder where it comes from, that level of unhappiness, and although I'm tempted to suggest that it is because they follow Brighton, I'm very aware that there seems to be a burgeoning undercurrent of almost retro hooligan culture, even at Palace, and it does trouble me, sensitive flower that I am.

With Murray missing for the second leg, Ian Holloway's only real option was to start Wilbraham, unless he was to change the team's shape completely, and the first half followed a similar pattern to that at Selhurst, yet somehow Palace looked more in control, playing with just a little more belief, while by contrast Brighton weren't

quite firing. For the first time in a while, Jedinak and KG were looking composed and solid in midfield, and even Gabbidon at the back was looking less like the pub player I had taken him for. At half time, the safest bet would have been 0–0, extra time and penalties, and the guessing game of who would take them began. Garvan, if he was still on, certainly; Kevin Phillips, for sure, and definitely Jedinak; Wilf, maybe; Bolasie? Please, no!

Kevin Phillips

The second half had barely started when Zaha broke from deep and played a perfect ball into the path of Jonny Williams, one on one with the keeper. He glanced up and picked his spot precisely, and it looked for all the world like the opening goal, but the net didn't even flutter as the ball almost kissed the post on its way past. A big miss for Williams, and potentially hugely costly, but from that moment it was Palace who had the edge, and they went on to play the most perfect half of football, and the most satisfying for the fans, for many a year. Brighton were denied the lead when Speroni flicked Barnes' effort on to the bar, followed soon after by Moxey's emphatic goal-line clearance, while at the other end Jedinak was about to tap in when he was dragged to the ground from behind, a stone cold penalty which was completely missed by all the officials. Whatever the final result, there was no denying that these two games were fantastic value, and every single Palace player put in a massive performance. Unsung team players such as Ward, Moxey and KG were playing magnificently, but ultimately it was the star man Wilfried Zaha who repaid the years that Palace had put into his development with the goals that put Brighton firmly in their place. He had been breathtaking on the ball at times, but it was Yannick Bolasie who turned on the magic to set up the first goal, leaving Calderon with twisted blood, then going back for more before delivering for Zaha to head home in front of the away section, continuing his dive in ecstatic celebration. How perfect that it should be Wilf again for the second, burying Brighton's dreams with a turn and shot reminiscent of Ian Wright in his pomp. Ian Holloway's celebration dance – another instant YouTube classic – together with his singing 'you ain't as good as you thought' expressed perfectly the mood of fans and players alike, together with a little gloating that the conceited Gus Poyet had got his come-uppance.

The danger now was that Palace might go in to the final feeling just a little too cocky, but over the course of the season Watford had proved themselves deserving of their place in the playoffs, and worthy favourites. Moreover, their manager Gianfranco Zola was a class act, quite a contrast to Poyet, whose typically ungracious reaction to Palace's victory prefaced the famously messy end to his adventure with Brighton.

It had been so long since we had been to Wembley that in a way the result wasn't the important thing, and although in the media the build-up was all about how many millions the game would be worth to the winners, for the fans it was all about just being there to enjoy it, win or lose. As ever, there were many who were fearful of making it to the Premier League, knowing that surviving more than a single season would be tough, as it is always bound to be for any promoted team, although historically fewer than half of the teams who go up come straight back down. I've never understood why any fan wouldn't want at least a season in the sun, and however crass one feels the Premier League circus is, surely the whole point is to get there and have a peek for yourself every so often.

For me there was none of the nervous tension that I had felt before the Brighton game, and I just relished the whole ritual scramble for tickets, deciding what to wear and how to travel, and when we woke up to a sunny day it all just felt right. At my age I should have prepared myself for disappointment, but I really didn't see the need, and all the way up the vibe from the red and blue throng was the same. Some serious drinking had gone on at strategic points around town, and I dropped in to a couple of pubs around Marylebone to continue my 'Promotion Special' leafleting campaign, feeling every bit as confident of the outcome as I claimed to be, although there were a few who thought I might jinx it by being so presumptuous. Inside Wembley, it was a splendid sight to see the Watford half glowing gold in the sunlight, while in the shade of the Palace end a mix of reds and blues was spattered with the odd bit of claret and a rumbustious knot of black identifying the Holmesdale Fanatics, Palace's very own self-styled mini-Ultras.

As a game of football, nobody could claim that it was a classic final, with both Palace and Watford starting cautiously, appearing reluctant to hurry things along, and for over an hour neither keeper was troubled.

The unfortunate KG had limped off despondently early on, forcing Ian Holloway to bring on Stuart O'Keefe, and although Zaha showed some typical brilliance on the ball, by and large it was a performance more in keeping with Dougie Freedman's creed than Ian Holloway's, and as a team Palace looked back to their very best defensively. Damien Delaney, in particular, reminded us how good he had looked when he first arrived, and alongside him Gabbidon oozed quality. At the sharp end, Aaron Wilbraham was all effort and even a little finesse, but when the few chances fell to him, he either froze, bewildered at finding himself with the opportunity to etch a place in Palace folklore, or clattered the ball straight at Almunia in goal. That bluntness was kind of what was expected of Wilbraham, but when O'Keefe put Zaha through on goal in injury time, Wilf showed the same indecisiveness and missed a massive opportunity to seal promotion and grab all the headlines. It should have been a killer goal at the death, much like David Hopkin in 1997 – or even Claridge for Leicester the year before – at the old Wembley, but when the whistle went shortly afterwards, Zaha looked completely and utterly distraught. His team mates tried to console him in the huddle as they prepared for extra time, but he looked shattered, defeated, and in despair.

Since Watford had looked inexplicably flat, and in truth really quite a poor side, the odds had swung in Palace's favour, but the worry was that the goal wouldn't come, despite the introduction of Phillips and Moritz. With the early forced substitution of KG, the expected impact of bringing on Bolasie was precluded, and the game started to feel increasingly as if it would go to penalties. Moreover, after that missed goal opportunity, Zaha's body language indicated that, although he had shown some

astonishing skills earlier, his contribution had run its course. We had been privileged as Palace fans to witness the burgeoning of a footballer of such rare talent as Wilfried Zaha, who had an abundance of the qualities needed, such as skill, commitment and strength, but who unquestionably also had that touch of alchemy that sets the truly great players apart. Somehow Zaha found the legs to take on Cassetti down the left and the merest touch took the ball past the Italian, who as he lunged to bring down his man knew that there would be no arguing about the penalty decision. From my position perched high above the halfway line, it at first looked like a slightly soft one, but in fact it was as clear a penalty as you will ever see, and there were few protests. Suddenly a fairly pedestrian game had turned into one of high drama, and to add to the plot it was Kevin Phillips who took on the responsibility, in front of the Watford end, against the team who had given him his first professional contract aeons ago. Without fuss, and apparently without nerves, Phillips simply did what he does, and buried it beyond Almunia to send Palace up after one of the most exhilarating and enjoyable seasons for many years.

There were a few small scares along the way, but Palace saw out extra time safely, and were undoubtedly worthy winners on the day, which must have been dreadfully disappointing for the Watford fans, whose team really let them down when it mattered. By contrast, the Palace players had all showed enormous character to recover from the late season wobble to progress through the playoffs without conceding a goal, and grind their way to promotion. Zaha's stunning performances against Brighton and Watford will long be remembered, as will Kevin Phillips' contribution at the age of 39, but every single member of the squad can look back on the season with great pride. Joel Ward's goal line clearance to deny Watford an equaliser, Speroni's scoop away from the feet of Deeney, O'Keefe's almost psychotic command of midfield were all highlights of the final, but every player deserved to hold the trophy aloft having done their bit throughout the season. Peter Ramage had given way to Gabbidon after a howler at Ipswich, but soaked up the plaudits every bit as much as Glenn Murray, on crutches, and Paddy McCarthy, who hadn't kicked a ball all year. Perhaps this was Freedman's legacy, that Ian Holloway inherited a group of players with a true team ethic, supported by owners whose motives were unimpeachable, and a set of fans whose tradition and passion was worthy of another tilt at the Premier League.

'*They said I lost the changing room. I know where it is, it's down the corridor on the left.*'
Ian Holloway

Ian Holloway

For a team like Palace, returning to the Premier League after a long eight years away, new signings during the summer are not only inevitable, but critical. It continues to be evident that promoted teams, even those who have shone in the previous season at a lower level, are unlikely to survive without major investment in the squad, and in players with proven experience at a high level. Which of the plethora of signings could be said to fit that description, even without the benefit of hindsight? Marouane Chamakh, for one, a star player for Morocco who had won the French League title with Bordeaux before spending a few less happy seasons at Arsenal. Apart from that you could just about make a case that Adrian Mariappa and Jimmy Kébé fitted the bill, having been relegated with Reading the previous season, likewise Barry Bannan and Cameron Jerome, bit part players at Villa and Stoke, but Palace's headline signing, beating the previous transfer record for the club, was the young prospect from Peterborough, Dwight Gayle, who only just over a year prior had been playing

in non-league for Bishop's Stortford. Of the other summer signings, one could have filled a lengthy 'where are they now?' article only a few months later with the names of Jerome Thomas, Stephen Dobbie, Elliot Grandin, José Campaña, Neil Alexander, Florian Marange, Adlène Guedioura, Jack Hunt and the returning Kevin Phillips. By the end of an eventful season, they had all come and gone, leaving barely a trace.

Dwight Gayle

An independent research study highlighted the fact that: 'Palace have used 34 players in this or the previous two campaigns… This reflects poor strategic planning as many established professionals do not even have the right to participate in league games. This may prove detrimental for team spirit over the long term', and although Steve Parish took some umbrage at the report, the high turnover was definitely a factor in Palace's poor start to the season, and perhaps emblematic of Ian Holloway's haphazard thought processes, although by his account the majority of the arrivals were the result of undue pressure from Parish, and made without enough consideration. Let's give credit, though, for probably the best bit of business that summer, the loan signing of Jason Puncheon from Southampton.

With Murray out long term, and Zaha having joined Manchester United, the team that started the season was weakened further by the absence of the injured Bolasie, and they did remarkably well against a very good Spurs side, only losing to a dubious penalty awarded after an accidental handball by Dean Moxey, a decision that might have been correct under later versions of the handball rule, but not at the time. At least that's how Ian Holloway saw it, as did I, and the manager was later banned from the touchline for two games following his outburst at the referee. Holloway's contention was that officials constantly favour the bigger clubs, and although there were a good few decisions during the season that supported that view, it's more a combination of unconscious bias and an element of bullying by the more successful teams that exploits the weakness of some of the less competent officials. I don't buy in to conspiracy theories as a rule, and prefer to put it down to ineptitude rather than the hysterical charge of corruption, but the referee in question against Spurs was Mark Clattenberg, and his name may pop up in a later chapter.

A fair start to the season then, putting in a game performance against a class team, followed by a narrow defeat at Stoke, and an emphatic victory against Sunderland, and the early signs were good, or at least better than most expected. In between times, a very poor second string were dumped out of the League Cup at Bristol City, a game only remembered for Owen Garvan's goal with just about the last kick of his stuttering Palace career and appearances from new signings Elliot Grandin and Florian Marange, which turned out to comprise their entire Palace careers. Neither was seen again in a Palace shirt, and both disappeared into the wilderness, in Marange's case amid some acrimony.

The optimism and energy displayed against Sunderland soon began to dissipate, however, as a string of defeats started to expose the weakness of the squad, and although they could point to being on the wrong end of more highly dubious penalty decisions against Manchester United and Liverpool, a pattern was beginning to form, of plenty of endeavour, but little reward.

Jason Puncheon

One bright spot was the return of Bolasie, who had been sorely missed for the first couple of months, and he was able to make his first start in a midweek game at Selhurst Park against Fulham. Those evening games under floodlights often turn out to be memorable ones, and when Palace went ahead against their likely relegation rivals, Selhurst was rocking again. I was thinking that this is where the season really starts, it's all coming together, and José Campaña is starting to look the part in midfield. That feeling lasted all of ten minutes, until Fulham's Swiss international Pajtim Kasami sealed his place in Palace folklore with one of the best goals ever seen at the ground. Approaching the corner of the penalty area on the right, he cushioned a long pass on his chest and without looking let fly with a sublime volley over Speroni and into the far corner of the net, which had home and away fans alike shaking their heads in astonishment and admiration. The players seemed just as shocked to witness such quality, and didn't really recover, so that when Sidwell scored another stunning volley from distance just before half time it felt like they had thrown in the towel already. As it turns out, on the sidelines, the busy voices in Ian Holloway's head had come to the same conclusion, and the team sleepwalked through the second half – without Campaña, who had been given the hook during the interval – ending up losing 4–1.

Marouane Chamakh

Disjointed, lacking a clear identity, not actually rank bad as such, nevertheless it was clear that something needed to change to get the team more focused, but it was still surprising to me, and apparently to Steve Parish, that the manager had decided that he didn't have the energy to carry on, and without that spirit and vigour, Ian Holloway isn't Ian Holloway. Perhaps the subtext was that the rash of new arrivals had destroyed the spirit of the squad, and that the manager didn't have the respect he needed from some of them, but by his own admission he was worn out, and

for once the euphemism of a manager leaving a club by mutual consent seemed genuine. Holloway later hinted that he had fallen out with the chairman over broken promises, but whatever the reasons, for all that he was totally steeped in the world of professional football, and as much as he relished fostering his reputation as an eccentric, Holloway clearly also had other more meaningful dimensions to his life, and made a swift and emphatic decision to move on. Although his time at Palace had been brief, it was certainly unforgettable.

Assistant manager Keith Millen stepped in as caretaker, not for the last time, while the process of identifying a new manager dragged on longer than is usual, but with ten games played Palace were looking doomed, with only three points earned, and even the most blindly optimistic among us were resigned to another very brief stay in the top division. However, some spirited performances under Millen, and at long last under a new manager, saw Palace briefly out of the bottom three and showing a bit of belief. That new man turned out to be Tony Pulis, who had done an outstanding job in getting Stoke promoted to the Premier League and keeping them punching above their weight for several years. He came with a reputation as a dour pragmatist, whose considerable achievements at Stoke failed to excite the fans, despite them making it to the Cup Final and getting into Europe, but whose great quality was the ability to avoid relegation, and Palace gave him the chance to cement that reputation. In fact, Pulis went way beyond that immediate goal, and steadily sorted out the team, adding some important players to the squad. After a fair Christmas period, the highlight of which was Dwight Gayle's goal of quality to get the points at Villa Park, and the low point Puncheon's stratospheric penalty miss at Spurs, a couple of quiet wins in the New Year saw Palace ease away from the bottom three, and a real turning point came in February, when three new faces appeared for the first time against West Brom. Two of them – Joe Ledley and Tom Ince – scored in the 3–1 victory, and defender Scott Dann fitted in seamlessly at centre back alongside Delaney. Although Tom Ince never really lived up to his early promise, having been voted The Football League Young Player of the Year ahead of Wilfried Zaha, both Ledley and Dann became crucial components in Palace's extraordinary renaissance under Pulis, and turned out to be exceptional signings. The West Brom game was a joyous one, and with Glenn Murray finally coming back into contention and Bolasie finding his best form, there was a positivity among the fans that perhaps they hadn't fully expected when Pulis arrived. The cauldron of noise initiated by the Ultra-lite Holmesdale Fanatics that Selhurst Park rightly became known for over the next few years had started to be noted as a refreshing contrast to the sterile atmosphere at some of the bigger clubs, whose sense of entitlement saw their soulless stadiums fall silent when things weren't going as expected, whereas the Palace fans relished and celebrated the role of underdogs, aware that they were interlopers among the elite, and knowing deep inside that they weren't likely to stay there for too long.

Victories proved hard to come by, though, and by early Spring there were still ten teams seen as possible relegation fodder, with Palace still very much among them, so going into the game against José Mourinho's Chelsea, who were four points clear at the top, having destroyed Arsenal 6–0 the week before, there was a palpable sense of dread. However, Palace surprised us all by putting in a performance of composure and confidence which fully deserved all three points, albeit thanks to an enormously enjoyable own goal from the odious John Terry, nodding home a cross from Palace's makeshift left back Joel Ward.

Joe Ledley

Tony Pulis had managed to create a team able to match the rest of the division on its day, and key players such as Speroni and Puncheon were now blossoming, while Joe Ledley in midfield oozed a composure and authority that raised everyone else's game. Remarkably, the Chelsea result kicked off a run of five straight victories that saw the Eagles comfortably move up the table, on the way halting Everton's charge towards a European place with a thrilling and convincing 3–2 win at Goodison Park.

With safety assured after beating West Ham, there was one more piece of high drama to come, just when the season could have fizzled out, as Liverpool came to Selhurst Park for an evening game which they simply had to win to be in with a chance of pipping Manchester City to the title. More to the point, having slipped up against Chelsea the week before, they needed not just points but plenty of goals, and at 3–0 it was clear that they were calculating whether six goals might be enough, or should they go all out for the 9–0, like in 1989. I'm not quite sure why it was so lovely to see them fall apart that night, perhaps it was the enduring sense of injustice that they had robbed Palace of a place in Europe so long ago, or perhaps it was just a response to Brendan Rogers' hubris, but it will go down as one the great nights at Selhurst, even though for us it was just a fairly meaningless end-of-season point. The score was still 3–0 approaching the last ten minutes, and Palace appeared to have at least subdued the opposition, but when Damian Delaney surprised himself with a long distance belter the tide turned, and suddenly the home side were on fire, urged on by their ebullient fans. Two minutes later Bolasie tore through the Liverpool defence to set up Gayle for a clever finish to make it 3–2, and with full time approaching, it was apt that a sublime piece of skill from Murray saw him chest the ball into the path of Gayle for an extremely cool equaliser, a supreme example of a striking partnership that we never really saw enough of. Is it mean-spirited of me to have enjoyed the inconsolable tears of Luis Suarez at full time quite so much? Yes it is, but who cares? Exceptional player as he was by any standards, and one of the very best of his generation, he was also one of the most grotesque cheats the game has seen, and although there was still a slim prospect of Liverpool overhauling City for the title, Suarez knew it was over. Some wag referenced Liverpool's comeback from 3–0 down against Milan many years earlier to win the Champions' League in Istanbul and dubbed the game 'Crystanbul', which has stuck, and it was indeed one of the great Palace memories in recent years.

The supposedly dull and regimental Tony Pulis had taken on a club in real trouble, and forged a proper team offering a blend of organisation and entertainment, but above all spirit, typified by the captaincy of Mile Jedinak, and remarkably they ended the season in 11th position in the table, the second best in the club's history. Julián Speroni was one of several players to prove their worth at the higher level, winning Player of the Year against stiff competition, Tony Pulis deservedly won the award for Manager of the Season, and it was hard not to look forward to having him the helm for what would surely be a bright future.

Tony Pulis

2014-15

'I think good people sometimes do bad things.'
Iain Moody

Tony Pulis went into the summer break with his stock at an all-time high, his reputation enhanced by the manner in which he had turned Palace around, going beyond just surviving and surprising many by moulding a team with some elan. One can only imagine the warm glow as he sat in Brazil watching the World Cup and reflecting on his unlikely trophy, albeit one awarded by the Premier League's sponsors rather than by fellow managers. Perhaps he allowed himself to dream of greater glory than could ever be imagined at clubs such as Palace or Stoke, with relatively frugal budgets and realistic levels of ambition. He clearly took umbrage at the level of influence that Steve Parish had over transfer dealings, and not for the first or last time, the two egos of the manager and chairman were unable to happily coexist. Pulis had clearly decided to leave before asking that a £2 million bonus for staying up, written into his contract and due a few weeks into the new season, be paid early, and Parish obliged, seemingly unaware that his manager was already planning his exit. It took a couple of years for a High Court ruling to force Pulis to repay the bonus, plus another £1.7 million on top, and it turned out to be a very costly and ham-fisted attempt at deceit on his part. A key piece of evidence which did for him was that on the day that Pulis claimed there had been a 'heated players' meeting' with Parish present, the chairman was able to prove that he had been at a hairdresser's appointment, a detail that has such a powerful ring of authenticity. Case closed, m'lud.

And so the cycle of crisis management began again, with Keith Millen stepping up as caretaker for the second time, but this time without the protracted recruitment process that had seen Pulis eventually take the job after Holloway's departure the previous season. A strong candidate appeared to be Malky Mackay, but that was scuppered when Cardiff's owner Vincent Tan proved the old adage that revenge is a dish best served cold. The previous season, after Mackay had fallen out with Tan and left the club, his sporting director Iain Moody had turned up in the same mysterious role at Palace, and later was at the centre of accusations that the Cardiff team to play Palace had been leaked to Moody. That seemed to blow over at the time, but now the Welsh club sent a dossier to the FA alleging that Mackay and Moody had shared a series of racist, sexist and homophobic texts while at Cardiff, and Moody promptly disappeared from the Palace payroll. To his credit, Moody didn't try to squirm out of it by excusing the texts as harmless banter, seeming to show genuine remorse for his actions, and not simply for getting caught out.

Martin Kelly

The choice of Neil Warnock to return to Selhurst Park smacked of exasperation, and perhaps disenchantment with the quaint idea of long-term planning, and probably the most compelling thing Warnock had going for him was that he was available.

Not many Palace fans loved Warnock's self-serving schtick the first time round, but the general response was a weary shrug and an acceptance that he would do, I suppose.

In fact, under Warnock, Palace made a fair start, and very briefly found themselves in the top half of the table, before slipping back down towards their rightful place in the bottom three, but the performances reflected the fact that the manager seemed to lack any real identity or personality, and it was hard to get away from the feeling that both manager and players were treading water. However, one outstanding piece of business was to persuade Wilfried Zaha back from Manchester United, initially on loan, and then later as a permanent signing, at a bargain price. It took a little while to rebuild Zaha's confidence, as he had never been given the chance to prove himself at Old Trafford once David Moyes had taken over from Alex Ferguson. It had been heart-breaking to see a player who we all knew to be potentially world class struggling in the big wide world, even when spending time on loan at Cardiff, and we just wanted to give him a big hug and welcome him home, which we were happily able to do. That was a huge signing, and whether or not Neil Warnock had much to do with the capture a couple of days later of James McArthur from Wigan, let's give him a little credit for a highly significant addition. McArthur had impressed for the Latics as they won the FA Cup the previous season, but once they had been relegated, he seemed to be on his way to Leicester before Palace stepped in, and McArthur went on to become the cornerstone of the Palace midfield for many years to come.

Less successful additions to the squad included Zeki Fryers, who disappeared without trace shortly afterwards, and the returning Andy Johnson, a massive hero from a decade ago, but unable to add much on the pitch this time around. The strangest decision, though was letting Glenn Murray go out on loan to Reading, denying us the chance to see him reunited with Bolasie and Zaha until his return in the New Year, and leaving the squad with three strikers in Gayle, Chamakh and the new man Fraizer Campbell, proud owner of one England cap, but destined to disappoint. Oh, and Kevin Doyle on loan.

James McArthur

By the early years of the decade, the use of Twitter by footballers had become ubiquitous, and the dangers inherent in having a means of direct expression without the useful filter of reflection and consideration were illustrated when Jason Puncheon had accused Neil Warnock of being a crook in quite explicit terms earlier in the year. This followed Warnock's fairly scathing assessment of Puncheon following his dreadful penalty miss at Tottenham the previous season, and it appeared unlikely that the two would now be able to work together happily, but in fact Puncheon's fine form continued under the new manager, and performances and results were decent, Palace looking like a fair mid-table team for much of the time. A particular highlight was a 3–1 defeat of Liverpool, still apparently reeling from their collapse a few months previously, with Mile Jedinak's wonderful free kick for the third one of the best we'd seen at Selhurst. The uncontrived image of the Palace captain reeling away to celebrate in the rain, tugging at his shirt and letting out a scream of delirium from beneath his burgeoning beard has become iconic in the truest sense of the word, and whenever fans bemoan the absence of the kind of much-lauded 'passion' personified by players like Jedinak, it is this single image that comes to mind.

Pape Souare

That exceptional afternoon proved to be Warnock's last win as Palace manager, and by Christmas it had become apparent that the team was drifting towards relegation, and that Warnock wasn't looking like inspiring or revitalising his players. Following a limp home defeat by Southampton on Boxing Day, Steve Parish acted swiftly, and not many Palace fans, I suspect, would have mourned Warnock's departure. They had seen how good these players could be at times under both Pulis and Warnock, and with the return of Zaha they should have improved even further, but a certain spark was missing, and the

managerial search began yet again while Keith Millen kept the seat warm for the third time in just over a year.

This time, however, Millen had barely got himself comfortable before Alan Pardew was announced as the new manager, leaving Newcastle to return to his spiritual home. Utilitarian as a player for Palace in Steve Coppell's team, Pardew had sealed his place in the mythology of the club with his winning goal against Liverpool in the extraordinary 1990 Cup semi-final, and had by now become an experienced and sporadically successful manager, famously being given an unheard of eight year contract at Newcastle, but developing a fractious relationship with their characteristically demanding fans. Despite having won both meaningful Manager of the Year awards in 2012, he never really won over the proudly parochial Toon Army, who continued to see him as an obliging stooge to the obnoxious owner, and the time seemed right to sever his always fragile links with the North East.

Although Palace had dropped into the bottom three, Pardew's assessment that it wouldn't be too hard a job to improve results was spot on, as the midfield triumvirate of Jedinak, Ledley and McArthur was developing nicely, Bolasie and Zaha were often outstanding, and thankfully Glenn Murray returned from his spell away on loan. Although Bolasie and Jedinak were away for most of January, the latter captaining Australia to victory in the Asian Cup, the team immediately responded to the new manager, the wins started coming, and there was a restored sense of confidence, as we had seen under Pulis. The January transfer window saw the arrival of left back Pape Souaré and, bafflingly, the QPR squad player Jordon Mutch, as well as South Korean international Lee Chung-yong, but most importantly the decision was made to complete the permanent transfer of Zaha, at a bargain price. It had been reported that Tony Pulis' resistance to signing Zaha had contributed to his falling out with the chairman, but clearly Alan Pardew had no misgivings whatsoever, and it's difficult to fathom why anyone would have had any doubts. It's equally difficult to understand why Manchester United let Zaha slip through their fingers, or why England did, as both would have benefitted hugely from a player in his prime, but as Palace fans, we were the lucky ones.

Wayne Hennessey

Pardew's job had undoubtedly been easier than Pulis' rescue mission, but it was still a remarkable achievement to finish the season in 10th position, and to have cast aside the inferiority complex that can curse perennial also-rans such as Palace. Coming from behind to beat Spurs set the pattern in Pardew's first home game, and for the rest of the season it felt that whatever happened, and whoever the opposition, Palace were always likely to score goals, with Jason Puncheon having his best season creatively, Zaha and Bolasie let loose and Glenn Murray showing his quality at the top level. Beating the reigning champions,

Manchester City, thrilling as it was under the Selhurst Park floodlights, wasn't as big a shock as it may have felt previously, and it was almost expected that we'd get another result at Anfield as the season drew to a close and Steven Gerrard said farewell to the home fans after a glorious career at Liverpool. Palace spoiled Gerrard's party with another 3–1 victory, but what we didn't know was that we had witnessed Glenn Murray's last league goal in a Palace shirt.

It was fitting that this turned out to be the second best ever finishing position in Palace's long history, as it was such an enjoyable time to watch our team, to witness the atmosphere generated by the Holmesdale Fanatics, to be dazzled by the audacity of Zaha and Bolasie, to wonder at the spectacular growth on the chins of Joe Ledley and Mile Jedinak, and to feel that we had a manager with a real devotion to the club, and a plan for success to maybe even rival that of Steve Coppell.

2015-16

'I remember coming off the FA Cup final disappointed. I felt I could have done better... on one decision in particular where I could have played an advantage, I should have played an advantage.'
Mark Clattenberg

One of the most difficult aspects of football management is having the nous to sense and anticipate a player's impending decline and start to replace them even when it might seem premature. One could argue that this was the case with both Glenn Murray and Julián Speroni, but to my mind both decisions were plain wrong, and not just for sentimental reasons. Granted, sentiment is hard to avoid when it comes to Speroni, as few players have had such a powerful bond with the fans over the years, but although some cracks had started to appear before Speroni was granted a testimonial game against his previous club, Dundee, neither of the two goalkeepers suddenly ahead of him in the pecking order – Wayne Hennessey and new arrival Alex McCarthy – were demonstrably an improvement on one of the very best keepers of my time following Palace.

Equally, in the case of Murray, even though it was a generous offer from Bournemouth that prised him away at the age of 32, he left a good two or three years too early, and again none of his replacements could hold a candle to him in any aspect of the craft of the centre forward. Connor Wickham, Patrick Bamford, and later Emmanuel Adebayor, all for one reason or another fell way short and as time went on the error grew more and more evident. Bamford was a curiosity indeed, as he never showed anything in his few Palace appearances to suggest that he would go on to become a striker of genuine quality on Leeds' return to the Premier League five years later. Put bluntly, he looked pretty rubbish in a

Palace shirt, but perhaps his public school background contributed to the negative perception of the Mumford & Sons of football.

Yohan Cabaye

I wasn't paying attention when the term 'marquee signing' came into common usage, but I can't recall its use in South East London before Yohan Cabaye's arrival. I'm pretty certain it wasn't in currency when Lombardo came to Palace, and it still has a rather contrived ring to it, but I guess it's stuck now, and the signing of Cabaye fitted neatly into that category. The French international had played for Pardew at Newcastle before a big money move to Paris St-Germain, and his signing was an announcement of serious intent by Palace to start considering themselves permanent tenants of the Premier League, rather than just lodgers. Indeed, Cabaye played his part with a fine goal in the first games of the season, and Pardew's team carried over the impetus from before the summer break with their best start for many a year, and after three wins from the first four games sat in second place, sandwiched between Manchester City and the eventual champions, Leicester. The third of those wins came at Stamford Bridge, not a ground where Palace ever expected to come away with much. Indeed the only previous league win there came in the dark days of 1982, when both teams were in the Second Division, and the winning goal came from Jerry Murphy, one of the remnants from the Team of the Eighties that never was. This time, Chelsea came up against a Palace side playing with confidence and verve, and perhaps with some of Cabaye's undoubted class rubbing off on players such as Puncheon, Zaha, Bolasie and even Bakary Sako, but the winning goal came from Joel Ward with a memorable diving header, although why he found himself in the centre forward position was a mystery. However, it was indicative of the optimistic approach to games under Pardew that made it a great time to support Palace, and saw him spoken of as a likely candidate to succeed Roy Hodgson as England manager, which really didn't seem fanciful at the time.

Bakary Sako

Despite the odd dip in form, Palace breezed through the autumn months with a spring in their step, with some wonderful moments to celebrate, such as Zaha responding to the predictably incessant boos to win another decisive penalty against Watford, and Lee

Chung-yong's cracking winner to light up a dour game at Stoke, which turned out to be his one really memorable moment for Palace. Another victory at Anfield almost felt commonplace, but there was a growing sense of hubris among the fans, who had too easily convinced themselves that their team was heading for a European place at long last, and although the year ended with Palace in fifth spot, the inexorable slide down the table came soon enough, without any identifiable turning point. A dreadful run of 14 league games without a win was only leavened by a stealthy run of FA Cup victories, but by the time Palace had reached the semi-final, they had plummeted down the table, and James McArthur can't have been the only person pondering Wigan's fate of winning the Cup and being relegated in 2013.

All this time, in the background, negotiations had been going on to sell a large stake in the club to two American investors, Josh Harris and David Blitzer, and a deal was finally done, leaving Steve Parish as Chairman, but with an injection of cash earmarked for developing the ground. Having no apparent connection to, or real interest in football or South London, despite declaring in eye-rolling corporate language that 'Crystal Palace has a storied legacy, a bright future and we're proud to become a part of it', the two stayed very much in the background, silent partners to the point of invisibility.

Although the long run of games without winning was beginning to be a worry rather than a real crisis, nevertheless Palace were continuing to play adventurous football, with a well-rounded squad of players, and while Murray was sorely missed, Bolasie's wayward shooting had started to improve and Zaha in particular was outstanding, although he remained inexplicably overlooked by England's manager, Roy Hodgson. There was a wealth of midfield talent to choose from, plus Jordon Mutch, but one player who had somewhat lost his mojo was Jason Puncheon, until the game against Norwich in April which gave Palace their first league win since December. Palace and Norwich went into the game as the two teams sitting just above the relegation places, so it was massively important for both, and indeed the Canaries went on to be relegated, while the three points for Palace all but guaranteed safety. What stands out in the memory, though, is Puncheon's raw emotion at scoring his first goal of the season, and the team celebration that followed, in front of the Holmesdale Fanatics in the corner of the ground. Hats off to whoever first spotted the similarities between Raphael's Renaissance masterpiece 'The Deposition of Christ' and the image of Puncheon cradled by his ecstatic teammates, his face a perfect illustration that 'Joy and woe are woven fine'.

With relegation worries behind them, Palace could now turn their minds to the Cup semi-final against old rivals Watford, having beaten Southampton, Stoke, Spurs and Reading on the way. This was to be Palace's first trip to Wembley since that epic playoff victory against the Hornets, and everything about the day turned out to be glorious: the weather, the journey, the atmosphere, and of course, the result. It was always likely that Zaha would inflict more pain, and although he did run Watford ragged, it was an early goal from Yannick Bolasie that set Palace up to dominate the game. It was almost a carefully planned and executed re-enactment of Pardew's goal against Liverpool in the 1990 semi-final against Liverpool: a corner from the left (for Andy Gray, read Cabaye), a headed near post flick on (for Thorn read

Delaney) and a decisive header from close range from Bolasie. Although Deeney equalised in the second half, it wasn't long before a beautifully controlled downward header from Connor Wickham sealed the tie with a full half hour to go, thirty very comfortable minutes with Watford offering minimal threat, and by the final whistle most of their fans had already slunk off home.

Scott Dann

For a supporter of a club like Palace, never destined to pack the trophy cabinet, to have seen your team play in one FA Cup Final in your lifetime, as I did in 1990, is perhaps as much as you could wish for, but now we had another chance to win something real, and an opportunity for revenge against Manchester United. Even more meaningful for me, it was the chance to share that rare experience with my son, who really had no choice but to support Palace, although my daughter still fails to see the attraction. I would take both of them regularly as infants into the commentary box, usually with the promise of sweets, and they would pay little attention to Dennis Bergkamp or Alan Shearer or Michael Owen running around in front of them, as they focused on their colouring in. I persisted with both of them over the years, and at least one of them now shares this particular passion, although still neither will willingly listen to Bob Dylan.

The thrill of reaching Wembley has certainly been diluted a little with the semi-finals now also taking place there, but the gap between the two games was just about long enough for the excitement to build again, and by matchday the anticipation was every bit as all-consuming as it had been 26 years earlier. Although it's true that the FA Cup doesn't any more grab the nation's attention as it did in the days before there was a massive surfeit of live football on television, if you're a fan of one of the teams involved it is as huge an occasion as it ever was, and for clubs like Palace, who have no interest in the money-spinning European competitions, it is the most glittering prize they can aspire to, and has lost none of its sheen. Although still dominated by the big teams, every so often the competition comes alive again for neutrals when it is won by a team like Coventry, Wimbledon or Wigan, and this time Crystal Palace had a realistic chance to add their name to that elusive list.

As before, United went into the game as clear favourites despite having had a pretty poor season under their unloved manager Louis van Gaal, but we knew that we had enough talent in the team and had shown enough excellent football at times during the season, to make a real game of it. I had an extraordinarily strong feeling that this was going to be our finest hour, that we would at last see Palace lift the Cup, and equally that we might never see that again. In 1990's thrilling final, Ian Wright had put Palace 3–2 up before Mark Hughes' cruel late equaliser sent the game to a tortuous replay which United just about deserved to win, but there was no sense of injustice involved, except perhaps for the

dubious bending of the loan rules for their goalkeeper. You're right, I should be over it by now!

The most difficult decision for Alan Pardew concerned who to start in midfield, and it was Puncheon who was sacrificed in favour of a more defensive trio of Jedinak, Cabaye and McArthur, with Bolasie and Zaha wide and Connor Wickham alone down the middle. With a settled back four of Ward, Delaney, Dann and Souaré, Palace went into the final in good shape against an under-achieving Manchester United team. It was all set up for Zaha to exact revenge for the shabby way he had been treated at Old Trafford, and to do what Ian Wright so nearly did for Palace in 1990, but ultimately the names we'll remember from this final are those of Wayne Rooney and Mark Clattenberg. The years were catching up with Rooney, the best English footballer of his generation by far, but this had forced him back into a midfield role in which he was outstanding, every touch from him throughout the game oozing class, and showing up not only Palace's midfield, but throwing into sharp relief the contrast between him and his own sub-standard teammates.

Just as we could do nothing against such a wonderful player, we couldn't legislate for the possibility that Mark Clattenberg, supposedly England's finest referee, would lose his nerve on the big occasion and have such a stinker. Early on in the game, Connor Wickham latched onto a beautiful through ball from Delaney and was pulled down by the flailing Chris Smalling, but Wickham's strength saw him recover his balance and take the ball forward, with Zaha unmarked on the penalty spot and an opening goal all but certain. However, Clattenberg had panicked and blown the whistle far too soon before the advantage was apparent, and although Wickham put the ball in the net, the defenders had heard the premature whistle and breathed a huge sigh of relief. It was obvious that the referee knew he'd messed up, but unforgivably he repeated the error just before half time when Joel Ward set off on a John Pemberton-like run down the right touchline and was fouled by Rojo, but again Clattenberg blew the whistle just as Ward had gained the advantage, and Palace were robbed of another chance by inept refereeing.

The second half continued with United just about having the upper hand, but it all changed when the tiring Cabaye was replaced by Jason Puncheon late in the game. He had only been on a matter of minutes when he won a corner with a teasing cross from the right, virtually his first touch of the game. His second was to take the corner, easily headed clear by Fellaini, but when Joel Ward returned the ball swiftly to the unmarked Puncheon, he controlled it and volleyed home past De Gea, who had been fairly untroubled up to that point, but stood no chance against the power and accuracy of Puncheon's finish from a narrow angle. What a moment that was, with just over ten minutes to go: of course, the fans went nuts and Pardew went a little mad with a curious celebratory wiggle, not quite a dance, but who could blame him, as we all thought we had one hand on the Cup. Forget Clattenberg, forget Rooney, this was the moment that Jason Puncheon, 'one of our own', was to become a true South London legend.

We were ecstatic in the ground, but mostly incredulous that at last we were seeing our team win a major trophy, but Wayne Rooney had other ideas and in less than three minutes our dreams were in splinters. The United captain picked up the ball and as he weaved his way diagonally forward,

waiting for an opening, he saw off the feeble challenges of six different Palace players before dinking the ball to the far post where Fellaini chested it down to Mata for a devastating equaliser. It was that moment from Rooney that made all the difference on the day. Palace did well not to crumble after such a psychological blow and had a couple more half chances to finish it in 90 minutes, but as the game went into extra time with both teams having used all three substitutes, two very weary sets of players continued to give absolutely everything, without any thought of slowing it down and playing for penalties. Smalling was uncontroversially sent off for wrestling Bolasie to the ground as he was sent clear down the left, and there were decent chances for Zaha, Bolasie and Gayle to win it, but it was United's Lingard who finally got the goal that always looked like coming as the game opened up. It was an instinctive volley worthy of winning any game, and if it had been a scrappy goal or a defensive error it would have hurt more, but in the end it felt like Palace had just been edged out in a thrilling game, and although I would have loved it to have gone to penalties, there was little to complain about, notwithstanding the referee. The atmosphere inside Wembley was wonderful, as it had been for the semi-final, and in a strange way the final result didn't matter quite so much, as Palace had put in a magnificent performance, one to be properly proud of, and for those three short minutes that elusive trophy was ours. One day, perhaps one day soon.

2016–17

'I'm not putting you under pressure to win, lads, but I am saying, just don't lose'
Sam Allardyce

Despite reaching the Cup Final, Palace's alarmingly swift decline throughout the previous season was a worry, and although they managed to hang on to Wilfried Zaha despite some stirring from Spurs during the summer, Pardew agreed to release two players who typified the very best of Palace's character and personality as a team. Both were understandable, Aston Villa offering Mile Jedinak a new challenge, having slipped down the pecking order at Selhurst, and Everton offering silly money for Yannick Bolasie, but with those two players went some of the heart and soul respectively of the team. It had been a real joy to see Bolasie at his best in the red and blue, and Jedinak had typified what fans want from a captain, although there had always been a fair amount of carping at his lack of finesse. Less of a loss was Dwight Gayle, who had never quite clicked at the top level, and overall had disappointed, given the very high expectations when he came as Palace's record signing, much like Marco Gabbiadini many years before, and the drop to the Championship with Newcastle was a good move for him.

Sam Allardyce

Coming in the other direction was the former Spurs and England winger Andros Townsend, whose once sparkling career had foundered somewhat before being revived at Newcastle, and as a replacement for Bolasie he seemed to fit the bill. Other summer signings included the French goalkeeper Steve Mandanda, who was intended as an alternative to the increasingly shaky Wayne Hennessey, and West Ham's unflashy central defender James Tomkins, who most Hammers fans were very sorry to lose.

However, the big news was the arrival of Christian Benteke from Liverpool, for a reported £32 million that was treble Palace's previous record fee for Cabaye a year earlier. The Belgian international had been exceptional in three seasons at Aston Villa, and had started well at Anfield under manager Brendan Rogers, but had fallen out of favour once Jurgen Klopp took over, although Palace fans had seen a little of him when he won and scored a highly dubious 96th minute penalty to give Liverpool a victory at Selhurst a few months earlier. Benteke's impact wasn't immediate, but he very soon looked a class above any Palace striker in recent memory, barring Glenn Murray, and it began to look like money well spent when he started knocking in the goals for his club as well as his country. Townsend was also bedding in well, often swapping wings with Zaha, and with the crosses coming in to Benteke from both sides, his peerless ability in the air started to bear fruit.

A fair start to the season saw Palace sitting in the top half of the table with eight games gone, and it looked for a short while as if Pardew had got things back on track after three wins on the bounce, but the rot set in once Benteke missed a penalty against West Ham, heralding a run of six defeats that sent Palace hurtling down towards the relegation places. By the end of that run, the calls for a change of manager had become louder and more persistent, although I was among those who was enjoying Palace's cavalier style under Pardew and was completely convinced that he would turn things around with the quality of players available to him. I was still very much in Pardew's corner even after the infamous 5–4 defeat at Swansea which was the game above all others that probably sealed his fate. Coming back from 3–1 down against the side in bottom place, Palace were leading 4–3 as the clock ticked past 90 minutes but stood back and waved Swansea through to score two goals in injury time, in a game that encapsulated the best and worst of the Eagles under Pardew. Although that game wasn't quite the end for Pardew, sadly it was for Connor Wickham, who never fully recovered from the serious injury sustained that day, despite a succession of false dawns over the following five years.

Luka Milivojević

When the axe finally fell, Pardew became the sixth manager to either be sacked or to walk away in as many years, although he had lasted longer than most, and I still maintain that he should have been given more time, despite the record of only six wins from 36 games in the calendar year. Nevertheless, I will concede that, had he stayed, Palace would have more than likely scored the most goals for a relegated team, so it's probably a good job on balance that I'm not in charge after all. There was much speculation over the influence that the American investors had on the decision, with their only apparent interest in the club or the game being the imperative of staying in the Premier League, but it was telling that in no time at all Palace had turned to Sam Allardyce, a man with an unfair Pulis-like reputation for primitive, pragmatic, survivalist football. For those of us who had thoroughly enjoyed Pardew's open, risky style, the portents were ominous when Steve Parish declared: 'We hope a change will change things. We all bought into the decision to play a more expansive style of football. We all believed in it. That hasn't worked. It's no one's fault. The players have been running their socks off for Alan, the spirit is good. But now we're going to wind the dial back the other way.'

We had gone from the man who would be England manager one day to the man who was England manager for one game. Allardyce's appointment by the FA had been curious in the first place, given the shadow of previous allegations against him, but now he had been taken in by a newspaper sting during which he discussed ways to get round the rules on the third-party ownership of players, the outlawed practice described by some as 'indentured slavery'. If this lack of wisdom on his part wasn't bad enough, Allardyce was also caught mocking the way his predecessor Roy Hodgson pronounced the letter R, and he left the position with a 100% winning record and his reputation no better or worse than it had been before. We will never know whether, had Allardyce stayed in the England job, he would have seen the light that Hodgson refused to and realised that Wilfried Zaha would have been a major asset to his country in the build up to the 2018 World Cup, and might just have added the spark that England needed to go that bit further, and even won the thing.

As it was, Gareth Southgate donned the blazer and made the disastrous decision to pick Andros Townsend for his first squad ahead of his far superior teammate, who was in the form of his life, and I imagine that was the final straw for Zaha, who decided to switch allegiance to the country of his birth, Côte d'Ivoire, who showed him the love he needed. In every other respect I'm a big fan of Gareth Southgate, having seen him grow from a boy in an oversized suit on the Wembley pitch in 1990 to a model professional for Palace, Villa and Middlesbrough, as well as for his country, but I still consider overlooking Wilf to be a huge, unforgiveable error. In a season without too many real highlights, Zaha was outstanding for Palace, and his exceptional solo goal against Hull was probably his best, but even that was surpassed by the one he scored for his country against Russia, which was further evidence that he could genuinely be considered world class, and a huge loss to England. Like most fans, I suspect, I'm not really all that bothered about the national team compared to my club, except if there's a Palace player involved, but manager after manager habitually tends to overlook players from lower status clubs, and instead pick whoever has been hyped as the real deal at Liverpool or Manchester United. The 2016–17 Palace squad included Martin Kelly, never more than a reliable but functional utility player, who won an England cap whilst at Liverpool, but who was nowhere near as good as Scott Dann or James Tomkins, players who never came close to being selected, even at their peak, although the latter did represent

Great Britain at the London Olympics. Of course there are exceptions – Peter Taylor among them when Palace were in the Third Division – but not all that many over the years.

Although Allardyce wasn't easy to warm to, given Palace's predicament he seemed a pretty sensible choice, but for a couple of months things got progressively worse on the pitch, the nadir coming at home to Sunderland when the away team went 4–0 up before half time. It's not very often over the years that we have heard booing from the Selhurst crowd, usually so vocally supportive even in the face of defeat, but on this occasion it seemed the only reasonable response. Throughout the team, from Hennessey to Benteke, nothing went right, and usually reliable players such as Delaney and Ledley had become inexplicably hopeless. Mercifully the Mackems didn't add to the score in the second half, but the humiliation was complete, and with Palace now second from bottom and sinking fast, Big Sam might have been kicking himself for taking on a team with apparently so little appetite for the fight. The heart that Mile Jedinak bought to the midfield had gone with him, Puncheon's star was on the wane despite him wearing the captain's armband, and neither Cabaye nor McArthur ever looked able to really dominate in that area, but the signing of Serbian international Luka Milivojević was a master stroke that proved the catalyst for Palace's unlikely revival, and survival. Once he had bedded in, Luka displayed much of the steel that we missed from Jedi, and with a little more panache.

There had been an obvious gap on the left side of defence since Pape Souaré's serious injury following a car crash in September, and although Joel Ward had done sterling work there, with Martin

Kelly less convincing at right back, it was good to see the arrival of a proper left back, Patrick Van Aanholt, along with Leicester's Jeffrey Schlupp, who it turned out could play anywhere. However, along with Milivojević, the other major factor in Palace's transformation was the loan signing of centre back Mamadou Sakho from Liverpool. Unfancied at Anfield by Jurgen Klopp, much like Benteke, the French defender bought real quality to the defence and was a considerable upgrade on the heroic but creaking Damien Delaney. Compare their respective approaches to distributing the ball from the back: the abiding image of Delaney with the ball at his feet is him nudging forward towards the halfway line, looking at the options, then playing the same ball every time, a left footed angled hoof/pass towards the opposite corner, whether there was a team mate there or not; Sakho, on the other hand, loved to get himself out of a tight spot and thread a short or long ball through the eye of a needle to build through midfield, and although he was always prone to be over ambitious and drop a critical clanger, overall the very good far outweighed the very bad, and he quickly became crucial to Palace's transformed defence.

The real turning point, and a memorable moment, came at West Brom, when Andros Townsend, whose form had been patchy, won the ball just outside his own area and took it all the way upfield into the opposition box before a couple of stepovers and a left-footed finish ended with him collapsing onto his back with a mixture of exhaustion and huge relief. That moment was reminiscent of Puncheon's crucial goal against Norwich the previous year, and this time it lifted Palace out of the bottom three and inspired a run of six wins in eight games, which remarkably included the scalps of Chelsea, Arsenal and Liverpool.

The transformation from the team that had been thrashed by Sunderland was complete: Zaha was no longer having to carry them alone, Benteke was scoring again, even Hennessey was playing the odd blinder in goal. Each of those three games was massive in the context of the season overall, and few would have expected any points, let alone the maximum nine. Benteke's sublime dink over the Chelsea keeper, Cabaye's finish in the convincing 3–0 rout of Arsenal, and Benteke's casual brace against his old team at Anfield were particular highlights, and any one of those results would have kept the fans happy for a while in any season, but to have all three in the same month was beyond belief.

Mamadou Sakho

One would have expected after that run that safety was assured, but with Tomkins, Dann and now Sakho out injured, a makeshift defence struggled as the goals dried up again, but everything came together with a convincing 4–0 demolition of Hull, which sent Marco Silva's team down and kept Palace up, with the scenes at Selhurst almost more delirious than when hammering Arsenal. The longest that Palace had ever stayed in either the old Division One or Premier League previously was four years, and so Allardyce's achievement was to cement their most successful sustained spell in their history. The familiar pattern had repeated itself, with first Pulis, then Pardew, now Allardyce performing a pretty miraculous salvage job, but wouldn't it be nice to have the odd season without all that drama? Maybe that's what makes following Palace frankly more fun than supporting a team that's never really in jeopardy, and over the years the excitement of promotion campaigns has been what has given us so many great moments, something that is missed by staying safely in the top division. One Cup Final every two or three decades isn't quite enough, although one or two every year can't be great fun either, which is only one of the reasons I'm so glad I'm not a Chelsea fan, like so many of my South London contemporaries.

seemed honest at the time, as he stated: 'I want to be able to savour life while I'm still relatively young and when I'm still relatively healthy enough to do all the things I want to do, like travel, spend more time with my family and grandchildren without the huge pressure that comes with being a football manager.' Perhaps he had seen enough of his family by the time he took the Everton job six months later, but once again Palace were in the market for a new manager, hopefully one who might stay a little longer.

Jeffrey Schlupp

Sam Allardyce had won over the doubters, who could now see that he was far more complex and thoughtful than his characterisation, and some of the football that his team were now playing was among the best we had ever seen – only in patches, admittedly – so it came as a huge shock when he decided to walk away just two days after the season's end. His reason

'The worst manager in the history of the Premier League... Frank de Boer... seven matches, seven defeats, zero goals... If he (Marcus Rashford) was coached by Frank, he would learn how to lose'
José Mourinho

Well, while the details may be slightly askew – it was only four league games with the Dutchman as manager – the sentiment is hard to disagree with.

After 45 years away from the top division, Huddersfield Town had scraped through the promotion playoffs and reached the pinnacle under the likeable German manager David Wagner, but surely were quaking at the thought of their first game, facing the Total Football of the new incarnation of Crystal Palace. Managed by one of the all-time greats of Dutch football, Frank De Boer, and including three players with caps for the Netherlands – Patrick Van Aanholt, Jaïro Riedewald and Timothy Fosu-Mensah – Palace were set to channel the spirit of Johan Cruyff at Selhurst Park. With a front three of Benteke, Zaha, and the rising star on loan from Chelsea, Ruben Loftus-Cheek, we home fans were rubbing our hands with glee at the prospect of a cricket score. Of course, the Terriers won 3–0, and the furrows on De Boer's brow grew deeper than ever.

One could see how Steve Parish might have persuaded himself, or been persuaded that with the luxury of the whole summer to recruit a new manager, Palace could for once plan positively rather than react to another crisis. The plan involved bringing in a man who had, on top of his peerless achievements as a player for Ajax, Barcelona and his country, also managed Ajax to win four consecutive titles in the Dutch league, and whose only slight blip had been a brief unsuccessful period at Inter Milan. These

were credentials that would have turned any dreamer's head, and along with the rest of us that was still a large part of what motivated the Palace chairman. The single best thing about De Boer's appointment was the arch manner that Palace's social media heralded his arrival as Cruyff's representative in SE25, with a plume of white smoke emanating from the Original Tasty Jerk takeaway next to the ground, but it was all downhill from there.

Jaïro Riedewald

Wilfried Zaha was injured in that first game, Benteke was the only fit senior striker, and De Boer persisted with a confused version of a back three with two reluctant wing backs in the ensuing defeats to Liverpool and Swansea, before simplifying things against Burnley, but losing again. Not only were Palace pointless after four games, but they hadn't managed a goal in that time, and the entire team looked shellshocked and drained of any confidence. It was obvious from what was happening on the pitch that something was fundamentally wrong behind the scenes, but it was still a shock to see De Boer given the elbow quite so swiftly. During that period the curious arrival of Dougie Freedman back at the club as Sporting Director was probably a sign that Parish was already deeply worried by the apparent bad blood between the new manager and several of the senior players. Steve Parish had been sold a pup, and by his own admission had made a big mistake, but to his credit he recognised his error and took complete responsibility, and following the fourth defeat in a row De Boer's sacking was really just a formality. The poor run of results made it easier for the chairman to do what he had already decided needed doing, and while De Boer's 77 days at Selhurst isn't the shortest managerial career in the Premier League, it remains one of the most infamous.

The interlude between managers was briefer than ever, and although many suspected that Dougie Freedman would complete his unlikely rehabilitation by stepping in, it was Roy Hodgson that the club turned to in an admission, even a declaration, that a team like Palace needed above all to focus on the basics in order to compete. At its heart, what makes football the beautiful game that it clearly is, the greatest team game ever invented, is its essential simplicity. Score goals and stop the other team scoring. Through all the attempts by journalist, commentators and analysts to make it more complicated, or to elevate their self-esteem by making it sound more sophisticated, that's ultimately all that matters. Of course there are different approaches, formations and tactics, and by all means give them a label if it helps you to understand what you are watching, but football is an art rather than a science. What does it matter what your possession stats are, how many yards various players have covered, or what your xG rating was (you tell me!), did you score goals and stop the other team scoring? Not only are those the only statistics that matter a jot, they're the only ones that I, as a fan who loves nothing more than watching the game live, care about. In over

40 years of commentating on Palace games at the ground with just a microphone and a notepad, I never felt lost without Optasports' offer of 'one-line data-driven insights to help shape pre-match narratives, highlight key in-game moments and provide insights for highlights and social media content after the final whistle'. I would hope that language, rather than numbers, conveys the game to the listener, with all its nuance, individuality and beautiful unpredictability intact. Who said 'dinosaur'? Is that me or Roy Hodgson you're referring to?

Roy Hodgson

Roy Hodgson was destined to one day end up back at Selhurst Park, where he had watched the team as a boy, and had played in the youth team alongside his contemporary Steve Kember, although he never graduated to playing professionally. It was as a manager that he made his name, first in Sweden, where he won multiple league titles with Halmstad and Malmö, before successfully taking over the Swiss national side, and managing Inter Milan among countless other clubs and countries. Later in his career he worked wonders at Fulham, taking them to the Europa Cup final before going to Liverpool, which didn't work out so well. The next stop was West Bromwich Albion on the way to finally taking over from Fabio Capello as England manager. Always a thankless task, Hodgson's record with England was decent, but he will always be remembered for presiding over the humiliating defeat by Iceland which knocked England out of the 2016 Euros, and with his retirement from the England job most assumed that we had seen the last of him as a manager as he approached his 70th year. Not only was he visibly shattered by the Iceland result, he clearly had little patience with having to deal with the media, comprised of journalists who were on the whole so manifestly his intellectual inferiors, and the time seemed right to put his feet up.

Patrick Van Aanholt

Thankfully for Palace, Hodgson decided that he didn't want to leave the game with Iceland as his legacy, and with his reputation dented, so he took on the challenge of repairing the damage done by De Boer, which even to the most blindly optimistic of us looked barely possible. The task was very clear, with the sole objective being to stay in the Premier League, and Hodgson was joined by his right-hand man at England, Ray Lewington, a veteran of the Palace dugout from Alan Smith's days,

in what appeared an unlikely quest. Indeed, a further three games into the season with still no points and no goals, new records were being broken each week: the first team ever in the top division to lose the first five games without scoring; the first in any division to lose six without scoring; the only team in Europe's top twenty leagues not to have scored a goal after seven games; no goals in eleven out of twelve Premier League games, spanning the end of the previous season and the start of this. I'm sure there are many more, but the key point was the inability to score, Benteke still being the only proven striker in the squad, with Wickham still injured and Fraizer Campbell let go by De Boer. After losing 5–0 to Manchester City and 4–0 to United, the top two in the table, the next game was against reigning champions Chelsea, and to make matters worse, Benteke was now likely to be missing for several weeks, leaving Palace with Freddie Ladapo the only striker available, and he was clearly a long way off this level.

At least Zaha was finally back to fitness, but the chances of getting anything from the Chelsea game were vanishingly small. Roy Hodgson opted to experiment with Zaha and Townsend – hitherto both out and out wingers – as a front two, and not for the last time it became apparent that Benteke had more often than not just been getting in the way, a literal waste of a shirt. Remarkably, Palace appeared full of confidence going forward and forced their first goal of the season, albeit an own goal from Chelsea's defender Azpilicueta, and although Chelsea soon equalised, it was Wilf who showed strength and composure to score the winner before half time, and although Palace had to see out the second half with a few scares, they always just edged it and fully deserved the points. Mamadou Sakho was now back permanently and played a big part, and even Speroni returned in goal for the injured Hennessey, who hadn't been able to do much right all season. Milivojević and Cabaye were at their best, and of course Zaha was sensational. It was a great feeling to celebrate victory at Selhurst Park once again, despite still being stranded at the bottom of the table, but at last there was crumb of hope, with enough poor teams within realistic striking distance, although that notion was still a minority view.

Christian Benteke

The next home game, against West Ham, was almost more of a turning point, despite only being a 2–2 draw. From 2–0 down, it was the dramatic manner that Zaha rescued the point with the last kick of the game, digging himself out of an impossible position to get his shot away in the 97th minute, that gave hope that things might start to go Palace's way at last and that maybe we weren't entirely doomed after all. Despite the long list of injuries and the psychological scars inflicted by De Boer, Roy Hodgson had got to grips with what was needed to get his players performing again, as they had for a spell under Sam Allardyce, and although Jason Puncheon's influence had diminished rapidly, Ruben Loftus-Cheek was really looking the part,

one of those players who you can just tell would one day play for England. Indeed, that call came surprisingly soon, as Gareth Southgate gave him his full debut following his good form for Palace, instantly making it highly unlikely that Chelsea would let him go permanently.

Palace now embarked on a run of games where every point was crucial, as they steadily narrowed the gap on those around them, and after a dogged run of eight games unbeaten, finally clawed their way up the table in a season where probably a dozen teams looked in danger of relegation at some point. During this spell, the midweek trip to Brighton was memorable not for what turned out to be a drab, goalless game, but for the astonishingly incompetent policing of a fixture that was bound to be troublesome, given the bad blood between the two sets of fans. Beautifully elegant stadium that it is, the planning of how to get fans to and from the ground via the inadequate Falmer station was never properly thought through, and to schedule the Palace game in the evening was asking for trouble. All was made worse than it needed to be, though, when the Sussex Police decided that this was an episode of Life On Mars, and all Palace supporters making the trip needed to be treated like old-school hooligans from the 1970s. It's clearly the case that among the wannabe Ultras attaching themselves to the club, there are a few that look for trouble, but the police decided to kettle the fans around Brighton, ensuring that they missed the kick-off, then the gates were closed after a few jumped the turnstiles and hundreds of fans with tickets for the game forced back onto the train. I had made it through just as the game started, probably a minute before it kicked off outside, and irritated as I was by the jumped up Casuals letting off smoke bombs in my ear, the police's claim that they had found knives and knuckledusters was of course repeated as fact by the press, and later proved to be a bald-faced lie, but 'Falsehood flies, and the Truth comes limping after it', and the damage was done.

Around this time, Steve Parish announced ambitious plans to expand the capacity of Selhurst Park by spending up to £100 million on an extension behind and above Archibald Leitch's original edifice from 1924, and although the architect's impression looked a lot better thought out than many similar projects, the addition of 8,000 extra seats seemed hardly worth the effort, and indeed the focus was really on increasing the potential for corporate events. It was obvious to anyone who knew the ground well that just appending something new and shiny out the back wouldn't really fix any of the issues that make the Selhurst Park matchday experience the anachronism that it is, and which we would surely miss in any case. As luck would have it, the club had overlooked the fact that Sainsbury's still owned a crucial bit of land that Palace needed, and they hadn't thought to mention their plans to the supermarket chain, so a project that was meant to begin construction in 2018 was, at the time of writing, no nearer starting.

Draws were becoming the norm on the pitch, but Palace really needed to convert some of these into wins if they were to have a hope of reaching safety, and one memorable chance came at home to Bournemouth, with the score at 2–2 on 90 minutes and the game entering injury time. Wilfried Zaha was brought down in the box and we prepared for Luka Milivojević, who had already scored a penalty in the game and was now established as hugely reliable from the spot, to seal the three points. However, Christian Benteke, who had completely forgotten how to score

following his wonderful first season, wrestled the ball from Luka and insisted on taking it himself. The Serb had not yet been given the captain's armband, but one would have expected him to stand his ground nonetheless. The crowd could see what was going on, and were livid with Benteke even before he stepped up and limply ushered the ball goalward, making the save easy for the goalkeeper. It was unforgivable by the Belgian, desperate for personal glory in what had been a dreadful season for him, and his relationship with the fans justifiably never recovered.

Three points would have lifted Palace off the bottom spot, but after beating Watford in the next game, they were at last out of the bottom three, for a day at least, and followed up with a 3–0 triumph at Leicester, Zaha again the architect of both victories. Remarkably, from an impossible position after seven games, in less than three months Roy Hodgson had lifted Palace up to 14th spot, and given them hope of survival, although they remained one of about ten teams still at risk of relegation. To have done that with so few options up front, and with continuing disruption to his defence, who seemed to be taking it in turns to pick up serious injuries, was testament to his outstanding abilities as a manager, and one of those injuries, this time to Joel Ward, presented a first team opportunity from nowhere to a modest young man called Aaron Wan-Bissaka from the youth team. From his very first appearance, a tough baptism against Spurs, Wan-Bissaka showed a startling ability to time his tackles to perfection, and it was clear that Palace had almost accidentally unearthed a rare talent, who very soon was being spoken of as potentially world-class, by me at least. Whoever he faced attempting to go past him, he filled you with confidence that he would stop them with his long legs and utterly intuitive anticipation, and we hadn't seen anyone tackle like him since the days of Doris. That's not to put Paul Hinshelwood in anything like the same league as Wan-Bissaka, but his focus on the fundamentals of defending certainly reminded me of that stalwart of the Team of the Eighties.

The return fixture against Brighton turned out to be another highlight in the most enjoyable season for years, largely since Zaha scored a brace of goals, including another header against them after saying before the game: 'I just want to beat them, then they can just be quiet'. Wilf just gets it.

A 5–0 rout of Leicester featured the most wonderful team goal of the season, involving Loftus-Cheek, Cabaye, McArthur and Zaha, and Milivojević even showed forgiveness to Benteke, generously allowing him to take a penalty which he just about managed to score, despite falling over. After that Palace swaggered to the end of an extraordinary season, not only safe, but finishing in 11th place. Hodgson had repaid the faith shown in him, and proved that sometimes the old ones are the best.

2018-19

'Do they need to break my leg before someone gets shown a red card?'
Wilfried Zaha

Roy Hodgson and Ray Lewington's triumph had been to not only rescue the club from a seemingly impossible situation, but to restore to Palace a real identity, and the fans recognised in Hodgson a genuine shared love for the club. His reputation had been fully repaired following the unhappy England experience, but if anyone thought he might quit while he was ahead, they misunderstood how completely absorbed by football Hodgson still was. He now had a chance to build a legacy at his boyhood club, and to shape it according to his principles. He had worked with the players he inherited, and with the club being governed with supreme financial caution the days of big money signings were at least temporarily a thing of the past. Christian Benteke's first season had been superb, but he had soon become an expensive spare part, Mamadou Sakho was a great asset, but Johan Cabaye had run out of steam, and never quite achieved what he was capable of in his heyday. Palace could have probably got another season out of him, but he rarely lasted 90 minutes anymore and moved on to play in Dubai, then back to France. The disappointment of losing Cabaye was tempered by the excitement at picking up Max Meyer, one of several players over the years to be burdened with the 'German Messi' label, on a free transfer from Schalke. Meyer's youthful promise had led to four full caps for his country, and a glance at his highlights reel showed a midfielder with the right mix of defensive aggression and attacking skill to make him an ideal replacement for Cabaye.

There had been a little transfer activity with Dougie Freedman back at Selhurst, and the hope was that he had helped unearth a few young gems from Europe with the signing of Polish defender Jaroslaw Jach, Swedish midfielder Erdal Rakip, and a desperately needed centre forward, Alexander Sørloth. Any of them might have blossomed, but sadly none of them worked out, and they became footnotes in Palace's history, along with Meyer, who ultimately proved to fall way short of the hype.

Max Meyer

More successful new arrivals were Cheikhou Kouyaté, the Senegalese captain from West Ham, and Spanish goalkeeper Vicente Guaita, both highly experienced, and ready to hit the ground running, together with Swansea's Ghanaian international Jordan Ayew. The son of the legend of African football, Abedi Pele, Ayew seemed an odd signing for a team so desperately in need of goals, which had never been his forte, and it was never quite clear what his natural position was: somewhere up front probably best describes it. Benteke had only scored three goals in his woeful second season, and appeared drained of all confidence even before injury kept him out for much of this, his third and worst at Palace, yet the manager had no confidence in the young Norwegian international Sørloth, on the face of it a like-for-like replacement at centre-forward. Indeed, it wasn't until Michy Batshuiyi came in on loan in January that there was finally a genuine striker who knew where the goal was, as once again the season's top scorer turned out to be Milivojević, mostly from the penalty spot.

Cheikhou Kouyaté

As well as a reluctance to pick Sørloth up front, Roy Hodgson had a bit of a blind spot when it came to his goalkeeper, keeping faith with the nervy Hennessey and leaving Guaita on the bench for the first half of a frustrating season all round. Although never in the bottom three all season, the previous year's miraculous finishing position of 11th never looked achievable, and whereas the Herculean task of survival after De Boer's brief spell had bought with it jeopardy and much excitement, the priority now switched to not getting into trouble in the first place. Solid in defence, solid in midfield with the trio of Kouyaté, Milivojević and McArthur, and relying as ever on Zaha for any creative spark, it became a season more to be endured than enjoyed. The love that the fans felt for Roy Hodgson began to fade a little, with many frustrated at his perceived stubbornness in ignoring Sørloth and Meyer, although the latter was given plenty of chances to

make his mark, mostly from the bench, and never threatened to take on the mantle of Cabaye. There seemed to be a joyless air around the club, and an absence of smiles, personified by Ayew's perennially miserable visage, whether it spread from the fans to the players or vice versa, and it wasn't helped by a succession of hard luck stories. Many good performances went unrewarded, and a couple of early results set the tone, losing at home to Liverpool thanks to a characteristically theatrical dive by Mo Salah, and away to Watford despite dominating much of the game but succumbing to their highly cynical targeting of Zaha which should have seen Capoue sent off. That would most definitely have been the outcome had VAR been in place yet, and a clear handball by Lacazette led to Palace being robbed of a deserved victory over Arsenal, another incident making the case for VAR which, to be absolutely clear, I think is an awful idea.

Jordan Ayew

Zaha's dismay at the treatment that he was getting from opposition players was compounded by Watford captain Troy Deeney's admission that 'you take it in turns kicking him', and similar treatment at Huddersfield, which couldn't stop

Wilf scoring a glorious winner, prompted him to complain loudly about the lack of protection he was getting from referees. Of course, this drew plenty of criticism from sections of the media who bought in to the notion of Zaha being a habitual diver, which is emphatically untrue. In the time that Zaha has played for Palace, I witnessed a few players dive, and condemned it every time. Townsend, McArthur and Cabaye were all guilty, and Ayew had an extraordinary and tiresome knack of falling over and convincing the referee, but I can honestly say that I have never seen Zaha take a dive. Conversely, I have never seen a player fouled so often and the referee give nothing, which is why he appeared so petulant and so frequently hard done by. I have to ask myself how I would have felt about Zaha were I an opposition fan, and I dare say it would be hard not to lazily go along with the uninformed narrative. There are other players with a similar reputation who got a fraction of the abuse that Zaha endured, Salah being a case in point and Jack Grealish, with slightly less justification, but the key difference is that Zaha found it hard to control his emotions or hide his feelings, when we wished he would just shrug it off and get on with the game rather than sulk. That's easy to say when you're not the one in fear of someone breaking your leg every time you get the ball, but this season in particular it had a negative impact on his game, and he started to sometimes go into his shell, fearful of the cloggers at last. The low point of Zaha's season came at Southampton, when another foul on him by the weaselly Ward-Prowse went unpunished and his frustration at having been targeted all game led to a harsh yellow card, but this soon turned to red once he had pointedly applauded the referee, demonstrating that sarcasm can sometimes be a more heinous sin than trying to injure an opponent.

Vicente Guaita

Among a succession of decent performances but poor results during the first half of the season were two games that displayed Palace's schizophrenic nature: a win over Burnley during which Palace managed an unprecedented 29 shots, followed immediately by an abject defeat at Brighton. However, there was one game that shone out, and gave us renewed enthusiasm and belief that anything could happen. Palace travelled to Manchester City just before Christmas to face a team that had won all nine home games, scoring 33 goals along the way, and Palace's last two trips to the Etihad Stadium had both finished as 5–0 defeats. There was some encouragement to take from their most recent encounter at Selhurst Park, when Palace had nullified City and were denied victory by a late penalty save, but that game apart there was little to suggest that there were any points to be had on this occasion. Still strikerless, and with Zaha alone up front, Palace held out stoutly for nearly half an hour before Gundogan scored the first of what was surely going to be a hatful. Schlupp soon equalised, though, and just minutes later Andros Townsend scored the goal of this or any other season with a volley from distance that left even the scorer in a complete state of shock. What made it the goal of the season for every impartial fan was not only the sheer beauty of way the ball was struck, but the context of the game, which turned out to be the only one that City didn't win at home all season on their way to the title. As if that wasn't enough, Palace scored a third with an inevitable Milivojević penalty and Palace came away with a most unlikely 3–2 victory, and a goal worth watching over and over again for years to come. We haven't had too many of those over the decades, and it was a bit of much needed light in a period of gloom.

From there, the season picked up as Guaita eventually came into the side and Batshuiyi filled the gaping hole up front, while a half decent FA Cup run came to an end with defeat in the quarter-finals, but what made the season was Palace's outstanding form away from home. In winning 3–2 at Arsenal, Christian Benteke scored his only goal of the season, his first for nearly a year, and Palace were mathematically safe with several games to go, finishing with a flourish by hammering Bournemouth 5–3 to finally give the home fans some cheer at the end of a season where it had been in short supply at Selhurst Park.

That final game was notable for several reasons: Palace's two best-ever right backs in Nathaniel Clyne and Aaron Wan-Bissaka facing each other; Wilfried Zaha's furious determination to stay on his feet and set up the final goal for Townsend; and emotional farewells to Jason Puncheon and Julián Speroni, whose departure was not exactly premature, but very sad nonetheless. Although finishing 12th, a slight dip from the previous year, Palace nevertheless achieved their highest Premier League points total of 49 and would go again for the seventh time in a row, making this easily their most successful period in the top division. Yet this wasn't enough for some fans, many of whom had now begun to feel entitled to be challenging for honours, forgetting what a terrific achievement it was for a club like Palace to still count themselves among the also-rans.

2019–20

'…there is a risk that, if we go too early, people will understandably get fatigued and it will be difficult to sustain this over time'
Chris Whitty, Chief Scientific Officer, 9 March 2020

This was the season that the Premier League introduced the Video Assistant Referee, and more words have been written and spoken about VAR than probably any other aspect of the game in recent years, so I may as well add to the noise. Everyone seems to have a view on the merits of using technology, often citing the introduction of goal line technology (GLT) as evidence of its effectiveness. Certainly, if GLT had been around in 1980 then Clive Allen's Palace goal tally would have been one more, or in 2009 then Freddie Sears would have at least the one goal to his name. Not quite enough to make a convincing case for it, but overall GLT is hard to argue against, as its sole purpose is to answer a binary question: over the line or not?

The great mistake made by enthusiasts for VAR is to assume a similarly scientific function, which is simply not the case. If the purpose of VAR is to eliminate mistakes made by officials, the reality has been that it completely undermines the referee on the pitch, introduces another couple of fallible and subjective human beings into the decision making process, and leads to utter confusion. If the scope of VAR was genuinely limited to dealing with 'clear and obvious' errors, and stuck to the principle of 'minimum interference, maximum benefit' then it might be more palatable, but in its early incarnation its effect was to drain the game of so much joy and spontaneity. Certainly, referees have always made mistakes, some clearer than others, but consider the Lacazette handball for Arsenal which cheated Palace out of victory in 2018 and the Victor Lindelof

handball that presented Palace with a penalty against Manchester United in 2020. The former was plain for everyone in the ground to see except for the officials, and the latter was almost impossible to detect even under the utmost slow-motion scrutiny. Of course, part of the problem is with the rules around handball rather than with the use of VAR, but as a football fan, rather than just a Palace fan, I can honestly say that I accept that the referee made an honest mistake that went uncorrected with Lacazette, and that winning a penalty from the Lindelof incident felt completely wrong.

Think also of the many offside decisions that have gone both for and against Palace, and where the inadequate technology has claimed a degree of accuracy that it clearly doesn't possess. Even if it did, I would still much rather rely on the naked eye to determine offside. It's part of the game that we love to be righteously enraged by poor decisions, and there's little doubt that VAR would have spotted David Hopkins' handball leading up to Dougie Freedman's goal against Stockport in 2001, with the club possibly never recovering from dropping into the third tier. For that reason alone, I'm against, and I wish that were my last word on the subject.

Once again there was much talk in the summer of Wilfried Zaha finally moving to a bigger club, and this time it was fans of Arsenal and Everton who got over-excited at the prospect of seeing Wilf play for their team, as both were in the doldrums, neither of them living up to their own view of what big clubs they were. As much as I loved seeing Zaha flourish at Palace, I would have been very happy to see him playing for Real Madrid or Barcelona, but Everton? Instead, it was Aaron Wan-Bissaka who attracted a realistic bid from Manchester United, and after a magnificent season and a half in the red and blue, he went with the fans' blessing, as £50 million was a more than fair price.

Andros Townsend

The questions around the extent of Palace's ambition to do any more than simply survive another season were probably answered by the continuing lack of eye-catching signings despite proceeds from the sale of Wan-Bissaka, notably the inability to add to the forward line after the departure of Batshuiyi and Sørloth and the continuing decline of Christian Benteke. Perhaps the hope was that Connor Wickham would at last be fit to challenge Benteke at centre forward, but beyond signing Ayew permanently the most potentially exciting addition was Spanish midfielder Victor Camarasa, who had stood out in Cardiff's relegated team the previous year. He was lauded as the player who would provide the creativity that the midfield so sorely lacked, and which Max Meyer had failed to deliver, but as it turned out the favoured trio of Milivojević, McArthur and Kouyaté continued to provide the usual solid core, augmented by Schlupp and the newly arrived James McCarthy from Everton, who was always destined to join McArthur in South London, the two of them having

played together at Hamilton Academical and Wigan. Camarasa made no impact and his season-long loan was cut short, whilst Meyer continued to disappoint despite many fans clamouring for him to be used more, but clearly neither player impressed Roy Hodgson enough, and neither came close to filling the Cabaye-shaped hole in midfield.

Stupidly optimistic as I always am, even I found it hard to believe that the season could result in anything but relegation without any real strikers, and although of course Roy Hodgson had better judgement than all of us fans put together I remained perplexed by what he saw in Jordan Ayew, who had worked extremely hard in his first season, running around and getting fouled a lot, but wasn't the player we needed to score goals. Then again, I though exactly the same when Andy Johnson came from Birmingham. It was Ayew, though, who kick-started Palace's season with a coolly taken goal to give them the lead at Old Trafford on the way to a 2–1 victory, and he scored again in the next game to beat Aston Villa and move Palace up to fourth in the table, their highest position for some time. Further goals followed at West Ham and Arsenal, and Ayew was now a guaranteed starter, with a half fit and hopelessly ineffective Benteke warming the bench. That Arsenal game saw an illustration of VAR at its best, when Zaha was brought down in the box and the referee booked him for diving, which in previous seasons would have been enough for the keyboard warriors to go to town with the same old abuse of Wilf. Mercifully, on this occasion whoever was sitting watching a monitor many miles away couldn't dispute what everyone in the ground already knew, that it was a clear penalty, and it was gratifying to see the referee humiliatingly make a show of withdrawing the red card. I half expected Zaha to applaud sarcastically and get sent off again.

Almost unheralded, Palace had also signed the Chelsea and England stalwart Gary Cahill as cover at centre back, but with a string of injuries to Dann, Sakho and Tomkins, it was Cahill and Martin Kelly who ended up playing more games than any of them. Cahill had won countless honours with Chelsea and gained 61 caps for England, yet never seemed to have become a household name, despite being probably the country's best defender for many years. He had always struck me as resolutely old school, and I'd always particularly admired his lack of conspicuous tattoos, which set him apart from almost all his contemporaries, so I was delighted when he signed a contract for Palace at a time when many expected that he might retire. It turned out to be quite a coup, although it did nothing to reverse Palace's position as the oldest squad in the Premier League.

Gary Cahill

Against everyone's expectations, Palace continued to hang around the top half of the table by cementing their reputation as a tight defensive team, relying heavily on the counter attack and Zaha in particular,

with draws becoming the norm. Heavy defeats were few and far between, as were resounding victories, and by now Palace had become regarded, in their seventh consecutive season, as Premier League fixtures. Sections of the crowd had started to become a little bored with the caution of it all, and started to turn against Roy Hodgson, berating him for not picking Meyer, not picking Riedewald, sticking with a defensive midfield, and numerous other perceived crimes against Palace's birthright as relegation fodder. The few highlights of a largely turgid season came courtesy of that man Jordan Ayew, who surprisingly but justifiably ended up as Player of the Season, also winning the Goal of the Season award hands down, for his memorable effort against West Ham on Boxing Day. Palace had been going through another drab spell, and in the previous home game had rescued a point against a superior Brighton team only with an equaliser from the hated Zaha, and the West Ham game was heading towards another draw when Ayew controlled the ball wide on the right, just in front of our new commentary position in the Old Stand. From there we had a wonderful view as Ayew took the ball towards the corner of the penalty area, bamboozled five defenders with a pirouette and a shuffle from one foot to the other, finishing with an elegant dink over the approaching goalkeeper. Coming so late in the game just made it more thrilling, and as special a goal as it looked at the time, repeated viewings confirm that it's possibly the best solo goal by a home player ever seen at Selhurst Park.

Ayew was also responsible for the goal that beat Brighton at their own ground, especially satisfying as it left them nervously flirting with relegation, and he scored again in the home victory against Watford, a bad-tempered game as always against a team whose main focus was on trying to get Zaha sent off, but who were heading down at last. With those back-to-back victories, Palace were now in 11th place, virtually safe from relegation already after 29 games, and just four points off sixth place, surely heading for their best season under Roy Hodgson, perhaps their best ever in the Premier League. What we didn't yet know was that it would be a long time before we could savour the special Selhurst Park atmosphere in person again, and that Watford game was the last game I went to at the time of writing, more than a year later. If I never get to see Palace again, I'll feel just a little cheated that the last goal I witnessed in person was scored by the sour-faced Jordan Ayew, well taken as it was.

Just two days after the Watford game, the whole of Italy went into lockdown as a response to the rapidly spreading Covid-19 virus, while in the UK the Government was keen to let not only the Cheltenham Festival go ahead, but the scheduled football programme as well, including a game between Liverpool and Atletico Madrid, stating that 'there's no reason for people not to attend such events or to cancel them at this stage'. Both events were later judged to have caused increased suffering and death that otherwise wouldn't have occurred, and it is to the great credit of the football authorities that they reacted far quicker to the threat posed by what was by now officially a global pandemic than did Boris Johnson's shameful government. Even after the weekend's football programme had been cancelled, the Prime Minister was still only offering vague suggestions that people should avoid pubs, clubs and theatres, while allowing them to remain open, and it wasn't until the end of that week that the government took any decisive action to limit the spread of the disease.

During the months that followed, football at first seemed the least of our concerns, as deaths from the virus reached the thousands, then the tens of thousands, but it wasn't long before the possible resumption of the game behind closed doors was being discussed in great detail, with Liverpool in particular appalled by the prospect of the rest of the season being cancelled altogether, as they had been coasting towards their first title for thirty years, and their solitary success in the Premier League. Although Scottish football was wisely called off for the season, and the planned European Championships postponed for a year, English football was so beholden to the broadcasting companies, and so reliant on that income, that the season eventually resumed under the cloak of 'Project Restart', with Palace's chairman Steve Parish among its most vocal advocates. It made little sense from the perspective of the science, with handshaking apparently not allowed, but players continuing to celebrate goals by clambering all over each other as usual, but there's no doubt that it was a popular decision for a large proportion of the nation pretty well obsessed by the game. With nine or ten games for teams to play once the season recommenced in mid-June, the schedule was packed tight, and every game was televised live, so that quite soon it had reached saturation point for players and viewers alike.

The restart coincided with a powerful show of solidarity by players throughout the leagues with the Black Lives Matter movement, in the wake of the murder of George Floyd in the USA, and in the context of a continuing environment of racism, keenly felt by many of Britain's black players. It was a subject very close to many Palace players, with Andros Townsend's father a prominent and vocal figure in the Kick It Out organisation, Patrick Van Aanholt a vociferous contributor to social media on the subject, and Wilfried Zaha one of many victims of disgusting racist abuse online. For the remainder of the season, and the one that followed, players routinely took the knee to keep the debate at the forefront of people's thinking, although after a while it was Zaha who broke ranks and in his usual honest and forthright manner declared that the gesture had become a hollow one, and that he would 'continue to stand tall' to highlight how little was actually being done to address the problem by anyone in authority. Of all the players who might have taken that stand, Zaha was one whose sincerity could never be in doubt.

Tyrick Mitchell

Another player worth listening to on the subject was the captain of Burnley, Ben Mee, when some numbskulls hired a light aircraft to carry a banner repeating the phrase 'all lives matter' that had become shorthand for 'I am a racist and proud of it'. When asked about the game straight after his team had been beaten 5–0, he instead spoke emotionally to condemn the stunt, and distanced himself and the club from a small minority who 'need to come into the 21st Century and educate themselves'. His spontaneous and heartfelt reaction must

have made the vast majority of Burnley fans immensely proud, and perhaps Mee had done his bit to educate as well as shame those responsible.

Palace won the first game back to make it four wins in a row and pass the 40-point safety barrier far earlier than usual, but effectively the season had ended for Roy Hodgson's team, who trudged through the last eight games, picking up a single point on the way to the conclusion of a season that might have seen them challenging for Europe, but instead fizzled out. We were able to watch every minute of the players going through the motions during that miserable run of games, and really could have done without it. Despite the feeble fag end of the season, there had been things to celebrate, among them Guaita's excellence in goal, Ayew's sharpness up front, and glimpses of a couple of promising youngsters in Tyrick Mitchell and Brandon Pierrick, but in the end it turned into another season of treading water, which in the context of what was going on in the world, was not to be sniffed at. There was even the odd hint that Benteke was starting to remember how to play football, but let's not get ahead of ourselves.

2020–21

'We've talked for so long about wanting to welcome the fans back, but no sooner do I get the chance to welcome them back that I'm going to be waving goodbye to them… Goodbyes have never been my forte, I'm much better at hellos than goodbyes'
Roy Hodgson, May 2021

Ebere Eze

As we approached the final game of the 20–21 season with more than enough points in the bag, unusually there were two things still to play for. The first was to gain the point needed to ensure that Palace finished above Brighton yet again, despite the Seagulls having had a season when everyone seemed to agree what lovely football they played for a side flirting with relegation. The second was the chance to ruin Liverpool's season by denying them the three points they needed to sneak into a Champions League qualifying place. The enjoyment derived from all but destroying their chance of winning the league on that famous night in 2014, which had come to be known as Crystanbul, was still fresh in the memory even seven years later, and it would be a fitting if somewhat belated revenge for Palace having been robbed of their own European place by Liverpool

in 1991. Only a few weeks on from the debacle of the proposed European Super League, it was also a chance to teach one of the Entitled Six a lesson in humility, or preferably humiliation, after they had pulverised Palace 7–0 earlier in the season, but don't forget that after the 9–0 hammering in 1989, Palace had exacted revenge by beating Liverpool 4–3 to reach the Cup Final. One further sub plot was that, as Roy Hodgson's last game, there must have been just a small and very private part of him that really wanted to prove a point to the club that never really made him welcome in his short time as manager.

With the country still in ever-shifting versions of lockdown, the new season had started a month later than usual, but with grounds still empty, and the Palace players appeared well rested, allaying fears that the dreadful form from just a few weeks earlier would carry over. With the transfer market naturally quieter than usual, it was a pleasant surprise to see Palace sign QPR's young rising star Eberechi Eze, perhaps a gamble at a reported £16 million, but indicative of the need to start reducing the age of the squad. With Tyrick Mitchell showing promise at left back, and right back Nathan Ferguson signed from West Brom, it started to look like there was a plan of sorts, but the most encouraging signing was the return of Michy Batshuiyi on loan again from Chelsea. The Belgian had shown his instinct for goals in his previous spell, and his arrival meant the end of Palace's interest in Conor Gallagher, also from Chelsea, as two loans from the same club were not permitted. It appeared a good call, since despite Benteke showing flickers of form, Jordan Ayew and the ever-injured Connor Wickham were the only other options up front, and the squad was already well off for midfielders.

Wilfried Zaha started as he meant to carry on with the winning goal against Southampton, and then scored two more to help secure another victory at Old Trafford against a mediocre Manchester United team who somehow went on to finish runners-up in the Premier League. After Townsend's early goal, Zaha extended the lead with a penalty, dubiously awarded for handball and then missed by Jordan Ayew, but ordered to be retaken after De Gea edged off his line. Rather than let Ayew have another go, Zaha took control of the situation as he was wearing the captain's armband for the first time, and showed great composure to score from the spot, wrapping up the victory late on with a characteristically powerful drive from the edge of the box to make it 3–1. It was thrilling to see Zaha performing so well against the club that served him so badly, and the signs were that this was going to be a season to remember.

James Tomkins

In between those two victories, a second string Palace once again went out of the League Cup at the first hurdle, which had become the norm in recent seasons, this time against Bournemouth. After a goalless game, the penalty shootout turned into an epic with all 20 outfield players scoring to make it 10–10, Palace's scorers including Jaroslav Jach, Ryan Inniss and even Mamadou Sakho. It was now the turn of the goalkeepers, and after Wayne Hennessey saved from Bournemouth's Begovic, he had a chance to win it and salvage at least a little respect from the fans, which had been in short supply. Of course, he lashed it over the bar, and although it was Milivojević whose miss was then the decisive one, it's Hennessey's that people will remember and mock, a little unjustly as I'm convinced the ball brushed the top of the bar on its way into orbit.

The season to remember turned out to be anything but that, and after such an excellent start, Palace settled into a pattern of the odd win, mostly against teams down at the bottom, and quite a few one-sided hammerings by teams near the top. This was unusual for Palace under Roy Hodgson, and to see his team thoroughly outclassed in games against Chelsea (4–0 and 4–1), Manchester City (4–0), Spurs (4–1) and Liverpool (7–0) was something we hadn't expected. Even worse were defeats to teams such as Aston Villa, losing 3–0 despite Mings being sent off in the first half, and West Ham, who deserved to win by far more than the 3–2 scoreline. That game against the revitalised Hammers illustrated the difference between a striker giving everything for his team, in the shape of the impressively energetic and honest Michail Antonio, and a passenger such as Benteke, who was still woefully off the pace and going through the motions, mysteriously keeping Batshuiyi and the newly signed Mateta on the bench. Despite so many low points, Palace spent almost all of the season in around 13th place, eventually finishing 14th for the second successive year, but with an improved points total of 44, a long way clear of relegation.

Let's focus on the positives, though, and there were indeed some peppered throughout almost a whole season played in empty stadiums. Eberechi Eze was eased gently into the side, but once established it was clear that he was destined to become an exceptional player, hopefully with Palace, but certainly at the top level. He first grabbed the attention with an absolutely sublime goal against Sheffield United, taking the ball from deep in his own half to the edge of the opposition box before casually and precisely passing it into the net. It's fair to say that he wasn't greatly challenged by any defenders on the way, but there was an ease and grace about his movement and control of the ball that was to become familiar as the season went on. He scored four goals in total, each of them memorable, and somehow it seemed like more, but what was undeniabe about Eze was what a sheer joy he was to watch. Commentators not used to lavishing praise on any but the big name players found themselves purring about Eze's quality on the ball, and for Palace fans it was refreshing to have not only someone who could share the creative burden with Zaha, but someone who appeared equally at home at the club, proper South London, and exceptionally cool. It's to be hoped that he makes a full recovery from the cruel blow of an Achilles injury suffered right at the end of the season, just as he was being considered for England, but he'll be worth the wait.

With all the established centre backs taking turns once again to suffer lengthy injuries, Cheikhou Kouyaté did a sound job in defence, where he played the majority of the season, and Tyrick Mitchell grew into the left back role, but for me the revelation was Joel Ward at right back. Although Nathaniel Clyne had by now made a welcome return, Ward defied those who had written him off in his ninth season at the club and even in a period when Palace conceded far too many goals, he set a wonderful example of dedication, bravery and loyalty, which made him my Player of the Season, although that accolade officially went to Guaita. For a short while it looked as though Jaïro Riedewald might establish himself in midfield following an injury to James McArthur, but despite some flashes he revealed himself to be no more than a useful squad player, highlighting how important the often unlauded Scot was to the team, and how much he was missed during this difficult season.

Jean-Philippe Mateta

Unquestionably the highlight of the season came on a Monday night in Brighton, a game sandwiched between two abysmal performances against Burnley and Fulham, when the clamour for Roy Hodgson to be replaced by the failed Chelsea manager Frank Lampard was at its peak. In the home tie earlier in the season Palace had somehow sneaked a point against Brighton with their only shot on target, a Zaha penalty, and this time their opponents were even more dominant in a game where the statistics for once do tell a meaningful story. Brighton attempted 25 shots to Palace's 3, had 75% possession and 13 corners to none for

Palace, and by any criteria deserved to win comfortably against a really poor opponent. What an absolute delight it was, then, when Jean-Philippe Mateta, making a rare start in his first season, put Palace ahead with an elegantly disdainful backheel at the near post, very much against the run of play. Brighton equalised and poured on the pressure in an effort to get the three points that would have moved them above their London rivals in the table, while Palace offered nothing going forward, somehow clinging on to the point until deep into stoppage time. At long last Palace mounted a final attack, Townsend went down the left and swept a hopeful cross to the far post where Benteke kept his eye on the ball and buried a perfect volley low and wide of the keeper to win three points that nobody could claim were deserved. Benteke had been pretty awful all season yet suddenly became a world class striker, the result left Brighton in peril near the bottom, and the only thing that could have made it more perfectly hilarious would have been a Lewis Dunk own goal.

Disenchantment with Hodgson reached fever pitch when he was unapologetically proud of the lack of ambition in the following 0–0 draw against struggling Fulham, but that point was followed by another drab goalless draw against an even drabber Man United, and safety was looking beyond doubt once again. Some fans couldn't see this in the context of Palace's history, that this was the club's most sustained success ever, instead focusing on the fact that there had been precious little entertainment, which was true enough. If they had been paying to go to the ground, they would have had more of a point, but the lack of crowds and a compressed schedule played a big part in the torpor of the team, and it was sad to see so much abusive vitriol directed toward Roy Hodgson on social media by some of the halfwits and dunderheads whose opinions it's now hard to avoid. It is so tempting to respond to some of the idiocy, but so much better not to engage at all. As the saying goes, 'never argue with an idiot; they'll drag you down to their level and beat you with experience'.

For so much of the season there had been speculation not only about the huge number of players coming to the end of their contracts, but about Roy Hodgson's own future, a question which he consistently and patiently batted away by saying that he would choose the right time to tell people what was on his mind, but it came as no great surprise when, with Palace mathematically safe, he revealed the news, 'hardly world-shattering' as he put it, that he would leave as manager, although reluctant to commit himself to the concept of retirement from football at the age of 73. The announcement came before the penultimate game against Arsenal, which apart from the Spurs game back in December was the first time a limited number of fans had been back at Selhurst for over a year, and it gave those who were lucky enough to be there the chance to give Roy Hodgson a fitting and emotional send off, and to thank him for four years during which we were lucky enough to support a club managed by such a true gent.

Although that Arsenal game ended in defeat, as did Roy's swansong at Anfield, the players had kept going right to the end, and unlike the dismal previous season's ending, couldn't face the accusation of 'being on the beach' already, all the more admirable as so many players were coming to the end of their contracts and faced an uncertain summer. For some of them it was time to move on, as the club turned its gaze to the future.

The Players

Goalkeepers

John Jackson was without doubt the finest goalkeeper ever to play for Palace, and one of the best in the country. He was not only capable of making miraculous saves, but produced them week after week until one came to take them for granted. He saved so many certain goals that, without him, Palace would never have stayed in the First Division for as long as they did, and his loyalty to Palace probably denied him the chance of playing for England, although he did turn out once for a representative Football League side. It was often said that if he had been born anywhere but England he would certainly have played for his country, but I would argue that only Gordon Banks was his superior, and that Jacko should have been his understudy in the England team.

John Jackson

The worst decision that Malcolm Allison ever made was to sell Jackson to Orient in 1973, and I maintain that Palace would not have been relegated that season had he stayed in goal, instead of the younger and vastly inferior Paul Hammond. In his attitude to the game and his dedication 'Stonewall' Jackson was the model professional, the sort of player that any youngster should look up to and admire, and more than ever football needs more like him. There have been other goalkeepers, of course, and it is worth having a look at their claims, but since Jacko was my complete hero his is the one place in my dream team that is sacrosanct.

Paul Hammond had to bear the burden of Malcolm Allison's patronage in preference to Jackson, and after keeping goal after a fashion as Palace slid down through the Second Division spent the next three seasons alternating between the sticks with **Tony Burns**. Hammond was a competent technician when it came to positioning and handling of crosses, but rarely made saves out of the ordinary, while the more experienced Burns was at least a better shouter. After the blandness of these two, the contrast when **John Burridge** took over was enormous, and quite apart from his clowning he was also a very good player. Burridge was ever-present in the Second Division championship season of 1978–79, and his irrepressible enthusiasm had a positive influence on the young defenders in front of him. However much he enjoyed entertaining the crowd, he was fanatical about perfecting his own game, and anything that went past him made him furious, unable to accept that some goals just can't be helped. The circumstances of Burridge's departure were symptomatic of the chronic malaise running through the club after 1979, and although he didn't actually leave until following Venables to QPR, he had fallen out over his contract long before that, and was replaced in the team by **Paul Barron**, from Arsenal. Barron was by no means as bad as his reputation would have one believe, but he had the bad luck to play for Palace during one of their worst ever periods, and he could have been Dino Zoff for all the difference it would have made.

After Alan Mullery had sold Barron to West Bromwich Albion, **David Fry** played out the rest of the 1982–83 season, but Mullery then went out and bought another Arsenal reserve, the bird-watching Scotsman **George Wood**, who only missed three games in the next five years before his ignominious end in 1988. Wood was never the quickest of players, but he was better than his immediate predecessors, and played consistently well until quite near the end. In his final season he was increasingly being blamed for a number of goals, particularly away from home, but the final straw for Steve Coppell was the disastrous 4–4 result at Leicester, Wood shouldering the blame for throwing away three points. After Wood had conceded 13 goals in five games, Coppell took decisive action and bought the England Under-21 keeper **Perry Suckling** from Manchester City, with Wood going to Cardiff. Suckling was quicker, sharper, more agile, and above all younger than Wood, and being a local boy the fans took to him at once. He had trouble with his kicking leg which meant him missing most of the first half of the 1988–89 season, and although **Brian Parkin** did a good job in his place, Suckling's return coincided with a run of good form that ultimately lifted Palace towards the play-offs. Suckling played a heroic part in winning promotion, and it was hard luck on such a likeable character that he should become the butt of so many cruel jokes after Liverpool's 9–0 win the following season. It is to his credit that after Palace had spent £1 million on **Nigel Martyn** to replace him, Suckling didn't indulge in any petulant outbursts, but instead got on with trying to play his way back into form, and did a particularly good job by all accounts when on loan to West Ham.

In his seven seasons in goal for Palace, Nigel Martyn only missed a handful of games, and was a constant presence under Steve Coppell, Alan Smith and Dave Bassett, until he finally left for Leeds, then in the Premiership. When he had first arrived from Bristol Rovers, soon after Liverpool had hit nine goals past Perry Suckling, he already looked top class and he got better and better over the years at Palace, becoming possibly the finest keeper in the country, although a succession of England managers didn't quite realise it, as he only won three caps in his time in London. He went on to play for many years at Leeds, then at Everton, proving what a marvellous player he was, becoming a crowd favourite at both clubs, and winning plenty more England caps. By staying at Palace following two relegations from the Premiership he undoubtedly harmed his international career, but the comparisons with the great John Jackson don't stop there. My one encounter with Martyn sums up for me what a solid, unassuming character he was, happy to chat about a game that Palace had just lost to a stranger standing in front of him in a queue. This wasn't in a West End nightclub, or a swanky dinner dance, but in the Croydon branch of Argos, where I just don't expect to see my footballing heroes.

Martyn was a huge presence in goal, and his calm demeanour gave the defence in front of him great confidence. He didn't look too acrobatic, but had tremendous positional sense and you got the feeling that he studied the art of goalkeeping in great depth, and was always learning. There was nothing flashy, nothing archly eccentric like so many goalkeepers, but he was everything a goalkeeper should be: commanding, agile, and exceptionally strong. He made a few fumbles here and there, and his form dipped along with the team's when goal difference meant relegation in 1993, but before that he was part of probably Palace's finest ever defensive line that conceded only 41 goals on the way to finishing third in the pre-Premier League First Division. He did get sent off once, when a rush of blood brought him careering out of the box to poleaxe Wimbledon's Robbie Earle, but that kind of misjudgement was rare indeed. Martyn's sheer strength enabled him to make some memorable point blank saves as well as spectacular dives and penalty saves at full stretch, and because of his positioning and quick reactions, his fingertips were rarely too far from any shot that did beat him. The very last goal he conceded for Palace did leave him stranded, watching helplessly as the ball sailed past him, but Steve Claridge can be blamed for not hitting the ball as well as he should have.

Nigel Martyn

With cover so rarely needed for Martyn, **Rhys Wilmot** made only a few appearances, and **Neil Sullivan** and **Bobby Mimms** just one each. After Martyn left, Dave Bassett signed two new keepers and struggled to decide which was his first choice out of **Chris Day** and **Carlo Nash**. Neither was outstanding, but although Nash seemed to have done enough to retain his place in the Premiership, Steve Coppell signed the well-padded **Kevin Miller** from Watford, who had a reputation as the best keeper outside

the top division. Miller conceded 71 goals as Palace were relegated in his first season, but overall he wasn't dreadful. When he was good, he was no more than that, but when he was bad, he was indescribably so. His second season ended with Palace in administration, Miller in dispute over the imposition of a pay cut, getting ever plumper, and giving a scandalously bad impersonation of goalkeeping as Palace lost 6–0 at QPR on the final day, for which Palace fans have never forgiven him.

Next up in goal was **Fraser Digby**, a solid jobbing keeper throughout the year-long administration, to be followed by Arsenal's **Stuart Taylor** on loan, before Alan Smith signed Palace's first ever overseas goalkeeper, Latvian **Alex Kolinko**. What is it you want from a goalkeeper? Do you want spectacular or do you want safe? Very occasionally you might get both, but not often, and although Kolinko was capable of the most incredible reaction saves, two in a defeat at Watford among the best I've seen, he was just as likely to flap, fumble or collide with defenders and drop the ball. Kolinko was in and out of the side for a while, alternating with the safer but far less entertaining **Matt Clarke**, and got a black eye from Trevor Francis when he allegedly laughed at Clarke conceding a goal. After Kolinko eventually left under a cloud, and Clarke was forced to retire from football, **Cédric Berthelin** and **Thomas Myhre** took over temporarily, and by the time Iain Dowie's team made it to the play-off final against West Ham, **Nico Vaesen** was doing a fine job on loan from Birmingham.

After so long with a string of unexceptional goalkeepers, Dowie managed to bring in two new players ready for the Premiership who would turn out to be among the very best in memory. The Argentinian **Julián Speroni** got the nod ahead of Hungarian

Gábor Király for the start of the 2004–05 season, but after his gaffe against Everton and the four defeats that followed, his confidence was in ruins, and Király became first choice for most of the next three years. Where Speroni lacked confidence, Király had it in spades, and very soon the fans adored him. Goalkeepers are meant to be loco, and although he milked it, that's just what he was. He was easily recognisable by his baggy grey track suit bottoms, widely known as his lucky pyjamas, but there was more to him than attention seeking. The easiest of shots would prompt Király to spring through the air, grab the ball to his chest and roll over for no reason other than to show off, but beneath it all he was a fine all-round goalkeeper.

Like all the best keepers, Király had his nightmare moments, but as his reputation grew he kept Speroni waiting patiently in the reserves, until he fell out with Peter Taylor and went out on loan to West Ham, then to Aston Villa. Bizarrely, Taylor then tried **Scott Flinders** for two games, during which he conceded seven goals, then brought in **Iain Turner** on loan from Everton, who in turn was injured, meaning that he had no choice but to play Speroni. After just two games and some outstanding saves against Sunderland, Speroni himself was injured, so he had to wait until the very end of the season for Taylor to begrudgingly give him a chance, after which he barely missed a game. Having spent so long in the reserves, Speroni could have been forgiven if he had decided to move on, but he wasted no time in showing what he could do, making it impossible for Taylor to drop him. Király moved to Burnley, and the humble Speroni excelled, winning the admiration of the fans who voted him Player of the Year for three years running, and four times in total. Some of Speroni's saves were breathtaking, and he

soon earned a deserved reputation as the best goalkeeper outside the Premiership, so that for Palace to keep hold of him during administration was a major achievement.

Julián Speroni

After such a stuttering start to his career at Palace, over the course of 15 seasons Speroni went on to exceed John Jackson's goalkeeping appearance record and was virtually ever-present for 8 seasons in a row, along the way endearing himself to the Palace crowd with his humility, dedication, commitment to the club and community, and the incontrovertible fact that he was one of the game's good guys. Several of the most visually memorable banners created and displayed by the Holmesdale Fanatics were dedicated to Speroni with the byline 'Manos De Dios', and they reflected the real love that was felt for Jules.

As the rigours of a couple of seasons in the Premier League started to take its toll on Speroni, manager Alan Pardew prematurely elevated **Wayne Hennessey** to first choice goalkeeper, and Speroni was only used sporadically for the next four seasons until his retirement, but was always ready to step in when needed, remaining a vital member of the squad to the very end.

His testimonial match against his former club Dundee was a fitting celebration and expression of gratitude for the player who most would agree is aptly described as a Crystal Palace legend.

Part of the problem that Wayne Hennessey had in winning over the crowd was that he had usurped such a popular keeper, but beyond that he had an air of vulnerability that often seemed to drain the confidence from the defenders in front of him. At his best he was an excellent shot stopper, and his performances for Wales showed how good he could be, but for such a big man he didn't appear commanding in the air, particularly when defending corners, and had periods of indecisiveness that saw him blamed for rather too many goals conceded. It was always pleasing to see the odd spectacular game from him, just to silence some of the unjust criticism that was thrown his way, but it is true that he made more than his fair share of costly howlers, and that is probably how he'll be remembered, along with his plausible ignorance of major historical events.

For a short while Hennessey shared goalkeeping duties with **Alex McCarthy**, and neither was better or worse than the other, but after McCarthy moved on to Southampton, the French international **Steve Mandanda** was signed from Olympique de Marseille, and it was anticipated that he had everything it took to become a cult hero at Palace, as he had been in France. It didn't work out for him in London though, and we only saw him in goal for Palace on ten occasions, none of which left a lasting impression. Hennessey reclaimed his place in goal, with Speroni as back up for a season, until the arrival of **Vicente Guaita** from Getafe. We didn't know what to expect from the Spaniard, already in his thirties when he

arrived, and it took him a little while to get his chance once Hennessey was injured, but he immediately looked the part and established himself as Roy Hodgson's first choice. Although prone to the odd lapse, the fans were more inclined to forgive Guaita than they would have Hennessey, as he quickly became a popular figure, bringing a positive energy that had been lacking in that position and specialising in wonderfully crowd-pleasing fingertip saves. It's a great pity that he didn't come to Palace as a slightly younger man, but goalkeepers can go on and on, and he may yet be up there with John Jackson, Nigel Martyn and Julián Speroni as one of the all-time greats. All three will have their advocates as Palace's best ever goalkeeper, and strong cases can be made for all of them, but I will never abandon my first footballing hero, and I remain loyal to John Jackson.

Full Backs

One player stands out from all the others as an automatic selection for the left back position. **Kenny Sansom** was the best of the impressively talented youth team who won the FA Youth Cup for two years running, most of whom graduated to the first team, and the First Division. Playing in a side which concentrated on accurate passing and building patiently from the back, Sansom was the starting point for many of Palace's attacking moves. The basis of his game was his usually faultless first time control, which meant that each tackle or interception he made was not simply defensive, but also gained constructive possession of the ball. Uniquely for a Palace defender he was able to take the ball past opposing players and make space for himself, and at times he was hardly seen as a defender, because he was so often in attacking mode. Before he had established himself in the first team, he learnt an early disciplinary lesson when being suspended after using 'industrial language' in a youth game, but thereafter he had the good sense to keep his temper, confident in the knowledge that he was undoubtedly a superior footballer.

Ken Sansom

His first full season came after Venables had taken over as manager from Malcolm Allison, a season which ended with promotion to the Second Division thanks largely to an excellent defence. Over the next two years his form helped Palace climb back into Division One, and also made him an obvious contender for a place in the England team, where he became a fixture over the next nine years. After the 'Team of the Eighties' bubble had burst, his move to Arsenal – in exchange for Clive Allen – signalled the beginning of a rapid decline for Palace. The conventional wisdom is that Sansom needed his cut of the transfer fee to get himself out of a financial hole, being a notorious gambler, but as usual the fans were kept in the dark about the deteriorating atmosphere behind the scenes, which temporarily wrecked the club.

It is true to say that there are few genuine contenders for the left back position in this imaginary team, and the list of those who have filled that shirt is rather uninspiring, including as it does such functional players as **John Loughlan**, **Bill Roffey**, **Les Strong** and **Brian Sparrow**. **Stewart Jump** wasn't a bad player at all, but he seemed to be playing in the wrong position somehow, and **Terry Fenwick** was never a defender, although incredibly he went on to play as a centre back for England later in his career. **Paul Brush** played his part in Palace's revival under Steve Coppell before he submitted to recurrent injuries, and his successor **David Burke**, despite being prone to frequent and elementary errors, was at least a true left back, and contributed to some valuable goals when swinging crosses over from that side in the promotion year of 1988–89.

Early in the career of **Mark Dennis**, he was considered one of England's brightest young hopes, but he repeatedly ruined his chances with his violent temperament, and the great shame is that in the few games he played for Palace between injuries in 1989–90, he impressed the sceptical supporters as potentially an extremely good player indeed.

On the left of the stable defence of 1990–91 was **Richard Shaw**, who is hard to pigeonhole, as he played for long periods in midfield, and surprised everyone at how adept he became at centre back later in his career. Although naturally right footed, Shaw always did a good job on the left, despite a spate of own goals, and was certainly better than either of his successors, the disappointing **Paul Bodin** and **Lee Sinnott**. Erstwhile emergency striker Chris Coleman was tried before **Dean Gordon** came into the side from the youth team and eventually established himself as Palace's first specialist left back since Mark Dennis. Gordon announced his arrival with an unstoppable goal from a long range free kick against Forest, and later in the season galloped forward to score a stunning late equaliser against Derby, one that confirmed what a powerful weapon Gordon's left foot could be. When asked to step up for a penalty, Gordon took a very short run-up and only had to hit the target, as any goalkeeper foolish enough to get in the way risked life and limb. A good athlete, but totally one-footed, Gordon's strength was in getting forward, overlapping down the left to whip in crosses, or moving onto loose balls outside the area and having a crack. He scored some beauties from distance over the years, and even scored one hat-trick, with two penalties and a header, and when Palace played with a sweeper system he found himself in his element as an attacking wing-back.

When Dean Gordon was injured for a long period, **Jamie Vincent** seemed his natural heir, having looked good in his few appearances and scored a Gordon-like goal with his left foot against Southend, but instead he moved to Bournemouth and Dave Bassett brought Australian left back **Kevin Muscat** into the side. Muscat was not yet notorious as one of football's most appalling thugs, but we saw plenty of that side of him in his time at Palace, where he was also used at right back and in midfield. Once Gordon had eventually gone, the left back position was a problem which wasn't solved by the costly failure of **David Amsalem** or the on-loan **Jason Crowe**, and it was a great pity that Chinese international **Sun Jihai** didn't stay longer than one season, as he was improving rapidly.

Jamie Smith was tried at left back for a while, but with no money to spend Steve Coppell did well to get two very good players on loan to plug the gap. The first was the highly reliable **Terry Phelan**, who was as solid one would expect, and he was followed by an obscure Arsenal youth team player, **Ashley Cole**. Cole was outstanding from the start, and played a big part in helping Coppell's young side survive the post-Goldberg administration season. For a short while we thought that Palace might be able to keep him, but Cole's performances at Selhurst Park had put him in the first team reckoning at Highbury, and he was soon way beyond our reach.

Perhaps it is unfair to compare Cole with his successor **Craig Harrison**, but Harrison didn't pull up any trees before **Steve Staunton** came on loan for a short while, his most memorable contribution being an extraordinary goal past the stranded Tranmere keeper from nearly the halfway line. Next up at Number 3 was **Danny Granville**, an improvement on Harrison, but an unremarkable player, although he did have something of a renaissance under Iain Dowie before losing his place to **Gary**

Borrowdale. Granville and Borrowdale alternated for a while until **Tony Craig's** short spell was ended by the arrival of **Clint Hill**. Brought in by Warnock to toughen up the team, Hill would have fitted well in Iain Dowie's boxing-fixated side, and mostly stayed just the right side of the line between uncompromising and plain dirty. Mostly.

All the while that Hill was at left back, **Lee Hills** could never establish himself after progressing from the youth team, but with Hills injured, George Burley started his season with **Julian Bennett** on loan from Nottingham Forest. **David Wright**, **Matt Parsons** and even **Edgar Davids** all had a turn at left back, before Dougie Freedman signed **Dean Moxey** from Derby, against whom he scored a stunning left foot goal which got me thinking about the good old days of Deano. Moxey looked the part as a proper left back in the mould of Dean Gordon in many ways, and was similarly one-footed, but was replaced for a while by the wonderfully versatile Norwegian **Jonathan Parr**, who was equally adept on either side of defence or midfield, and was voted Player of the Season at the end of his first year.

Once back in Premier League the left back position proved problematic and was unresolved for a couple of season, with **Adrian Mariappa** and **Joel Ward** often played there out of their natural positions, but with the signing of the Senegalese international **Pape Souaré** from Lille it looked as though Palace had fixed the problem, as he grew into the role during a very consistent second season under Alan Pardew, and was part of the settled back four that made it all the way to the Cup Final. After crashing his car on the M4, Souaré was out injured for a year, and at times it seemed that his career might be

over, but despite eventually getting back to playing, he was released and Palace found themselves once again struggling at left back until the arrival of **Patrick Van Aanholt** and **Jeffrey Schlupp** at the same time. Either could play there, but it was PVA who made the shirt his own, getting forward to score some fine goals and linking well with Zaha, while Schlupp turned into the ultimate squad player, who could be relied on to do a good job wherever he played, generally across the midfield. Van Aanholt was at times patchy in his defending, but the good far outweighed the bad, and it wasn't until he was injured that Roy Hodgson was forced into bringing through **Tyrick Mitchell** from the youth setup. Mitchell immediately impressed with his defensive focus, and in his second season he came more into the picture as Van Aanholt's contract began to run down, While not as immediately eye-catching as Wan-Bissaka had been a couple of seasons previously on the right, nevertheless Mitchell gave the impression of a player who could go a long way in the game, and become an established Premier League defender.

At right back, of course **John Sewell** must be considered strongly, more for his qualities as a captain than for anything else. With his upright bearing and his always immaculate appearance, he appeared to belong to another era even at the time of his greatest success, leading Palace to the First Division for the first time ever in 1969. Unusually, perhaps uniquely for a team skipper, Sewell made a point of never arguing with the referee, and took pride in the fact that he had never been booked. Most of his few goals came from the penalty spot, but his aimless punt against Gary Sprake in his final season with Palace, 1970–71, was one of the most memorable goals ever scored at Selhurst Park, and ensures his place for ever in Palace folklore. Sewell's successor, **David Payne**, did a fair job after being converted from midfield, but was always the ultimate utility player, and **Paddy Mulligan**, the Irish international, was injured so often that he rarely strung more than half a dozen games together. Mulligan's greatest moment at Palace was when he scored two of the five goals against Manchester United in 1972, the only time he scored for the club.

Peter Wall

One of my favourite players from the 70s was **Peter Wall**, who was with the club for eight years, although he broke his leg twice in that time, and missed long periods as a consequence. I always got the impression that Wall had more ability than he ever bothered to use, and that he sometimes felt that he should actually still be playing for his previous employers, Liverpool. Bought as a left back by Bert Head, by the time Malcolm Allison had taken over at Palace, a serious break sustained against Liverpool meant that Wall had been effectively replaced, first of all by Tony Taylor, and then by Stewart Jump and Jim Cannon. Although he made a brief comeback in 1973–74, the season when Palace slid straight down through Division 2, he was

then out of action again until the latter part of the following season, when he replaced Paddy Mulligan as right back, and stayed there during the famous cup run of 1976. Although naturally left footed, he appeared just as confident on the right, and even played a few games as a kind of sweeper, a job which would have suited him very well if he had been a bit quicker. He eventually left the club in 1977, to play in the North American Soccer League, where his languid and intelligent style would, I am sure, have been well appreciated.

There weren't too many other notable right backs for many years, with **Brian Bason**, **Gary Locke**, **Gary Stebbing** and **Steve Lovell** being among those who I wouldn't want to consider for too long. In fact, Steve Lovell became an extremely prolific goal scorer after leaving Palace, at a time when Alan Mullery was desperate for a decent forward, and he must have been cursing his lack of judgement, which the supporters did from the day he came to the club. A player who made the opposite transition, from striker to right back, was the distinctive looking **Paul Hinshelwood**, whose puny frame and curly hair earned him the nickname, derogatory at first, but ultimately affectionate, of 'Doris'. Hinshelwood was a fixture in the team that won the Second Division title in 1979, and as promotion was built on a remarkably good defensive record, he must take his share of the credit along with his colleagues, Sansom, Cannon and Billy Gilbert. His main strength, though, was in going forward, and although he didn't score too often, occasionally the ball would fall nicely into his stride as he galloped towards goal, and he would let fly with a fierce shot. Just like Sansom on the left, Hinshelwood was the starting point for a good deal of Palace's attacking manoeuvres, having received the ball from Burridge, but he did not have

Sansom's talent for close control, so the longer ball up the touchline was more usual on that side of the field. What endeared Doris to the fans was not his playing ability, but his dogged determination to overcome his failings as a defender. Faced by a fast and skilful winger, he would crouch a few yards off his man all the way down the touchline, staring intently at the ball, until he was shown just enough of it to attempt the tackle. The lunge, when it came, would more often than not miss the ball and connect with the legs, but his fouls were always of a clumsy, even comical nature, rather than what you would call dirty. The vogue for Crystal Palace players at one time even earned Hinshelwood two England Under-21 caps, but effective though he was when things were going well, he was never more than an ordinary, if eccentric player, and after staying through the upheavals of the early 1980's, he was sold by Mullery to Oxford, and replaced by Gary Locke.

All of Palace's right backs from then on until the arrival of **John Pemberton** were being used in that position as a makeshift measure, and arguably the best of them was **Tony Finnigan**, really an attacking midfield player who was sold prematurely to Blackburn, and who could have done a better job in midfield than either Glenn Pennyfather or Alan Pardew. Gary Stebbing was a player who never looked comfortable whatever position he played in, although he had shown promise as a youth – even playing for England – and he was always the target of abuse from a frustrated crowd, which left him bereft of confidence. **Henry Hughton** was another player more at home in midfield, and never the equal of his more famous brother Chris, and John Pemberton will always have a place in our hearts for his burst down the right which lit the touch paper for Palace's startling 4–3 victory against Liverpool in that Villa Park semi-final in 1990.

The experienced **John Humphrey** was brought in at right back to replace John Pemberton that same year, and he played a major part in Palace's improvement in a wonderful defence alongside Eric Young, Andy Thorn and Richard Shaw. Although already pushing 30 when he arrived from Charlton, Humphrey was as fit as anyone in the squad, had a calm, solid look about him, and impressed straight away. Strong in the tackle, and always keen to get forward, in possession of the ball he was always looking up, trying to find an opportunity to play a long angled pass for Wright and Bright, and a hoof was a rarity for the unfussy Humph. Equally rare were goals, but his second of only two for Palace was brilliantly thumped in from distance against Wolves, all the more memorable for being scored by Humphrey. He was untouchable at right back until Alan Smith sent him out on loan to Reading for three months in the middle of the 1993–94 promotion season, not long after that Wolves scorcher, but to the fans' delight he returned to play his part in winning the title.

Having made it back to the Premiership, Alan Smith experimented with new **signings Darren Pitcher** and **Darren Patterson** at right back, but neither imposed themselves and Humphrey ended up playing half the season after all, but it wasn't until his replacement **Marc Edworthy** arrived the following year that Palace had another decent player in the No. 2 shirt. Edworthy developed quickly after joining from Plymouth, and betrayed his origins as a winger with his penchant for beating his man and taking the ball forward through the middle, although he was too often caught out of position. At times he would be used as a sweeper in the absence of Andy Roberts, and this role suited him well, but he didn't always convince defensively. Edworthy played a vital role in Smith's promotion side of 1998, and was one of the better players as he captained the side that went straight back down, but one of Terry Venables' most unpopular decisions was to prefer **Dean Austin** at right back, and Edworthy didn't hang around, moving on to Coventry. Edworthy was the sort of player that one could see staying at a club like Palace for many years, and he was a great loss.

Partly because he replaced the popular Edworthy, and partly because he was nowhere near as good, the crowd didn't take to Dean Austin at all, and he lost his place for a while to **Jamie Smith**, with **Sagi Burton** also getting a few games. A single moment, scoring the winning goal at Norwich, repaired Austin's fractured relationship with the crowd, and he became a fixture for the next few embattled years, earning respect at least, if not adulation, from the grateful fans.

Joel Ward

Under Steve Bruce, then Trevor Francis, Jamie Smith was again preferred at right back before the arrival of **Curtis Fleming**, past his prime, but a wholehearted attacking full back, whose Palace career was cut short by injury. Into the side came **Danny Butterfield**, and eight years later he

was still there, despite a few interruptions along the way. Butterfield had been billed as a right-sided midfielder when he arrived from Grimsby, but he was at his best in defence, often getting forward in support down the right, and putting in some very good crosses. Over the years he had hit a few spectacular goals, his first from a tight angle against Ipswich being especially glorious, and he was often used in midfield or at centre back, but in Butterfield's final year at Palace Neil Warnock put him into the side for an FA Cup replay against Wolves as a makeshift centre forward. Wolves were in the Premier League, and Palace were in administration, but Butterfield scored not just a perfect hat-trick, but the fastest in Palace's history, scoring with his head, his right, then his left within just six minutes. Ridiculous.

The players who had filled Butterfield's boots in the intervening years included **Emmerson Boyce**, an improving defender from Luton, who was one of Dowie's best players in his year in the Premiership, and **Matt Lawrence**, who came in for constant abuse, but gave his all for the cause, as well as writing an unusually witty and entertaining column in the match day programme. Finally Butterfield had to win his place back from **Nathaniel Clyne**, which he did for a period, before Clyne settled into the first team and became one of the best full backs ever at the club. As always seemed likely from the first time he stepped up from the youth team, Clyne went on to play for England after he had left Palace for Southampton, then Liverpool, and as well as his obvious quality as a player, he endeared himself to one part of his native city at least with his 'South London is ours…' tweet following a victory over Millwall. It was a huge loss when Clyne left, but **Joel Ward** was a more than capable replacement, and quickly became valued for his athleticism, dedication and reliability, retaining his shirt unchallenged as Palace rose to the Premier League again, and continuing to excel even when asked to fill in at left back for lengthy periods.

During those first few years back in the top flight, under a succession of fire-fighting managers, Ward's cover at right back was provided by **Adrian Mariappa** and the all-purpose **Martin Kelly**, before Frank De Boer bought in the fleet-footed **Timothy Fosu-Mensah** on loan, but it wasn't until an injury crisis under Roy Hodgson that another youth player was catapulted into the first team against Spurs, and proved a revelation from his very first game. Few had heard of **Aaron Wan-Bissaka**, a Croydon boy who had been with the Academy since the age of 11, and had started out as a winger, but from the very first sighting it was obvious that he was a rare talent. There have been a few players over the years that from the very first could be identified as future England internationals, and although Ashley Cole, Nathaniel Clyne and Ruben Loftus-Cheek have proved me right, Ben Watson was one I got wrong, and at the time of writing Wan-Bissaka hasn't yet played for his country despite developing into one of the best defensive right backs in the world. Although he only played seven games in that first season, each appearance cemented his reputation as the best tackler we had ever seen, with his preternatural timing and positioning, and it was extraordinary to know with utter certainty that if anyone tried to take him on down the wing, AWB would come out on top. He continued his outstanding form the following season, and it isn't hyperbole to state that he was already world class, so that Palace fans knew that we couldn't hang on to him if a richer club came knocking, and indeed he went to Manchester United for a huge fee with our blessing and gratitude

for having witnessed such a talent. In Wan-Bissaka's final game for Palace, a thrilling 5–3 victory over Bournemouth, it was good to see him up against Nathaniel Clyne, now on loan at the Cherries from Liverpool, to my mind our two best ever right backs facing each other on the same pitch.

Aaron Wan-Bissaka

In summary, the choice at left back for my dream team is obvious, and perhaps indisputable by anyone who ever saw Kenny Sansom in a Palace shirt, but right back is more vexing. We've been well served over the years with the likes of Peter Wall, John Humphrey, Danny Butterfield and Joel Ward, but Clyne and Wan-Bissaka stand out as top class players who could hold down a place in most teams. As I write, and with Clyne having returned late in his career, I have to say that Aaron Wan-Bissaka just edges it, as it's so unusual that one can get excited about going to see a defender play.

Centre Backs

If you want to know the definition of 'craggy', you need look no further than **John McCormick,** a tall, red-headed Scottish centre half, and a perfect example of the species. Big Mac was ever present in the 1968–69 promotion side, along with Jackson and Kember, and kept his place until being dropped to accommodate Bobby Bell in 1973, at the age of 36. Although physically very tough, he was by no means a dirty player, and set an example to his colleagues with his supreme application to the job. When heading a ball either in defence or attack he seemed to use every muscle in his body for maximum power, and was the last player ever to let his head drop if things were going badly. No one would claim that he was the most skilful when in possession, but his timing in the tackle was always accurate and efficient, and his positional sense compensated for the occasional waywardness of his partner, Mel Blyth. As a traditional 'stopper' he was one of the best, and would have deserved a place in any Palace side since.

John McCormick

Mel Blyth was in fact deposed as centre back for a while by yet another Scotsman, **Roger Hynd**, but after playing in midfield for much of the 1969–70 season he won his place back when Hynd was temporarily switched to the forward line. Blyth liked to play his way out of defence, but the execution didn't always match the ambition, and he often found himself getting into trouble. Nevertheless, the contrasting styles of Blyth and McCormick made for a good mix, and the two of them stayed together until McCormick's retirement, near the end of Bert Head's time in charge. Blyth continued on and off throughout Malcolm Allison's first, disastrous year, before being sold cheaply to Southampton in the same week that **Ian Evans** arrived from QPR. His move to The Dell renewed his enthusiasm and there he played the best football of his career as a member of the side that beat Palace in the FA Cup semi-final, going on to collect a winners' medal. Two years later he came back to Selhurst Park on loan, ironically to fill the gap left after Ian Evans' awful injury, before giving way to the next No.6, **Billy Gilbert**. Blyth's reputation was completely the opposite of John McCormick's, both on the field and off it, and he was always likely to get into trouble with referees, once being sent off in a game against Everton for elbowing the niggling Alan Whittle, then playing for the Toffeemen. He escaped further punishment from the FA Disciplinary Commission due to doubt about the evidence, as the referee reported that Blyth had used his right elbow to strike the blow, whereas Blyth insisted it was his left. After a newspaper had run an article about his playboy image, quoting him as saying '..my Saturday night ends late on Sunday morning – it's devoted exclusively to birds and booze', he was given the programme space normally devoted to Bert Head's thoughts to put the record straight, and he expressed his disgust that the article had 'made me out to be some kind of raver', although it certainly had the ring of truth. Blyth's fellow central defenders after McCormick were a fairly motley bunch, with Allison's supposed star of the future **Derek Jeffries** being the best and **Bobby Bell** probably the worst, with the hard man **Roy Barry** somewhere in between, but when **Ian Evans** succeeded Blyth, Palace at last had a really good central defender in the team.

Ian Evans

Evans came as part of the package with Terry Venables, and it was a bold move for a player with such an obviously bright future to drop down to the Third Division, but we were glad that he did. For the next three years Evans was the key player in a Palace team that, although unable to climb out of Division Three, played good, entertaining football to big crowds, and surprised everyone by reaching the last four of the FA Cup, which was no fluke. Initially partnered by Derek Jeffries, with **Jim Cannon** at left back, Evans was clearly a player of great ability, but once Cannon joined him in the centre he looked superb. Both players were ever-present, together with Kenny Sansom, in Terry Venables' first season as manager, when Palace finally made it back to the Second Division, and they looked set to go straight up to the First the following year until Evans broke his leg against Fulham, in a tackle with

George Best. Evans' recovery was painfully slow, and by the time he was fit again, Billy Gilbert had established himself in the side, and Evans finished his playing days at Barnsley, before coming back to Palace in 1984 as Steve Coppell's assistant.

Jim Cannon had made an impact in his first ever game for Palace, when he scored the second goal in the victory against Chelsea that signalled Allison's arrival, but it took him a couple of years, playing mainly at left back, to establish himself in the first team. He really matured when he played alongside Evans, and by the time Billy Gilbert came into the side Cannon was one of the team's senior players, at the age of 24. In nearly 15 years of service, under a total of seven managers, Cannon was often the one player who could be relied on to perform consistently well, and after a while it was difficult to imagine Crystal Palace without him, his 568 league appearances giving him a club record that is unlikely to be beaten. Although he was often touted as a potential Scottish international, he was probably just short of that level, but as a club player he was the type that is invaluable. When he was feeling confident he would set off on a gallop that took him into a shooting position, which was only occasionally successful, but most of his few goals came from headers, and he was always a danger at the far post from corners. His best remembered goal, though, was the fourth against Ipswich in 1979 that sent Palace to the top of Division One, the day that both he and his team were at their peak.

Cannon's regular partner for some seven years was Billy Gilbert, a straightforward player with few frills, although like everyone else in Venables' team of 1979 he had the confidence early in his career to play a quality of football that later gave way to a more basic defensive strategy, depending rather more on intimidation. Gilbert had long spells of very good form with interludes when nothing would go right, but his final season at Palace was his best for a long time and I for one was sorry to see him go to Portsmouth, although things were in such a state under Alan Mullery that one could hardly blame him for wanting to get away. When Coppell took charge, then, one of his many problems was finding a replacement for Gilbert – although **John Lacy** was on the staff, he wisely looked elsewhere – and after **Chris Whyte's** too brief sojourn, and experiments with **Gavin Nebbeling** and **Gary Stebbing**, he persuaded Chelsea's Titan **Micky Droy** to form a formidable team with Jim Cannon. Although this was only a short term solution, the difference that Droy made to the defence was a major factor in Palace's revival the following year, and it was typically shrewd of Coppell to give him the job at the age of 34.

Eric Young

After Droy had finally slowed to a halt, Gavin Nebbeling showed significant improvement in his game to win back his place, but was soon under threat from the former Spurs and Brighton player **Gary O'Reilly**, and these two vied for the No.5 shirt for the next three seasons, although

O'Reilly missed a lot of that time through injury. Both players were very strong in the air, but less sure of themselves on the ground, although to my mind O'Reilly was certainly the better player, as well as coming over as a thoroughly engaging character from his intelligent and articulate appearances on the radio. All this time Jim Cannon had been the one constant factor in a changing defence, but after coming close to promotion for three years running, Coppell decided that his skipper had served his purpose, and shocked some of his admirers by giving him a free transfer.

Jeff Hopkins was the player bought to replace Cannon, and he played a big part in Palace's promotion to Division One, but he was sometimes guilty of disastrous lapses of concentration, like his own goals against Swindon in the play-offs and Millwall in the First Division. After the 9–0 Nightmare at Anfield, a priority was obviously to spend some money on a centre half with some authority, and following protracted negotiation Palace landed **Andy Thorn**, one of Wimbledon's Cup-winning team who had used that opportunity to get away from Plough Lane, ending up at Newcastle. The prosaic reputation of that side worried those who hadn't seen Thorn play, but he quickly proved himself to be an excellent bargain, a player around whom an entire defence can be structured. Once he came into the side Palace always appeared likely to stay in Division One, and he acted as a talisman all the way to Wembley, raising the game of those around him, particularly Gary O'Reilly in the Cup semi-final and final.

According to reserve keeper Andy Woodman, **Eric Young** was 'a cold, blunt bastard, but not a bad bloke'. If you can't have a Bobby Moore or Franz Beckenbauer in defence, what you really do want is at least one cold, blunt bastard, and Young gave the team a hard centre that had been lacking with Gary O'Reilly. Young and Andy Thorn renewed their partnership from their days at Wimbledon, and for a few years the pairing was as good as any we had seen at Selhurst Park. Wearing a headband to protect his forehead during games, Young became known as 'Ninja', and was as fearlessly strong in the tackle as in the air, scoring a few goals as well as creating many more whenever he went forward to create havoc from free kicks and corners.

Young's style gave ammunition to those who put Palace's success down to their strong-arm tactics, and one might never have guessed that he was a trained accountant. Not averse at times to dishing out the odd elbow, I still never saw Young as essentially a dirty player, more a wholehearted and single-minded stopper, with more skill than many realised, but he met his match when Martin Keown's craven revenge attack put him out of action for five months. Young came back as strong as ever, became a regular in the Wales side, and was at the heart of Alan Smith's promotion-winning team of 1994, alongside fellow Welsh international **Chris Coleman**. By now we had seen the best of Ninja, and Smith ignored him for most of the following Premiership season, but there is no question that Young was one of the very best central defenders Palace have had.

Andy Thorn was perhaps the junior partner in the pairing with Young, but his contribution to Palace's excellent defence was just as valuable. His forays forward were a key weapon, with several goals coming from his near post flicks from corners, and it was his goal that knocked Liverpool out of the League Cup one famous night in 1992. Thorn was replaced at centre back

the following year by Chris Coleman, who at last found his niche after being used as a left back, and as an emergency striker for quite a spell. Once he had settled into the centre back role alongside Young, for a while his Wales team mate, Coleman looked a natural and his partnership with **Richard Shaw** the following season was equally effective despite having a very difficult time in the Premiership. While not as powerful as Eric Young in the air, Coleman was confident with the ball and read the game very well, but once Palace were relegated in 1995 he appeared to have become more interested in getting a deal with a Premiership club, eventually joining Blackburn, where he did reasonably well for a season before moving on to Fulham. Shaw himself had spent most of his time at Palace either at full back or in midfield, but despite his lack of height, he had become a very good reader of the game and surprisingly played some of his best football as a centre-back alongside Coleman.

Palace struggled to adequately replace Coleman and Shaw as they headed for the play-offs under Dave Bassett, and although Andy Roberts often did a fine job in defence, **Gareth Davies** – yet another Welshman – was in and out of the side, **Tony Gale** and **Jason Cundy** played a few games between them, and **David Tuttle** followed Bassett from Sheffield United to play alongside **Leif Andersen** for a while. Tuttle was passable, and Leif was certainly big, but dreadfully slow and cumbersome, yet between them they helped Palace to the play-offs. Tuttle never really had a decent partner at the back until **Andy Linighan** arrived from Arsenal, and although he was past his very best, the improvement in Palace's defence was considerable. As expected, Linighan struggled somewhat in the Premiership, and while the emergence of Icelander **Hermann Hreiðarsson** was promising, the record signing of **Valérien Ismaël** at £2.75million was a washout. Ismaël had been thrown into a relegation battle in a strange country and with a lot of strangeness going on all around him, and although he showed no signs of being worth the massive fee, he later went on to play at the top level in Germany for double-winning sides Werder Bremen and Bayern Munich. He was never given a chance in the team under Terry Venables, and was sold at a huge loss within nine months of arriving at Palace, leaving us to wonder what might have been.

Fan Zhiyi

Two of Venables' best signings, having dumped Ismaël and lost Hreiðarsson, were the Chinese defender **Fan Zhiyi** and Rangers' Australian **Craig Moore**, although it seems his transfer fee was never paid, and he returned later that season. Moore didn't look or behave like a typical centre back, and was a far better footballer than either Tuttle or Linighan, although a fearless tackler all the same, but a bigger impression was made by Fan, who was equally effective in midfield or at the back. Fan was the captain and star of China's national team, and an issue for the club was always going to be the amount of time he

spent with his country, but whenever he pulled on a Palace shirt he gave his all and could never be accused of being a mercenary just going through the motions. He had his rash side, gave away a few penalties and was sent off a couple of times – once for shoving the referee out of the way to get the ball back at QPR – but he played with total commitment and passion. Although only at Palace for three full seasons, there was something about him that chimed with the club and the fans, and it was a sad day indeed when Steve Bruce let him go.

As Palace scraped through administration Coppell gave chances to young centre backs **David Woozley** and **Richard Harris**, who had an almighty long throw and whose last start was in a 7–1 defeat at Huddersfield. Once the club was solvent again, though, it was time to invest in a good centre back, but **Neil Ruddock** wasn't it, starting slowly, and getting slower before his place was filled by a couple of loan players, **Andy Morrison** and **Matthew Upson**, and for the vital last couple of games, American World Cup defender **Gregg Berhalter**.

A regular at centre-back for Australia, **Tony Popovic** was one of Steve Bruce's first signings and although his season was rather fragmented he looked a strong, agile defender, with a natural air of leadership. His best period was possibly when he was paired with **Darren Powell** – Palace's first really big centre half in the classic mould since Eric Young – before losing his place to **Kit Symons**. Although Popovic was generally very popular with the fans, during his five seasons at Palace he wasn't always first choice, but was always ready to step back up from the reserves. He was a little erratic, and his elegantly executed back heel to score an own goal against Portsmouth capped a very difficult introduction to the Premiership under Dowie, who later dropped him for **Gonzalo Sorondo**. By that time, 'One Size' **Fitz Hall** was first choice at centre back, and **Mark Hudson** had made a permanent move from Fulham, while there was further competition for places from **Mikele Leigertwood** and the 'Peckham Beckham', **Darren Ward**.

Hall was one of the better performers in his first season, and initially formed a solid partnership with Darren Ward the following year, while Leigertwood turned out to be a useful utility player in a number of positions in defence and midfield, a little like Richard Shaw had been. Ward's form fell away, and Peter Taylor's preferred centre backs were Hudson and his own signing **Leon Cort**, renowned for the scarcity of his bookings throughout his career. Cort looked every bit as good as Hall had been, and was possibly Taylor's best purchase, but he wasn't rated by Neil Warnock, and was replaced at the back by **José Fonte**. Fonte settled in alongside Hudson, who was succeeded by **Paddy McCarthy,** a very similar player to Hudson, but perhaps a little more aggressive. Although Fonte had a reputation for being able to play the ball out of defence, we didn't see too much evidence, and both he and McCarthy were prone to basic errors at times, often found ball-watching as crosses were whipped in between them. To stiffen the back line, Neil Warnock signed Derby's notoriously brutal **Claude Davis**. In his time at Palace, Davis was at times a rock, throwing himself fearlessly into challenges, but at others was a liability; he could show deft skill to go past players, or he could let them in for a chance on goal with a complete howler. With Fonte being sold to Southampton, Davis got more games than he might have expected, or we might have hoped, but was eventually usurped the following season by the loan signing and proud owner of one England cap **Anthony Gardner**, unquestionably a

more sophisticated player than Davis, and less nerve-racking to watch.

Damien Delaney

During Dougie Freedman's first season in charge, with Paddy McCarthy at the heart of the team alongside Gardner, they were augmented by a series of defenders including **Peter Ramage**, **Paul McShane** and the Bulgarian **Aleksandar Tunchev**, all of whom played a part in stabilising the club after the recent traumas, but with McCarthy out injured for the whole of the following season, the permanent signing of **Damian Delaney** to play alongside Ramage proved to be a master stroke by Freedman. The experienced Irishman had become disillusioned after being released by Ipswich and was considering moving to the USA to extend his career when Palace offered him a short term contract, and he ended up staying for six years. Delaney belied his age time and again in a Palace shirt and although his emotional response to promotion at the end of his first season was enough on its own to cement his bond with the fans, he carried on with his wholehearted, no frills approach to the game in the Premier League to everyone's surprise, partnering first with **Danny Gabbidon**, then with **Scott Dann**, signed from Blackburn by Tony Pulis. Their partnership flourished, and although Dann's quality was appreciated at Selhurst Park he fell just short of being picked for England, but at his best was at that level.

The pairing of Dann and Delaney remains one of the most memorable in Palace's history, and either might be considered for any all-time team individually, but as their age started to show cover was provided by the even older **Brede Hangeland** for a short while before the arrival of **James Tomkins** from West Ham. This was quite a coup for Palace, since Tomkins had grown into one of the Hammers' most popular players over the many years he had played for his boyhood club, and himself hadn't been too far off an England call up, instead representing Great Britain at the 2012 Olympics. He soon impressed as a very accomplished defender, who got on with the job without any histrionics, but his time at Selhurst was punctuated by a series of injuries as he took his place in the queue for the treatment room alongside Dann and then the big money signing **Mamadou Sakho**, who had been a member of Brendan Rogers' Liverpool team that had stumbled in their title challenge a few years earlier at Selhurst Park. Initially on loan from Liverpool, Palace showed their intent by signing him permanently for a huge fee and eye-watering wages, but whereas he had been frozen out by Jurgen Klopp at Anfield, he became an instant cult figure at Selhurst Park. Alongside the quietly effective Dann or Tomkins, Sakho simply grabbed your attention, turning every challenge into a showpiece and never happy to keep things simple. His passing from the back was wonderfully incisive, something we hadn't seen before, but often his first touch left him needing to perform miracles to recover, which he did most of the time. Yes, he gave you kittens every time he tried a Cruyff turn in his own area or a completely unnecessary backheel, but he was an absolute beast whose wages became a burden as he started to spend far more time out injured than on the pitch, and he was sadly one of those released at the end of Roy Hodgson's time.

In stark contrast to the maverick Sakho, **Gary Cahill** was the epitome of an old school English centre half in the mould of Jackie Charlton, and Chelsea's decision to let him go at the age of 33 after having been a major part of their success over the years meant that Palace were able to sign a player who was still one of the very best defenders in the Premier League for nothing. A slight loss of pace was more than compensated for by Cahill's exceptional leadership qualities, although it's paradoxical that in his second season Palace conceded many more goals than usual under Roy Hodgson, in part due to a constantly disrupted defence in which **Cheikhou Kouyaté** was preferred to **Martin Kelly** as a stop-gap. For three or four years Palace had been unable to field an established pairing at the back, and over the years it's the partnerships that remain most memorable. McCormick and Blyth, Cannon and Gilbert, Young and Thorn, Dann and Delaney, all of these can be thought of as great partnerships, but who were the greatest individual centre backs? Sakho was objectively one of the best players, and terrific fun to watch, while Jim Cannon has to be on anyone's list of Palace favourites, but my short list comes down to the unique Fan Zhiyi, John McCormick, and the two players I love to imagine playing alongside each other, Ian Evans and Eric Young.

Midfielders

The main feature of Bert Head's successful team was a willingness to graft for each other, and while players like **David Payne** and **Roger Hoy** had this quality in abundance, the only outfield player who made his mark as an outstanding individual was the young midfielder from Croydon, **Steve Kember**. Although he was still only 20 years old in the promotion year of 1969, he had been a first team regular for over three years and there had never been any doubt that he was bound for the First Division, be it with Palace or with a bigger club. He had everything you could ask for in a midfield player, being both a tenacious ball winner and always intelligent and adventurous with his distribution, and the Palace team was built around his skills for the five years leading up to his sudden departure in 1971, when he was sold to Chelsea for a record fee of £170,000. This was a great shock for the team and the fans, but the truth was that since going up they had failed to make progress, and Kember had little choice but to leave if he was to stand a chance of pressing his claims for a place in the England team. The great shame was that he joined a Chelsea side in serious decline, and never made it beyond the national Under-23 team, because in the right environment he could have become one of the great players of the Seventies.

After rather fading into obscurity with Leicester, he answered Terry Venables' call to re-join his old club in 1978, and his experience and devotion to the cause was the single most important factor in Palace's successful push for promotion, although the kudos went mostly to the precocious youngsters, several of whom had benefitted years earlier from Kember's laudable interest in coaching juniors in his own time. It was no surprise that Kember was the fans' choice as manager after Dario Gradi was sacked in 1981, but he was given a pitifully short time in which to prove himself, being dismissed after six months and replaced by Mullery. I am sure I am not alone in thinking that someone who had done so much for Palace, and who had such an affinity with the supporters, deserved better treatment, although Kember's innate dignity prevented him from expressing any grudge against the club.

Steve Kember

There has been nobody since who I would consider so adept as Kember in every department, although there have been several midfielders to admire for their own particular qualities. Kember's successor in 1971 – who had also been his predecessor until 1965 – was **Bobby Kellard**; energetic, tough as old boots, and also a big favourite with the fans, but without the creative imagination that was so needed in that struggling side. Kellard in turn was superseded by two Scotsmen who were very disappointing in their different ways; **Charlie Cooke** had been a great player, but had little left to give Palace, while **Iain Philip** – at the time Palace's most expensive signing, at £115,000 – was a star of the future who came to nothing, lasting just a year before returning to Dundee.

Allison's first, woeful season in charge was characterised by indecision concerning selection that saw several inappropriate players used in midfield, including Mel Blyth, Jim Cannon, Derek Jeffries and Don Rogers, with only **Jeff Johnson** and **Mark Lindsay** looking vaguely at home. After **Terry Venables** had padded round for a few games, Allison's best period came when **Nicky Chatterton** combined with **Martin Hinshelwood** and **Phil Holder** in midfield, a solid, hardworking unit which nearly took Palace to Wembley, and should have won promotion in 1976. Holder, formerly with Spurs, was a pugnacious little footballer in the mould of Bobby Kellard, while Hinshelwood was infinitely more elegant, although desperately fragile. Chatterton was somewhere between the two of them, and although he also had frequent interruptions through injury, he was a fixture in Palace's team for five years, until finally being replaced by Kember in 1978, and moving to Millwall. Chatterton was typical of the kind of grafter that most good teams contain, very much a team player like David Payne or, latterly, Alan Pardew, who also scored his share of goals each season, and who managed to win most genuine fans over, despite being the 'boo-boy' for a while. For a couple of seasons Chatterton was required to do the running around on behalf of **George Graham**, known as 'Stroller', and never was a nickname more apt. Graham had been a member of Arsenal's double-winning side, and had once scored the winning 'Goal of the Season' on The Big Match, against Palace. He was undoubtedly a skilful player in possession of the ball, slowing the play down and opening up obscure avenues of attack, but he seemed to miss nearly as many games through suspension as through injury, and his cynicism as a player later found expression through the teams he went on to manage.

The most successful midfield combination of the Seventies was the one that formed the core of Terry Venables' Second Division Championship winners of 1979, comprising Kember, **Peter Nicholas** and **Jerry Murphy**, with the occasional contribution from **Terry Fenwick**. Peter Nicholas first came into the side as a makeshift defender, but once moved to the right of midfield it soon became obvious that he was set to become one of the game's natural captains; hard in the tackle and strong going forward, from early on he was spoken of as the heir to Terry Yorath's Welsh crown. His contemporary, Jerry Murphy, couldn't have been more different, and relied on the endeavours of Kember and Nicholas to allow him to practice his ambitious, audacious and often sublime skills. Murphy loved to show what he could do by delicately chipping the ball with backspin wherever possible, but although everyone knew what a good player he was, he ultimately let himself down because he wasn't able to graft in the same way as someone like Nicholas and consequently became stuck in a very deep rut at Palace, finally being almost the last of Venables' great team to leave in 1985.

When Palace went up in 1979, Venables' most important addition to the side was **Gerry Francis**, an exceptional player at one time with QPR, but by now significantly slower than he needed to be, although he was superb in midfield in that wonderful first half of the season, and still showed glimpses of genius. After everything collapsed the following year, Francis followed Venables back to Loftus Road, leaving the midfield in the hands of such players as the would-be boy wonder **Shaun Brooks**, the paunchy **David Price**, and the equally unremarkable **Steve Lovell, Gary Stebbing** and **Henry Hughton**. **Steve Galliers** offered little more than manic effort and a fearsome tackle, but matters only really improved when another former Wimbledon man **Steve Ketteridge** linked up with **Kevin Taylor**, and Palace finally started winning again in 1985. Ketteridge in particular would chase everything, and Taylor could play a bit of football, and with these two solid in the middle Coppell was able to build a simple, effective structure that continued to evolve along the same lines. Where Ketteridge was weakest was in going forward, and he was replaced by **Andy Gray**, by instinct a striker, but who looked a natural once switched to a creative midfield role. Gray's successful conversion meant that, with himself and Taylor both exclusively right-sided, Palace were on the look out for a new left-footer, and the man plucked by Steve Coppell from the obscurity of Crewe Alexandra – **Geoff Thomas** – was to prove one of his shrewdest buys. With Gray throwing himself all over the place and being generally flash, Thomas applied himself to the task of holding everything together in the middle, fiercely protective of the ball once in possession and organising those around him, which led to him becoming the obvious choice as captain after Jim Cannon had gone.

Thomas was an outstanding success in his first season, but was forced to miss the second half of the1988–89 promotion season with an injury, which left the midfield places to be fought out by Super **Alan Pardew**, **Glenn Pennyfather** and, most impressively, **Dave Madden**. Pardew's sturdy contribution was to grow in importance throughout the year, although he was never as powerful as Thomas, but as a creative force Dave Madden was the key player, often showing skills belying his status as a reject from Reading. Madden lost his place the following season after the return of the prodigal son, Andy Gray, but when Thomas was forced to play in defence his place went instead to Pardew, who held

on to it all season. Madden finally got a look in only at the very end of the season, and came on as a substitute in the two Wembley finals before leaving on a free transfer, but will mostly be remembered for his nerveless penalty against Blackburn in the 1989 playoff final.

Geoff Thomas

As the 1989–90 season wore on, with Andy Gray forced to play wide on the right wing, Geoff Thomas gradually began to come back to his best form, and showed some of his nicest touches in the Cup games, including a cracking equaliser against Portsmouth and some assured and incisive passing against Liverpool and Manchester United. This central midfield partnership of Gray and Thomas continued to serve Palace well following the FA Cup final defeat, and earned them both England recognition, although Andy Gray's involvement was limited to half a game for his country. They both had possibly their best seasons as Palace confounded everyone by finishing third in 1991, and with the maverick Andy Gray complementing Thomas's outstanding endeavour, the two of them dovetailed beautifully on the pitch. Thomas fully deserved his England place, and was an example to everyone with not just his relentless hard work and athleticism, but his strength in possession, vision when passing to the front men, and ability to arrive late in the box for powerful headed goals. Geoff Thomas was the best all-round midfielder I have ever seen at Palace, whilst Gray had a good range of skills as well as a dangerous long throw and powerful shot, but was very different in character to Thomas and more likely to fly off the handle. He was sent off following a scrap with the similarly undisciplined Dennis Wise in a game against Chelsea which Palace won at Selhurst Park, and was always prone to rash reactions, so Coppell finally had enough of his attitude. Feeling that Gray was not pulling his weight in training or in games, the manager put him up for transfer as a wake-up call and Gray sulked off to Spurs, which opened the way for first **Simon Osborn**, then **Gareth Southgate** to make the step up to the first team.

Unlike his fellow 'Bisto kid' **Simon Rodger**, Simon Osborn never really entrenched himself in Steve Coppell's side, ultimately appearing a little lightweight, although he later moved on to have a long and successful career at a number of other clubs, mostly at a lower level. On the other hand, once Gareth Southgate got his hands on the shirt, he kept it. Southgate had come through the youth system and into the first team initially as a right back, filling in for John Humphrey for a spell, but as he developed his best performances for Palace were in midfield, from where he went on to captain his club. His first goal on the opening day of the 1992–93 season against Blackburn was a stunning long range effort, but Blackburn's new signing, Southgate's future England colleague Alan Shearer had to go and trump it with two fabulous goals of his own. Although Palace were relegated that year, they bounced straight back under Alan Smith, with Southgate having

a superb season as captain, and bursting forward to score more terrific goals, none better than the outstanding solo effort against Portsmouth. Southgate caught the eye during his final season at Palace, and moved on to become an exceptional centre back for Aston Villa and England, but it was in Palace's midfield that he developed into a top class player.

Gareth Southgate

There were a number of bit part players in Palace's midfield during Southgate's time, such as the coltish and nimble **Bobby Bowry**, and **Ricky Newman** who played virtually a full season in the Premier League and scored three goals of quality, but neither really developed and moved on to have good careers at Millwall. **Darren Pitcher** was another utilitarian defensive midfielder who never really sparkled, although he scored a memorable cup goal against Wolves which left the ball satisfyingly lodged in the stanchion. He was guilty of some dreadful brutality in midfield at times, and his replacement **Ray Houghton**, arrived just too late to help Palace avoid the drop in 1995. Houghton was the wise head so desperately needed in Alan Smith's young side and one could see the quality that he brought straight away.

Houghton had done it all with Liverpool and latterly Aston Villa, and although he was 33 years old, he had more energy than any of the younger players and put them to shame with his work ethic. The previous summer he had scored a famous goal for Ireland in the World Cup to beat Italy, and for a struggling Premiership side such as Palace he seemed just the man for the job.

Houghton had an excellent second season, linking well with the newly arrived Dougie Freedman and another recently acquired Scot, **David Hopkin**. Having never quite made his mark at Chelsea, the signing of Hopkin by Steve Coppell turned out to be one of his very best, and he very quickly became a favourite at Selhurst Park with his wholehearted commitment and no-nonsense approach. Not the prettiest, with his wingnut ears, ginger hair and missing front teeth, all the clichés about Celtic warriors applied to Hopkin and if there was a loose ball to be won, he would make it his no matter who was in the way. He was destructive and creative in equal measure and scored a host of superb goals during his first two seasons, typically lashing the ball home with either foot with apparent disdain. His finest moment came with the last minute winner at Wembley against Sheffield United, by which time he had become a valuable commodity, and it was the greatest of shames that he moved on to Leeds straight afterwards.

Arriving at Selhurst Park at the same time as Hopkin was **Andy Roberts**, at the time Palace's most expensive purchase, from Millwall. Played sometimes in central defence, sometimes in midfield, Roberts was generally thought of as a sweeper, and during his first season he looked like he could develop into an England player in time. His goal against Leicester in the play-off final was about the first time he had advanced over the half way line all season, as his job was to pick up the ball deep and feed Hopkin and Houghton ahead of him. Often he could hit a sweet long pass up-field, or thread a delicate ground pass through an impossible gap, but after a while he seemed to become all about the style, and started to look slow and a little lazy, despite becoming team captain. He finally fell out of favour after a poor season in the team that included Lombardo, and made a surprise move to Wimbledon as the squad was just about to be dismantled.

By this time Simon Rodger had returned to the midfield, with a succession of mediocre players like **Carl Veart** and **Jamie Fullarton**, who had no place being in the Premiership, and **Neil Emblen**, the answer to a question nobody asked. Towards the end of that desperate season with Lombardo ostensibly in charge, Mark Goldberg, having failed to entice Paul Gascoigne, spent one of the millions that he never really had on **Sasa Curcic**, the talented but troublesome misfit from Aston Villa. For a while Curcic had gone missing – not for the first time – apparently to sort out a work permit, but it was telling that his Villa manager John Gregory wasn't too worried: 'He had to get some papers but if he has gone home he might have been grabbed to do National Service. To be honest, I'm not bothered about him.' The saga dragged on for some weeks, but once Curcic announced that he had just married a girl that he met in Asda, the problem with the work permit vanished, and he was free to sign. Tales of Curcic's unprofessional behaviour are legion, including how he went AWOL from Villa in order to have a nose job, and he was essentially a party animal with too much money and too many drugs to spend it on, but – and this remains a guilty pleasure – he was fantastic to watch, even more so when sporting his peculiar bleached goatee. A born crowd-pleaser, it came as no surprise to find out that since retiring Curcic went on to win Serbia's version of Celebrity Big Brother. Perhaps it was his reputation more than what we actually saw, but it seemed senseless at the time that players such as **Nicky Rizzo** and **Craig Foster** were playing while Curcic wasn't even on the bench, although we can now surmise why that was.

As Goldberg's fantasy crumbled, Steve Coppell soldiered on with the midfielders that were left, and Craig Foster deserves some credit, as well as **Steve Thomson**, but at the heart of Coppell's midfield for the most testing of years was Simon Rodger, until **Hayden Mullins** moved forward from central defence to become a highly accomplished player in the middle. Mullins was ready as soon as he made the step up to the first team, and from the start had a calm air that was vital at that nervy time. He was unflustered in possession, a good tackler, and always looking to play the ball to feet. Naturally defensive, and perhaps generally one-paced, he got forward to score ten goals in one season, and his performances never dipped, no matter what position he was asked to play in. He had a touch of class that was maybe wasted in a struggling team, but remained consistently one of Palace's best players under Steve Bruce and Trevor Francis, waiting patiently for Premiership football again until moving sideways to West Ham. A year later Iain Dowie took Palace up, beating Mullins' new team in the play-off final.

One of Alan Smith's first signings after Simon Jordan's takeover was **Jamie Pollock**, whose portly presence acted as ballast for Palace's slide down the table, and the return of David Hopkin was a disappointment, but Smith made his best acquisition when he signed **Aki Riihilahti**,

a Finnish international midfielder, from Norwegian side Vålerenga. He came straight into the team and made a key contribution to survival, scoring one of the goals that beat Portsmouth and playing in the last day victory at Stockport, but he really blossomed the following season under Steve Bruce. In a match day programme Q&A feature, Dougie Freedman was asked: 'If you weren't a footballer, what would you be?' and his answer was 'Aki Riihilahti'; Aki himself would be unlikely to take offence, highly aware as he was of his strengths and weaknesses. He was no Sasa Curcic; in fact you could say he was the antithesis of Curcic in every respect bar one, that the crowd loved him. Although categorised as a defensive midfielder whose job it was to break up play – and he was one of the best we've seen at that job – he wasn't the sort of player to hover around the centre circle, but would arrive late in the box to score some vital and memorable goals, inviting comparisons with Geoff Thomas. He was nowhere near as good on the ball as Thomas, but his relationship with the Palace fans bore comparison with his predecessor, and Riihilahti would certainly be pressing Thomas for a place in my dream team.

When **Shaun Derry** came into the side under Trevor Francis, the first impression was of a fairly ordinary midfielder, with a range of misguided hairstyles, who would graft away in a team whose ambitions didn't go beyond finishing in the middle of the table, and to me it felt like Derry fitted well with the general atmosphere of mediocrity prevalent while Francis was around. When Steve Kember took over, nothing had changed, and Derry was one of many players who looked so poor during the 5–0 defeat at Wigan that turned out to be Kember's last. Iain Dowie used him less and less, and by the end of the season he was generally on the bench, and not expected to have a role to play in the play-offs. For the final in Cardiff it seemed a most peculiar decision to replace the suspended Julian Gray on the left with Shaun Derry, whose appearances to date had all been deep in central midfield, but Derry's disciplined performance was a revelation, and I saw him in a different light at last. He soon moved on once Palace were promoted, but when Neil Warnock brought him back to the club three years later he immediately made a huge difference to the team, and made me wonder whether I hadn't really been paying attention before. He gave the midfield what it had been missing since Riihilahti, and although he wasn't as mobile as Aki, his energy and determination in the defensive role made him a natural to captain the team, which he did superbly as Palace recovered from the ten point deduction in 2010. Derry's passing could be patchy, but when he was on song he was more than just a destroyer, and did a lot of good work around the opposition box, although goals weren't his thing.

While Derry had been away, **Michael Hughes** had done a sterling job in the middle before falling out of favour under Peter Taylor, despite still having plenty to offer, and two youngsters had come through to become fixtures in the team. **Ben Watson** and **Tom Soares** really established themselves during Dowie's season in the Premiership, and continued as regulars under both Peter Taylor and Neil Warnock before both leaving for Premier League clubs. Watson, whose best performances earned him the fanciful nickname 'the ginger Zidane', had looked something special when we first saw him as a 17-year-old, but he took a while to develop into no more than a solid but inconsistent central midfielder, a good striker of a dead ball, and an excellent passer, but only on his day. He

started out looking as if he would become a great player and although at Palace he only ever became very good, it was wonderful to see him some years later score the winning goal in the FA Cup Final for Wigan. Tom Soares was a different type of player; tall, highly athletic, very occasionally willing to take players on and head for goal, but he spent a lot of time out of position as a wide player on the right, and I could never quite work out what he was doing, or why he was so often in the team.

Carl Fletcher was an honest, diligent player who was seen as one of Taylor's men and gradually dropped out of Neil Warnock's plans, **Nick Carle** was a creative midfielder who never really got going at Palace, and if Warnock thought that Palace were 'too nice' when he arrived, that was never going to be an issue with **John Oster**. French youngster **Alassane N'Diaye** was briefly the next big thing, ending up as a squad player, but one of Warnock's early signings, **Neil Danns**, eventually came good after being out injured for most of his first year. An energetic, busy player, who covered a lot of ground in all areas of the pitch, Danns got better and better throughout his difficult final season, and it was a great pity when he left for Leicester.

George Burley's brand new midfield pairing of **Owen Garvan** and **Andy Dorman** had no bite to it, and all we could say of the once-great **Edgar Davids** was that he really should have stayed retired. With the pressing need to erect a dam in midfield, Dougie Freedman turned to another of Burley's men, **David Wright**, who proved the key player as the defence shut up shop for the year, assisted variously by the promising **Alex Marrow**, and the commentator's nightmare, **Kagisho Dikgacoi**, whose contribution as Palace headed towards promotion in 2013 was immense but slightly undervalued. Alongside KG, as we preferred to call the South African, Dougie Freedman bought in an unheard of Australian who had been latterly playing in Turkey, and whoever spotted **Mile Jedinak's** potential deserves all our heartfelt thanks. Jedinak very quickly established himself as the defensive core of the midfield, and was the sort of utterly uncompromising player that fans are bound to adore.

Mile Jedinak

Although sometimes criticised for his passing ability, that would be to miss the point of Jedi, whose job was to bully the opposition, win the ball whether fairly or not, and give it to someone else with more flair, perhaps **Darren Ambrose** or **André Moritz**. The latter was another of Dougie Freedman's more successful signings who played an important part, along with KG and Jedinak, in Palace's success under Freedman and then Ian Holloway, but it was the Australian who really made his mark once Palace had won promotion, and he thrived at the top level, with both club and country. There was no messing with Jedinak, and one got the impression that whatever group he found himself amongst he would emerge as leader, and of course

he took the Captain's armband and wore it proudly for five eventful seasons before stepping down a division and moving on to Aston Villa.

With the failure of the physically frail **Jonny Williams** to reach his undoubted potential and the minimal impact made by the likes of **José Campaña**, **Barry Bannan** and **Jordon Mutch**, for a while Palace relied on a memorable midfield trio of Jedinak, **Joe Ledley** and **James McArthur**, collectively dubbed McJedley. While Jedinak remained essentially destructive, both Ledley and McArthur were wonderfully versatile both defensively and offensively, and for a spell under Alan Pardew provided a solid base for Zaha, Bolasie and Puncheon to flourish as we dreamed of Europe and Pardew dreamed of England. McCarthur's contribution to the team was often under-appreciated, but as a rule if he played well then so did the team, but if he had an off day it was usually bad news, and overall he made more of an impact in midfield than the slightly disappointing **Johan Cabaye**, although they are both up there among the best we've seen in that position. Conversely, I never really took to **Jason Puncheon**, despite his sporadic purple patches of scoring vital, ofttimes iconic goals and his avowed bond with the club as 'one of our own'. He bought us close to winning the FA Cup, it's true, and wore the captain's armband for a while, but his infuriating habit of trying to overegg the pudding and turning full circle with the ball before losing it cheaply became more marked as his Palace days came to an end, and he never fully recovered from the injury sustained in stopping Manchester City breaking away and scoring an undeserved winner at Selhurst Park after **Luka Milivojević's** missed penalty in injury time. The press acted as if Puncheon had murdered their darling Kevin de Bruyne with that foul, but he was fine to play just two days later, while Puncheon missed the rest of the season and never really came back. I should love him a bit more, I realise, but sometimes the spark just isn't there.

When Luka Milivojević signed from Olympiacos shortly after Sam Allardyce had become manager, he took a little while to bed in alongside Cabaye, but before long it became apparent that Palace had unearthed a midfield leader in the mould of Jedinak, albeit with a little more panache on the ball, and like Jedinak he was fearless when called on to take a penalty, scoring 22 and only missing 3 to date. Ill-used by Frank De Boer, the Serbian went on to thrive as skipper under Roy Hodgson and for three seasons was one of the most impressive players among the rump of the Premier League, and might have been at home at a higher level. Hodgson came to rely on a solid midfield built around Luka as the basis of his defensive, counter-attacking game, and over time some fans grew restless at the perceived lack of creativity, despite **Ruben Loftus-Cheek's** sadly temporary spell, and **Jeffrey Schlupp's** ability to drive forward with the ball, but hopes were high when **Max Meyer** joined on a free transfer. His showreel suggested a player in the mould of Cabaye, an all-round midfielder with a sharp tackle and incisive passing ability, but he proved to be essentially too lightweight for the English game and by the end of his time those clamouring for him to start had mostly fallen silent. The manager much preferred the supreme athleticism of **Cheikhou Kouyaté**, the captain of the Senegal national team who had spent four very consistent seasons at West Ham, and who followed his former team mate James Tomkins over the river. Augmented variously by **James McCarthy** and **Jaïro Riedewald**, the midfield of Milivojević, McArthur and Kouyaté wasn't the most thrilling, but was highly effective at implementing Roy Hodgson's renowned tactic of first of all stopping the usually superior opposition from playing.

Lastly, let's put **Eberechi Eze** in the category of midfielder, although he is one of those players a little hard to define, and hard to predict where he will end up. In his brief time so far, Eze has taken the eye wherever he has played, but some of his best moments have come when picking the ball up deep and effortlessly taking it far into the opposition territory, skating past bewildered defenders in a style reminiscent of Don Rogers. It may be that he'll play more on the wing, or as an out and out forward, but as long as he recovers well from his devastating Achilles injury everyone agrees that he has a massive future in the game, hopefully at Palace, for many years to come.

Geoff Thomas is probably the player that personifies one of the most glorious periods in Palace's history, and he would be the perfect captain for my dream team, but alongside him I'd love to see Steve Kember, a Palace man through and through, a crucial part of two promotion-winning teams, and objectively one of the very best in his position over the years.

Wingers

It is very difficult to discuss the relative merits of various Palace wingers since the term itself can be misleading, and I am using it here to embrace the whole range of wide attacking players, few of whom would have been regarded as true wingers in Stanley Matthews' day. If one was to be pedantic, then clearly players like Jim Scott, Bobby Tambling and John Craven could not be called wingers in the way that Neil Smillie or Alan Irvine could, but essentially their function was the same. Indeed, some people would claim that Steve Coppell himself was a wide midfielder for England rather than a winger, but the distinction is too fine to worry about.

Palace won promotion in 1969 using two wingers who also happened to be better than average goal scorers: **Mark Lazarus** on the right and **Colin Taylor** on the left. Both were stocky little players who looked about ten years older than they were, and Taylor in particular had an awesomely powerful shot when the goal was in his sights, scoring the winning goal in the famous 2–1 victory over mighty Leeds United in the League Cup. However, Taylor soon returned to Walsall, and Lazarus only played a handful of First Division games before moving on to Orient, leaving the fitness fanatic **Tony Taylor** as the only wide player until **Jimmy Scott** and **Bobby Tambling** arrived the following year.

Scott had the knack of dribbling past two or three defenders before falling over the ball or running straight into touch, and only managed a few goals in his short time at Palace, but the former England international Bobby Tambling was Palace's top league scorer during the 1971–72 season, albeit with only eight goals. His best goal for Palace was in the Anglo-Italian Tournament, against Luigi Riva's Cagliari side, when he somehow found the net with a swinging left foot shot from almost the corner flag, although some observers put it down as a fluke. Another previously prolific scorer whose goals dried up when he moved to Palace was the ex-Bolton winger **Terry Wharton**, and following him came **John Craven**, strong and direct and often the only player in the team who looked like he wanted to go forward, although it was sometimes difficult to fathom where Bert Head wanted him to play.

Don Rogers

At the same time as Craven arrived came **John 'Yogi Bear' Hughes** into the outside left position, and although he scored one of the great Palace goals of all time, against Sheffield United, he did little else between injuries before being sold to Sunderland, and was replaced by **Don Rogers**. At last Palace had bought a star name, if only from the Third Division, and Rogers was an instant success at Selhurst Park, scoring a goal in his debut that was a prototype for many others to come, although he played for less than two full seasons. His great asset was a burst of speed from a standing position that made a mug out of more than one apparently quick defender, and any ball played through for him to chase brought the crowd to their feet in anticipation of another spectacular solo run, finished off by rounding the keeper or arrogantly chipping the ball over his prostrate body. Having found himself with one of the First Division's most exciting and effective wingers, Malcolm Allison then hatched a cunning plan, which effectively converted Rogers into a central midfielder, and he was never the same exhilarating player again. It certainly wasn't that Allison had any great ideological objection to wingers, because he soon went out and bought a player with a similar style, right down to the crouch: **Peter Taylor** from Southend.

Vince Hilaire

Despite his brilliance, Taylor couldn't save Palace from dropping to Division Three, but he did all he could to drag them back up again, in the process earning himself rave notices and a call up for his country, and inspiring the 1976 FA Cup run to the semi-final. After two seasons stuck in the Third Division the lure of Spurs was too great for Taylor to resist, but Terry Venables, in his first season as Palace manager, finally won promotion using either **Rachid Harkouk** or **Barry Silkman** on the left, and these two alternated for a couple of seasons until the prodigious talent of **Vince Hilaire** forced him into the team, initially as a

centre forward, but then more usefully on the left wing. Hilaire was handicapped early on by the high expectations of him created by Allison's ravings and his own documentary on TV but he turned out to be every bit as good as hyped, and when forging links with Sansom and Murphy along the left touchline he was capable of the most extraordinary flashes of genius, with wonderful control and an uncanny ability to breeze past full backs, although the final cross was too often found wanting. The other criticism was that he was reluctant to have a go at goal himself, having torn the defence to shreds, but his real problem – strangely, for one so gifted – was a lack of confidence.

During the dark years of the early Eighties, **Neil Smillie** and **David Giles** were the two other wingers used by Dario Gradi, Steve Kember and Alan Mullery, but as the team crumbled around him Hilaire was for long periods the only good reason for going to watch Palace, and he finally left before Coppell arrived, probably having stayed loyal too long for his own good. If Palace had been successful in that period then Hilaire would surely have been in the running for England honours, but his career had gone steadily off course, and he was sadly never able to become the star that he should have been, although he continued to play brilliantly in patches.

Coppell's first winger, **Alan Irvine**, was extremely basic, very effective going forward down the right hand touchline and getting crosses in to the centre, but strictly limited to this function. The use of such a straightforward ploy was clearly to Coppell's liking, though, and Irvine was followed by **Neil Redfearn**, who added an element of defensive strength to the position that Irvine had lacked, and who was more willing to take up positions other than out wide, which rendered him more useful to the midfield as a whole.

Meanwhile, two very different players were vying for the left wing position, but it was eventually **Phil Barber** who was to become the manager's choice ahead of the more gifted **John Salako**. The fact that Barber was always referred to as 'Mr. 110%' betrayed the reality that his effort and dedication far outstripped his ability, but those are qualities not to be sneered at. Having come to Palace from Aylesbury, originally as a striker, Barber was the only survivor from Alan Mullery's squad to make it to the First Division with Palace, and his propensity for hard work obviously impressed Steve Coppell, who used him in a number of positions before he finally settled wide on the left, although you wouldn't call him a winger in the strictest sense since he was never blessed with great speed. Despite enduring years of scorn and abuse from the fans – and I was always one of his many critics – it was heartening to see Barber play his part in Palace's Cup run: scoring against Rochdale, setting up goals for Bright against Huddersfield and for Thomas at Cambridge and playing a tight marking game, almost as a left back, in the semi-final and final. He took the free kick that led to the first goal at Wembley, and to eventually come away with only a loser's medal after coming so far must have been especially distressing for Barber, knowing that he was unlikely to play there again in his life.

When Steve Coppell set about strengthening the side in 1990, one of the areas that he identified as a weakness was wide on the left, and when **Glyn Hodges** arrived from Watford, it looked like the end of the line for Phil Barber, who had toiled manfully for the past seven seasons. For all Barber's endeavour, Coppell needed more quality in order to progress in the top flight, and Hodges had a reputation as a skilful player and sometime Welsh international who had followed Dave Bassett from Wimbledon to Watford, and perhaps belonged in the top division. A South London boy, Palace seemed a good fit for him, but he disappointed in his first few appearances, and was regularly substituted, looking patently unfit. He did score one of the eight goals against Southend in the League Cup, but that was just about his only meaningful contribution at Selhurst Park before he was farmed out to re-join Bassett at Sheffield United that same season. In fact the best we saw of Hodges was the following year, when he scored a peach of a goal for United against Palace, and looked decidedly trimmer, but he has to go down as one of Coppell's first misjudgements since promotion to the First Division.

Eddie McGoldrick

Hodges' failure meant a stay of execution for Barber, but in what turned out to be an unusually settled side that finished third in the table, first choices on the wings were **John Salako** and **Eddie McGoldrick**, who provided the ammunition for Wright and Bright in the middle. Salako had come into his own during the previous season's cup run, but this was the year that he really began to shine, and started to score goals as well as create them. The beauty of Salako was that he could not only play comfortably on either wing, but would cross with either foot and this enabled him to keep defenders guessing. It wasn't too often that he would push the ball past the full back and gallop into the space, as his trademark was his close control and ability to change direction and run with the ball. Indeed, his tendency was to cut inside and head down the middle, and for a while he was used more centrally, and was a good finisher, even placing a deft header past Neville Southall in the ZDS final at Wembley. He did a good job in goal once, when Nigel Martyn was sent off against Wimbledon, and the part that he played in Palace's best ever season earned him a deserved England call-up. One particularly memorable goal was the long distance lob at Nottingham Forest, but early on in the 1991–92 season he jumped to head a ball goalward and as he landed his knee was bent backwards, causing what many feared would be an injury to end his career in football. His rehabilitation from surgery was long and arduous, but he came back fighting fit in time for the start of the next season and any fears that he might not be the player he was were soon dispelled, earning him a recall to the England squad, before injury once again put him out of action for another ten months. An articulate and telegenic player, it looked for a while as if his future would lie behind a microphone rather than on the pitch, but with tremendous determination he came back once again, and even scored a hat-trick in his first game back, going on to play a major part in Alan Smith's side that went up to the Premiership as runaway champions. As a key player during several of Palace's best seasons, and as one of the finest players to come through Palace's

juniors, he is generally fondly remembered, although not in contention as one of the great wingers.

On the other flank in 1990–91 was Eddie McGoldrick, a winger almost by accident. Some, and possibly McGoldrick himself, felt that his best position was as a sweeper, and Steve Coppell used him in that role when he thought the game required it, but having been a key member of the promotion side of 1989, at first his slight frame didn't seem equipped for the rigours of the top division. Although not blessed with Salako's range of skills, McGoldrick's close control made him hard to dispossess when he had his head down, and his final ball was usually accurate and inviting for the strikers. He also hit a scoring patch in 1992, mostly tap-ins and close range headers, and a fluke long range chip against QPR, and eventually earned international recognition with the Republic of Ireland. Always enjoyable to watch and a key player in Coppell's team for many years, it was still a surprise when he left following relegation, the surprise not being that he had gone, but that he had gone to a club as big as Arsenal.

When **Simon Rodger** came into the first team, at around the same time as Simon Osborn, he wasn't really identified as a winger, but it was evident early on that he had a talent for delivering the kind of balls with his left foot that Mark Bright in particular thrived on. That left foot was also a potent weapon at corners, where the near post flick on from Thorn or Young was still a favoured tactic. Throughout his long Palace career, spanning eleven seasons, 'Jolly' Rodger played in a variety of positions in midfield, as well as at left back, but for me his best performances were as a wide man. Wherever he was asked to play, Rodger was totally committed, and whatever one might have thought of his ability, he was one of the most industrious players at the club for many years. He saw countless managers and chairmen come and go, and each time it seemed as if his Palace career was over he would come back, from a year out through injury or from loan, as strong as ever. He joined Steve Coppell during his brief stint at Manchester City, and after he was released by Trevor Francis, joined up with Coppell again at Brighton, as befits a Sussex lad. If loyalty and dedication were the sole criteria, Simon Rodger would get into my dream team without question.

An exciting young winger who made a big impact early in his career was 'Ooh Aah' **George Ndah**, who made his full debut at Anfield in the League Cup together with Bobby Bowry, and was used only intermittently during the next five seasons. Skilful and quick, and deceptively strong, Ndah was beset by injuries and became a perennial second string, despite always causing the opposition problems when recalled to the first team. Another wide player who never really became established was **Damien Matthew**, who made a big contribution to the promotion push of 1994, but it was at that time that **Bruce Dyer** signed from Watford with a big reputation. Another player hard to pigeonhole, Bruce Dyer started out as a winger, but as he developed was used more and more as a striker, becoming a favourite of Dave Bassett down the middle. Dyer seemed to have all the attributes required, namely great strength and speed, but although he did have a couple of seasons where he scored plenty, for me he was never a natural striker and was better used wide on the right. If he had sight of goal, it was anyone's guess whether he would connect with the ball, and if he did, where it might end up.

When **Attilio Lombardo** arrived at Palace, it was a very exciting time indeed, and although it is now hard to disassociate that happy day with the implications of Mark Goldberg's involvement, at the time it felt like Palace were about to become a proper Premiership side at last. A seasoned international, and still winning trophies with Juventus, the bald-headed Lombardo was instantly recognisable, and easily the most famous player Palace had ever signed. I was so thrilled that I named my shiny, Italian scooter Lombardo in his honour. Although known as a winger, Lombardo spent much of his time at Palace more centrally, although in fact he was all over the place. He had a curious upright running style, but his footwork was so delicate and his passing and movement so subtle that he stood out a mile from a team that included Tuttle, Muscat and Fullarton. What we saw of Lombardo in the Premiership was exquisite, but he missed half the season through injury, and by the time he returned in March, Palace were already doomed. Bizarrely put in charge of team affairs rather than being asked to play Palace out of trouble, Lombardo was still loved by the fans despite the inevitable relegation. It was amazing that he stayed, and he started the next season well under Terry Venables, but Goldberg's financial collapse meant the end of his surreal and brief stay at Palace.

Among the plethora of new faces bought by Terry Venables – and there may have been other wingers in that cohort who never got a game – was the Australian **Nicky Rizzo**, memorable for scoring one terrific goal against Norwich but little else, and it was to be another couple of years before Palace signed any wingers worthy of the name. **Andrejs Rubins** was a compatriot of Kolinko from Latvia, who had a good run in the team after scoring a priceless long range goal against Leicester in the League Cup, and although he scored a similar goal against Liverpool in the semi-final, he never appeared robust enough for Division One, and melted away. **Tommy**

Black and **Julian Gray** were both young Arsenal players who hadn't quite made it, but both looked very good prospects at Palace's level. Initially it was Tommy Black who made the most impact on the right wing, but he gradually went backwards while Gray flourished. Steve Bruce used Julian Gray as an attacking wing-back for a while, but it was as a straightforward winger wide on the left that he became most effective, and had his own moment of glory against Liverpool, scoring a sweet volley and forcing an own goal to knock them out of the FA Cup in 2003. Gray had all the skill and speed required to play on the wing, and had a fair eye for goal, but he too often went missing in games. Sadly, the abiding image of a player who had some outstanding games for Palace is of someone sulkily thinking to himself 'I'm better than this lot'.

As Black and Gray's stars waned, **Wayne Routledge's** was in the ascendency. Having first broken into the team aged 16, it took him a couple of years to establish himself, but he played every single game under Iain Dowie, as the new manager dragged Palace up to the Premiership and swiftly down again, at which point Routledge was off. As a youngster Routledge was expected to have a future as bright as the other Wayne, his contemporary Rooney, and he was certainly talented with good close control and all sorts of tricks, but at times he seemed to have caught a bit of Julian Gray's attitude, so that when he signed for Spurs, before he had developed as far as he might have with Palace, it wasn't quite with everyone's very best wishes.

Fresh from winning Euro 2004 with Greece, **Vasilis Lakis** toiled for a while on the left, as did Germany's **Marco Reich**, but it was Routledge's replacement, **Jobi McAnuff**, who ensured that the loss of young Wayne wasn't felt too keenly. Far more direct than Routledge, and genuinely two-footed, McAnuff could comfortably switch wings or play down the middle and was the architect of many goals for Johnson and Morrison, as well as scoring some important ones of his own such as a winner at Brighton. At times brilliant, at others invisible, McAnuff was ultimately frustrating, as his ability was evident, but I never understood why he became persona non grata at Selhurst Park after he left. An eye-catching player in the Championship, but never making it at a higher level, in many ways his profile matched Palace's but he chose to pursue his dream of Premier League football at Watford, which didn't quite work out. McAnuff was a model of consistency however, compared to **Paul Ifill**, who, when he wasn't laid up with a bad back, seemed in his own little bubble on the pitch. He scored a few enjoyable goals, but was always just about to come back to his best, which never really happened. Nor did we see any of the talent that **Mark Kennedy** had once possessed, after Peter Taylor had brought him to Palace with high hopes, and once Neil Warnock arrived and demanded a bit of grit, he was on his way, along with another of Taylor's failures, **Stuart Green**. Green had scored one superb free kick against Leicester, but was too much of a lightweight to figure in any team put out by Warnock, who experimented for a while with first **Frank Songo'o**, then both **Victor Moses** and **Sean Scannell** on the wing, as well as giving chances to **Kieran Djilali** and **Kieron Cadogan**.

Chelsea's **Scott Sinclair** also came in on loan and featured in the play-offs against Bristol City, and would have been a superb signing if Palace could have afforded him. Instead, both Moses and Scannell, academy graduates with big reputations, were thrown in at the deep end, and both started to develop very quickly in positions that perhaps wouldn't be their first choice. There had always been a lot of buzz about Moses, who was just starting to really dazzle when he was sold to Wigan, but less had been expected of Scannell, and it was gratifying to see how he developed and strengthened over the next couple of years although he didn't really sustain that progress afterwards.

At the start of Neil Warnock's final season, he made possibly his best signing for Palace when rescuing **Darren Ambrose** from obscurity at Charlton. It would be reasonable to dispute the description of Ambrose as a winger, as it would be with Lombardo, but he did play the majority of his games under Warnock in a wide midfield role at least, often switching from right to left during the course of a game. Not on the face of it an archetypal Warnock player such as Shaun Derry or Clint Hill, Ambrose nevertheless had an outstanding first season, scoring 20 goals in all competitions. His goals weren't confined to spectacular long-range shots, as he got his share of tap-ins as well, but those were the ones that stick in the memory, especially the stunning free kick in an FA Cup tie against Aston Villa from an impossible distance. Nobody in the Palace squad could hit a ball as sweetly as Ambrose, be it a shot on goal or a long pass, although he could also have spells when his corners failed to clear the first defender. His form fell away slightly once Palace were faced with a scrap to recover from the ten point deduction, but despite it looking certain that he would follow Warnock to QPR, he played every game under Paul Hart, and it was fitting that he should score the vital second goal against Sheffield Wednesday to save Palace from relegation. In his second season, under George Burley, Ambrose never looked fully fit and missed a lot of games, but just

when you started to wonder whether he was actually on the pitch, he would pop up with another superb goal, such as the spectacular – and crucial – volley in the six-pointer against Sheffield United. In his final season at Palace Ambrose scored surely one of his best ever long range goals at Old Trafford in the League Cup, and the player who fed him the ball that night was the young **Wilfried Zaha**, just turned 20, whose performance during that game first caught the eye of Alex Ferguson.

Zaha had been at the Palace academy since the age of 12 and got his first senior start under George Burley, a skinny youth with obvious potential who scored a goal against Leicester at the Whitehorse Lane end and kept his place for the whole season, and little did we know that we'd witnessed the first start at Selhurst Park of probably the best player we would ever see. With Palace 3–0 up at half time, that was to be George Burley's finest hour, but Zaha flourished under Dougie Freedman and his audacious skills when played in a wide position throughout the season gave the fans some real excitement in a period that became another rather dour battle for survival, and already his soaring reputation made him a target for some corrective treatment by defenders – if they could get near him. Zaha's quality was soon recognised beyond Selhurst Park, and when he eventually left for Manchester United he had already sealed his place as a Palace legend with his two goals against Brighton in the playoff semi-final. It was more than we could dream of that he should return after David Moyes froze him out at Old Trafford, and we were lucky enough to see him continue to grow at Palace, becoming a truly world class player who stayed at his parent club year after year, despite constant talk of offers from elsewhere. Hard as it is not to turn this book into a paean to Wilf, Palace fans who have actually watched him play over the years will need no convincing that he is indeed, in the current sporting vernacular, the GOAT despite his imperfections. Well, just one imperfection, his undeniable petulance when sometimes we'd prefer him to shrug off the kickings and the weak refereeing and simply show them that he's just too good for you.

Wilfried Zaha

A key feature of Palace's promotion season in 2013, first under Dougie Freedman and then Ian Holloway, was the elegant simplicity of the team shape, with Glenn Murray down the middle and Zaha and **Yannick Bolasie** either side. Bolasie had been one of Freedman's signings at the same time as Damian Delaney, and although it was Zaha who was getting most attention, Bolasie was for much of the season his equal, as they swapped sides and bamboozled defences while Murray knocked in 30 league goals. Sometimes infuriating, but always highly entertaining, caution wasn't in Bolasie's repertoire but when he was on song he could be unplayable, with the confidence to take on full backs with some flamboyant moves, speed and terrific strength, but perhaps too often ending up with a ball lashed nearer the corner flag

than the goal. He continued to develop in the Premier League without losing any of his spontaneity but by the time Zaha returned, Murray was being underused and that trio was rarely given the opportunity to bring back the old days. Bolasie was sometimes used as a central striker, and although he did score one memorable hat trick in 11 minutes at Sunderland, goals were never really his thing, and when Everton came calling with an irresistible offer, it was a huge loss for the fans, whose love for Bolasie had continued to deepen.

Neither **Lee Chung-yong** nor **Bakary Sako** ever established themselves in the team, and only when **Andros Townsend** arrived from Newcastle did we have good options on both wings again. Townsend was a very different type of winger than Zaha or Bolasie, relying on close control and tenacity rather than blistering speed, but for a while he became a fixture on the right despite favouring his left foot, and was particularly effective once an in-form Benteke was in the middle. He also had a quite productive spell in a front two with Zaha, and for much of Roy Hodgson's time worked as hard defensively as going forward. Of course his astonishing volley against Manchester City will be remembered for a long time, but he'll also be looked back on as a real team player whose professionalism and dedication, together with an open and engaging personality, endeared him greatly to this fan at least.

It will come as no surprise that Wilfried Zaha is the first name on my own dream team sheet, but I'm torn when it comes to the other winger, with Peter Taylor, Vince Hilaire and Lombardo all in with a shout, but I know in my heart that nothing would thrill me more than seeing Don Rogers in a Palace shirt once again.

Strikers

By the late 1960s British teams had more or less universally adopted the 4–2–4 system, with the centre forward paired with a second striker, an evolution from the earlier inside forward, and the norm became to number these 9 and 10. Typically the 'Big Number 9' would be tall, strong, good with his head and happy to take 90 minutes of hard knocks. The number 10 tended to be slighter, quicker, usually more skilful and looking to profit from the knock-down or touch-off from his partner. This combination was evident at most successful clubs of the time, such as Gilzean and Greaves at Spurs, Jones and Clarke at Leeds, and of course Hurst and Hunt for England, although manager Alf Ramsey famously dispensed with wingers during the 1966 World Cup. At Palace, easily their most successful attacking partnership historically – that of Mark Bright and Ian Wright – is a perfect example of the system at its best, but we'll get there eventually.

Palace's centre-forward in Bert Head's promotion side of 1969 was **Bobby Woodruff**, a consistent scorer with good timing in the air and a notable long throw, but too gentle a soul to make his mark after helping the team into Division One. **Cliff Jackson** was originally a winger, and when he converted to centre-forward it was his speed on the ground above all else that made him dangerous, happy to let Woodruff get on with the job of challenging for the ball in the air. His best season was the promotion year of 1969, and he it was who scored the vital equaliser against Fulham after Palace had been 2–0 down, which he celebrated with his renowned 'gladiator' salute. He had a less happy time in the First Division, largely due to the fact that his new partner **Gerry Queen** was too similar a type of player, and neither of them had the muscle to cause problems to hefty First Division defences.

Gerry Queen was signed from Kilmarnock by Bert Head, who said of him: 'When I weigh up a player I look for just 8 attributes... Gerry has 7, which shows how highly I rate him.' He only averaged a goal every four games for Palace, and was unfortunate that he never had a good target man to feed off, ending his Palace days scampering around looking for scraps up front with **Willie Wallace**. Queen had the distinction of scoring in Palace's first ever game in the First Division, against Manchester United, and it was his goal that beat Liverpool in 1971, Palace's first league victory over that team. The goal which stands out, though, was in the Boxing Day game against Chelsea in 1970, when Palace were hammered 5–1, but Queen looped a long-range, wind-assisted googly past Peter 'The Cat' Bonetti from an implausible distance, to briefly give Palace the lead.

After Woodruff had left, only having played a few games in the First Division, there was no real target man until **Alan Birchenall** arrived the following season, as Palace's first £100,000 signing. Birchenall never looked as good as he was supposed to be, and although he always worked hard he spent most of the time with his back to the goal, knocking the ball down to nobody in particular, and was rarely in positions to score himself. Maybe he would have had more luck in a better side, but Chelsea didn't seem to miss him too much, although he epitomised their lingering swinging sixties image, claiming that he used to sing with Joe Cocker in Sheffield.

Following Birchenall were a succession of tiny forwards including Wallace and Derek Possee, although the long, thin **Ross Jenkins** earned the distinction of probably being Palace's tallest player ever after progressing from the reserves to the first team for a few games. Perhaps Palace gave up on him too hastily, feeling that he was too easy to knock off the ball, because when he re-emerged a few years later as the fulcrum of Watford's spectacularly successful airborne attack force, he had changed into a strong, aggressive and effective player.

Willie Wallace was one of Bert Head's least successful Scottish buys, and both **Derek Possee** and **Alan Whittle** had far bigger reputations than were warranted before they came to Palace. Whittle at least scored one terrific goal on his debut against Manchester United, and won a few penalties, but Possee simply wasn't the same player who had been so good at Millwall, and the two of them together up front were a dead loss, not just because they were so short.

Another graduate from the youth team, **Dave Swindlehurst**, was given an early chance by Malcolm Allison, and after a slow start improved steadily to become Palace's highest scorer of the 1970s, with a total of 81 goals. Swindlehurst's big asset was his all-round physical strength, and it was this rather than any agility that won him a lot of balls in the air, a good proportion of his goals coming from powerful headers, although he loved to try a spectacular volley from time to time. He once scored eight goals in a spell of nine games in 1975, and although he only scored one hat-trick – in the last game of 1977–78 – he was the only player who could guarantee a steady stream of goals throughout the season. He particularly benefitted from the service given by Peter Taylor on the wing, and his best season was when Palace reached the FA Cup semi-final in 1976, Swindlehurst scoring the winning goal in perhaps the greatest victory of that run, at Leeds United. He invariably scored in the key games, including one of the four

against Wrexham that hauled Palace out of the Third Division in 1977, and a goal in each of the last three games of 1978–79, victories that won Palace the Second Division Championship.

After Swindlehurst had established himself in the team, he had a variety of striking partners, the most of effective of whom were the heroic **Jeff Bourne** and the unlucky **Mike Elwiss**, and **Dave Kemp** had his moments, but Swindlehurst was undoubtedly at his best when playing alongside **Ian Walsh**. Walsh was from the vintage crop of youth team players that served Venables so well at the end of the 1970s, and he was a perfect foil to the big man, although never a great goal scorer. He was a very busy player, always looking for the ball in deep and wide positions, and for a small man he was pretty good in the air, notably when scoring the first goal against Burnley in the 1979 promotion clincher. Palace's success helped him to win a place in the Welsh national team, but Venables regrettably preferred to play his expensive signing **Mike Flanagan** in his place, and Walsh's appearances from then on were only intermittent, although he came in and out of the side for a couple of years before Steve Kember released him to Swansea.

Having spent so much money on Flanagan, a ponderous player who I for one never took to, Venables could hardly drop him when it was apparent that the partnership wasn't working, so it was Swindlehurst who paid the price, eventually being sold to Derby County. How Palace could have done with him in the years to come, and it wasn't until we we had been made to suffer such poor substitutes as **Tommy Langley**, **Ian Edwards** and **Chris Jones** that we really appreciated Swindlehurst's qualities, and yearned to have him back. I suppose some people would regard Swindlehurst's replacement **Clive Allen** as a classic English centre-forward, and there were certainly enough clubs willing to employ him as such over the years, but quite frankly all we saw during his time at Palace were glimpses of hints of a suggestion of his potential, his greatness remaining well hidden as he finished top scorer with 9 goals in a team destined for relegation in 1981, ahead of **Tony Sealy** and Ian Walsh with 5 each.

It wasn't until **Kevin Mabbutt** signed from Bristol City in 1981 that Palace at last had a really good forward, although he had to try his best with scant assistance from either Tommy Langley or Chris Jones. It is a great shame when you see a good player unable to exploit his talent because of injury, but Mabbutt was clearly fated never to make it to the top of his profession, Palace finally losing patience with him in 1984 after several false dawns. **Andy McCulloch** was another of Alan Mullery's unsuccessful strikers, and at least his successor – **Trevor Aylott** – almost reached double figures in 1984–85, his nine goals comparing favourably to the seven collected by the top scorer the year before, **Tony Evans**.

When Steve Coppell took over in 1984, he experimented with several partners for Aylott – Andy Gray and Phil Barber both having some success – but once the green but talented **Ian Wright** had found his feet there was no looking back. In his first season Wright scored some important goals after coming on as substitute, but his second year was a bit of a disappointment, with only nine goals from 42 starts, the expected rate of return for a Palace forward until then. After Mark Bright had been installed, though, Wright suddenly found a new confidence and began to play with abandon, and it was soon evident that here was one of the most naturally skilful players unearthed for many years, not just

at Palace, but in the English game. His haul of goals from then on tells part of the story, and there was no more delightful sight than Ian Wright pouncing on to a loose ball and lashing it into the net, but there was so much more to his game than that. He could devastate defences with a wicked burst of speed, but his most enjoyable trick was to bring down a high ball with his back to the goal, and with one neat flick control it, turn past the centre back and leave him sprawling in his wake as he bore down on the goalkeeper. Most memorably, despite returning from a broken leg he came on as substitute and scored two spectacular goals in the FA Cup final, which put Palace to within seven minutes of winning the Cup. His first goal that day was something extra special, and deserves to be remembered as one of the great Cup Final goals of all time. Wright should have been used earlier by England, and might have become England's answer to Toto Schillaci in the 1990 World Cup had he been selected by Bobby Robson, but even under Graham Taylor, Terry Venables and Glenn Hoddle he was too often overlooked.

Ian Wright

After Aylott's drawn out demise, both Andy Gray and Phil Barber had a go in the

No. 9 shirt, but Steve Coppell finally struck gold when he bought **Mark Bright** from Leicester City, for only £75,000. Bright had been in the shadow of Gary Lineker and Alan Smith at Leicester, and hadn't done himself justice when he finally got his chance in the first team, but Coppell saw something in him that others had missed, a keen intelligence in front of goal that more than made up for any deficiencies of speed or sharpness. Bright scored in his first game for Palace, a 3–3 draw with Ipswich, and spent the rest of the 1986–87 season fine tuning his partnership with Ian Wright, which produced spectacular results the following year when his 24 league goals made him Palace's highest scorer in a single season since the days of Johnny Byrne. He was a target man in the truest sense, with long clearances invariably aimed towards his handsome head, and he was rarely bested over the course of a game by any central defender. The fact that he demanded such close attention in turn created more space for his colleagues, but as well as setting up a good number of chances with little flicks of the head, and by holding the ball up to lay it off into somebody's stride, he proved beyond doubt a precious instinct for scoring.

Bright didn't score too many from distance, but put the ball across the face of goal and he would be there to force it home with some part of his body, his face animated with a delight that revealed him as someone who loved the game as much as the fans themselves. In contrast to a lot of big forwards, who often tend to have a violent edge to their game, Bright was a gentleman even when he went in hard, and it was completely uncharacteristic for him to stamp on a Sheffield Wednesday defender in 1989–90, for which he was deservedly sent off. Critics of Bright insist that he only did so well thanks to being paired with Ian Wright, but I would say that the benefit was entirely mutual, and that although Bright certainly wasn't as fast or as skilful as his partner, his other qualities made him one of the very best of his type in the English game at the time. Without doubt, Mark Bright's most memorable and spectacular strike was his unstoppable volley against Liverpool in the FA Cup semi-final, but he won many a lesser game with more mundane goals, and has to be considered among Palace's best ever traditional No 9s.

Anyone who succeeded Wright and Bright up front at Palace was bound to suffer by comparison, as the pair continued their wonderful partnership in the 1990–91 season, and Palace's surprise emergence as title contenders meant that their talent was being more widely acknowledged. This was their fifth season together at Selhurst Park, and both were at the peak of their powers and as thrilling as ever to watch. Where Wright had explosive speed, agility, and eye-catching ball skills, Bright's all round ability was always slightly underestimated, but each benefited from the other's presence, and in their own way they were both able to score any type of goal. Long range shots, tap-ins, headers, all were within their compass, but it was Wright who could make a goal from nothing, turn a player and be in on goal in a flash, or see half a chance from distance and subtly lob the keeper as he did on the way to a memorable hat-trick against Wimbledon. Supplied all season by Salako and McGoldrick on the wings, the fans were treated to the best entertainment ever witnessed at Palace, although much of the press couldn't see beyond Coppell's supposed route one tactics. That was one source of goals, certainly, but there was a great deal more to Palace that year, and it was a bitter blow when Wright and Bright were robbed of the chance of competing in Europe.

Once Ian Wright had decamped to Arsenal the following season, Mark Bright went on to prove that he was an outstanding striker in his own right, and was ever present in all competitions, scoring 22 goals. The problem of how to replace Wright, though, was one that took a while to solve, and with **Garry Thompson** having left, and problem child **Stan Collymore** proving a misfit, the squad was very short of forwards. Steve Coppell paid big money for **Marco Gabbiadini**, but it soon became clear that this was one of his poorer decisions. Gabbiadini was a stocky player who never really looked like making it at the top level however busy he was, and despite a handful of decent goals. His best performance came during Palace's 2–1 victory away to Liverpool where he darted in to score with a neat touch at the near post, and he looked best with the ball at his feet, which really didn't suit Palace's pattern at the time. He was by no means dreadful, but Coppell quickly realised his mistake and offloaded him at a loss less than three months after he signed, an embarrassing admission of failure, but the right decision all the same. Young **David Whyte** showed some promise and a good deal of enthusiasm during a spell alongside Bright, but the season ended with defender Chris Coleman up front. He actually proved to be a better partner for Bright than his immediate predecessors, but Palace didn't sign another proper striker until Bright himself was about to end his Palace days, moving on to Sheffield Wednesday, with **Paul Williams** coming in part-exchange.

The youngster signed from Millwall, **Chris Armstrong**, played two games alongside Bright without either of them scoring, but for his first appearance at Selhurst Park Armstrong was paired with Williams and straight away looked a real find, walloping a goal from close range, scoring a second with a header, and showing the kind of speed that had been missing since Wright's departure. Even better, he bagged another brace the following week at Everton, and could have scored even more in an outstanding performance. Armstrong had a good first season, but still Palace were deficient up front since Salako, who was looking like a possible solution in the centre, was badly injured. Paul Williams, despite good technical skills and a touch of elegance, wasn't robust enough, so Chris Coleman was again used sporadically in the front line as Palace slipped agonisingly out of the Premiership on goal difference. The following season was Armstrong's best, scoring 25 goals in all as Palace won the Division One title, forming a good partnership with Paul Williams and latterly **Paul Stewart**, and he netted his first hat-trick in the 5–1 demolition of Portsmouth, the best being a memorable flying header. The archetypal Armstrong goal, though, would see him cutting in from deep on the right with his long-striding upright gait, latching on to a through ball, outmuscling and outpacing the defender before hitting a daisy cutter or a rising shot inside the near post.

As Palace looked to make sure of promotion in 1994, it was clear that more power was needed up front, and Paul Williams made way for the on-loan Paul Stewart. Stewart made a real impact despite only three goals, and it would have been ideal to have kept him in the Premiership, but once again the problem of finding a strike partner for Armstrong who could operate at the highest level wasn't addressed soon enough. The hard working **Andy Preece** was never going to be the answer, although he started brightly enough, and by the time **Iain Dowie** arrived in January the rot had set in. Dowie was just the job, scoring a few vital goals in the league as well as memorable strikes against Wolves and Manchester

United in the FA Cup. The goal against Wolves summed up Dowie as he parried the ball with his face before volleying on the turn, and he even had a good chance against United to put Palace into the Cup final, but ultimately he had arrived too late to save Palace's season.

Dougie Freedman

Following relegation, Armstrong left for Spurs, and after a few games Dowie was also on his way, so Palace began the following season with Bruce Dyer as a striker before a brand new pairing of **Dougie Freedman** and **Gareth Taylor** tried their luck. It was Freedman who was an instant success, scoring 20 goals that year, but Taylor's experience was not unlike that of Gabbiadini before him. His failure to score a home goal and the impatience of the crowd led to him being dropped and then sold before the season's end. New manager Dave Bassett tried George Ndah as Freedman's partner for a while before settling on Bruce Dyer again, and with big **Jeroen Boere** offering little, it was Freedman who was left to score the goals that saw Palace into the play-offs. Freedman was completely unlike any of Palace's best recent strikers – Wright, Bright, Armstrong or Dowie – being slightly built and lacking killer pace,

but he perhaps had more real skill on the ball than any of them, and his goals were generally elegant, graceful and most of all subtle. Freedman liked to get the ball at his feet and tease the defender rather than push it forward and go hell for leather, as he had exceptional close control and it was impossible to read which way he would take the ball. Once he had worked himself into position, he had the widest repertoire of efficient finishes, using the toe-poke, volley, side-foot, and most pleasingly the delicate lob. Quite apart from his finishing, though, Freedman's positional awareness was second to none, and you could almost see how much he was thinking ahead. It was a great pity that Freedman was never paired with Iain Dowie, but he did form a good partnership with **Neil Shipperley** before losing his place under Steve Coppell and making a surprise move to Wolves.

Dave Bassett's signing of Neil Shipperley gave the forward line a real focus, and both Dyer and Freedman benefitted greatly from his presence as a big target man, although he was no slouch on the ground either, becoming Palace's best centre-forward of his type since Mark Bright. Shipperley and Dyer became Steve Coppell's favoured partnership as Palace progressed through the play-offs, which left Freedman on the bench more often than not, but back in the Premiership, Shipperley himself was replaced by Paul Warhurst, one of that season's many costly failures. Warhurst had somehow gained a reputation as a striker since converting from defence some years earlier, and had even been called into the England squad, but on the whole he looked very ordinary at Palace, and he eventually dropped into defence then out of the picture entirely once Venables had taken over. Juventus reserve player **Michele Padovano** cost Goldberg £1.7million for a solitary goal, and **Tomas Brolin**, although playing deeper than expected, failed to score at all, but by the end of the season Shipperley was at last supported by a striker of real quality in **Matt Jansen**.

Following a delicious goal against Villa, Jansen very quickly became a target for a number of clubs, and ultimately spent less than a season at Palace, but in that short time he caught the eye with his control, his speed and his finishing, as well as his attitude against a background of upheaval and financial uncertainty. He was a similar player to Freedman in many ways, but had a more showy style and scored some lovely goals before inevitably being sold to Blackburn, a great talent lost to Palace. Another young striker who showed glimpses of real promise was **Marcus Bent**, who was developing into a fine player before Venables came along, but one player who did make it was **Clinton Morrison**, who appeared as a substitute at the very end of the season and tapped home a late winner from a cross by Lombardo, not a bad way to start your career.

Although Dyer and Shipperley were initially preferred by Venables, Morrison came in to the side after a couple of months and developed over the season into the player that Dyer should have been. He had good body strength to hold off defenders, a great ability to get into telling positions in the box, and the asset that Dyer lacked, an eye for goal. Although Morrison's place was under threat from new signings **Matt Svensson** and the wooden **Lee Bradbury**, it was him that the fans loved, and he appeared to love them back. Morrison was soon first choice up front, and had a succession of partners who never quite stuck, including **Andrew Martin** and the willing **Leon Mackenzie**, but the best was **Mikael Forssell**, on loan from Chelsea. One could see why Forssell was so highly

rated, but also why he wasn't quite ready for Chelsea's first team, as he often seemed to need just a little too much time on the ball, or wanted to get everything in place before shooting, unlike Morrison, who was all about instinct.

Morrison and Forssell continued together under Alan Smith, but finally Dougie Freedman came back to help rescue Palace at Stockport, and the following season formed an astonishing partnership with Morrison. As Palace went top of Division One under Steve Bruce, Freedman and Morrison were in the best form of their careers, and bringing out the best in each other, but Trevor Francis felt the need for more muscle up front, and that was about all he got with **Ade Akinbiyi**. With Akinbiyi injured and out of contention, the next forward to usurp Freedman was **Dele Adebola**, who was poor at Palace although he went on to do a good job elsewhere, but by now Morrison had swapped places with Birmingham's **Andy Johnson**, and it looked at first as though we had been landed with a fairly ordinary squad player. After a hesitant start, Johnson's Palace career went from strength to strength following the hat-trick against Brighton, and if Freedman was the most skilful player at the club, which he was, then Johnson was the most hard-working and honest, despite a completely unfounded reputation for diving to win penalties.

When a well upholstered Neil Shipperley returned to Palace in 2003, he surprised everyone by having a fine season and scoring the play-off winner against West Ham, but back in the Premiership Iain Dowie decided to bring in a number of strikers to support Johnson, and they all flopped, leaving Johnson to plough a lone furrow up front. **Sándor Torghelle** was no better than Bradbury had been, **Nicola**

Ventola spent all season on the treatment table, **Iván Kaviedes** was a complete misfit, and **Wayne Andrews** was a long way from being up to Premiership standard, spending most of his time warming the bench. Back in the Championship, **Jon Macken's** unimpressive form heralded the return of Clinton Morrison, who was once again reunited with Freedman and, for the first time, Andy Johnson. That combination really should have stormed the division, but Palace didn't quite make it, which meant AJ moving onwards and upwards with Everton as Palace stagnated under Peter Taylor.

The fact that Peter Taylor's preferred strike force tended to be **Jamie Scowcroft** and **Shefki Kuqi** ahead of Freedman and Morrison sums up his time in charge, and their successor as the target man, **Alan Lee**, wasn't really any great improvement, although he did come to be appreciated more once he was leaving. It wasn't until **Craig Beattie** joined on loan under Neil Warnock that Palace had another centre forward to get excited about, but his time was all too short, as was that of the less robust but promising **Anthony Stokes**.

When Simon Jordan's house of cards finally collapsed in 2010, Palace were left with very thin resources up front indeed, and ten points deducted. **Freddie Sears'** loan had ended, with his only goal not even counting, **Stern John** was on the injury list after just one game, and Victor Moses had been sold, although Neil Warnock had rarely used him down the middle in any case. That left Alan Lee struggling with **Calvin Andrew** and **Sean Scannell**, who was himself not fully fit. Andrew was an asset to have available from the bench, as he would come on and chase every loose ball, jump for everything in the air, and generally charge around, but he never

looked like scoring goals. Nevertheless all three, together with Stern John returning at last, played a valuable part in the scrap for survival under Paul Hart, and Lee in particular deserves recognition for his effort, and even the odd goal.

George Burley's signing of **Pablo Couñago** didn't bear fruit, but he did well to entice the committed **James Vaughan** on loan from Everton and the veteran Norwegian **Steffen Iversen**, who together with **Jermaine Easter** did a solid job after Dougie Freedman took over as manager, but once **Glenn Murray** had signed from Brighton we at last had the sort of centre forward that every aspiring team needs if they are to push for promotion to the top division. From humble beginnings with Barrow and Carlisle in his native Cumbria, Murray had stealthily worked his way up through the divisions to be part of Gus Poyet's Brighton team that had just won promotion to the Championship, where they would at last get to play their old rivals Crystal Palace again. It seemed strange that Murray chose to leave a club with such clear impetus, but however he was persuaded to come to Selhurst Park, it proved to be a great decision for both parties. On the face of it a typical lower division journeyman, and a little slow at that, Murray turned out to be an absolute master of his craft, utilising strength, timing, positioning, focus and intelligence so that speed was never an issue. It actually took a while for us to see the best of Murray, despite the first season highlights of his goal against Brighton and his winner at Old Trafford, but his second season, with Zaha and Bolasie providing the service, was outstanding despite a serious injury keeping him out of the playoff final and out of action for the best part of a year once Palace had won promotion. In the Premier League, Murray's rehabilitation was understandably cautious, but he was every bit as good a player as he had been before his injury, although the various managers didn't necessarily see it that way, and despite a good offer from Bournemouth it was huge mistake to let him go, several years before his sell-by date, as he proved by returning to Brighton and helping them to promotion and survival in the Premier League. When he finally retired at the age of 37, his old mate from Palace and fellow northerner Peter Ramage put it succinctly and with enormous affection: 'Happy retirement you miserable sod'.

Glenn Murray

Few other strikers made anything like the same impact as Murray, with players like **Cameron Jerome**, **Aaron Wilbraham**, **Stephen Dobbie** and **Fraizer Campbell** all passing through without leaving much impression, although **Dwight Gayle** had his moments and **Marouane Chamakh** proved popular with the crowd despite hardly scoring any goals. **Connor Wickham** had his big moment at Wembley against Watford, and nearly another against Manchester United, but was mostly injured for five of his six years at the club, and when **Christian Benteke** finally landed in South London it looked like we had some real quality up front for the first time since Glenn Murray. For one season Benteke was peerless in the air, not only scoring 15 goals but forming a real focal point for the attack, and the huge transfer fee seemed well worth it. The Belgian had looked like one of the world's best strikers whilst at Aston Villa, and we saw a little of that side of him, but for some unfathomable reason he suddenly forgot how to score, his confidence drained away, and he spent three or four seasons making abortive comebacks from injury as the fans gave up on him, longing for Palace to cut their losses. His return to form at the very end of Roy Hodgson's reign perhaps vindicated the manager's faith in him, but was never enough to make up for the years when he played like he wouldn't get in a pub team.

While Benteke was struggling, **Alexander Sørloth** came and went, **Michy Batshuiyi** played a few games in two loan spells and scored a few important goals, and **Jordan Ayew** had one very good season before going back into his shell, while **Jean-Phillipe Mateta** was barely seen in his first season apart from that lovely back-heeled nutmeg against Brighton. If that's all he ever does, it was priceless and unforgettable.

No other striker even comes close to challenging Ian Wright for his place in my dream team, but although the obvious choice as his partner would be Mark Bright, who remains undervalued, I shall choose Dougie Freedman as the striker I'd most like to see alongside Wright, although Glenn Murray and Chris Armstrong would be wonderful too. Andy Johnson would have a strong claim as well, not least because I was happy to be so wrong about him, but I just love the thought of Wright and Freedman together, tearing defenders apart in their own very different ways.

Dream Team

So here's my dream team, the players I dream about watching when I close my eyes and think back on everyone I've seen play for Crystal Palace over the years. Or perhaps there are indeed infinite parallel universes, and in one of those, right now, these players are all in their prime, physically and mentally, and my commentary flows effortlessly, the words come easily, and all agree how witty, insightful and constantly fascinating this commentator is.

I'm not talking about the best players, necessarily, although a few of them probably are, but simply my favourites over the years, and those who have given me the most joy, the most excitement, the purest pleasure:

1. John Jackson

2. Aaron Wan-Bissaka

5. Eric Young

6. Ian Evans

3. Kenny Sansom

4. Steve Kember

8. Geoff Thomas

7. Don Rogers

9. Dougie Freedman

10. Ian Wright

11. Wilfried Zaha

Postscript (2021)

Fifty-two summers have come and gone (or to call them by their proper name, close seasons), but despite the huge changes the game has seen during that period, what lies at the heart of supporting a club like Palace hasn't changed a bit. I still look forward to every game just as much and need to know every result, every position moved up or down in the table, every formation and nuanced tactical tweak. I still get that buzz of anticipation that I might witness dazzling forward play or miraculous goalkeeping: once it was Vince Hilaire or John Jackson, Wilfried Zaha or Julián Speroni, and whoever it is in the years to come, as long as they are in Palace colours they will be doing it for us, the devoted fans. At the moment the club appears to be in good hands, but I can still dream of owning Crystal Palace, changing the colours back to claret and light blue and the nickname back to 'The Glaziers'.

The cycle of fifty-two years was of great importance to the Aztec people, who feared that the sun might not rise again, and would perform a 'New Fire Ceremony' to ensure the world's continued existence. All flames were extinguished, new fires lit, and dwellings were purged of objects linked to the past cycle. As I write this postscript something similar is happening at Selhurst Park, and it feels like the right time to look to the future rather than the past, and to conclude the Biased Commentary series, which I trust you have enjoyed reading.

And so we look forward to what feels like a wholly new era under new manager Patrick Vieira, one of the finest players of modern times, and with high hopes for some of the new signings and for several youngsters who might make the transition from the Academy over the coming years. The stability that Palace achieved during Roy Hodgson's time as manager has put Crystal Palace into an unprecedented position of perhaps being considered at last among the elite, on merit. I can't shake the feeling that this may be our zenith historically, and that soon enough we'll return to our natural state, bouncing between the top two divisions, but equally we could be about to see Palace reach further and finally win something. Either way, I'm very happy with what I regard as 'my' team, which has been of such importance in my own life since 1968, and which will remain so. Don't let's ask for the moon; we have the stars.

Chris Winter

July 2021

South East London

Chris Winter